IF THINGS ARE SO GOOD, WHY DO I FEEL SO BAD?

IF THINGS ARE SO GOOD, WHY DO I FEEL SO BAD?

You aren't alone. There's a growing crisis of discontent in America, but there's a way out...

GEORGE BARNA

MOODY PRESS
CHICAGO

All Scripture quotations, unless indicated, are taken from the *Holy Bible: New
International Version.*® NIV.® Copyright © 1973, 1978, 1984 International Bible
Society. Used by permission of Zondervan Publishing House. All rights re-
served.

Scripture verses marked (NKJV) are taken from *The New King James Version.*
Copyright © 1979, 1980, 1982, Thomas Nelson, Inc., Publishers. All rights reserved.

Scripture verses marked (KJV) are taken from the King James Version.

ISBN: 0-8024-9244-4

3 5 7 9 10 8 6 4 2

Printed in the United States of America

CONTENTS

ACKNOWLEDGMENTS

T his has been a particularly difficult book for me to write, given the many activities occurring in my life at the time the manuscript was to be completed. I gratefully acknowledge those individuals who played a special role in enabling me to convert the underlying concept for this book into a tangible reality.

My colleagues at the Barna Research Group (BRG) were faithful in carrying out their duties during my absences to focus on this book. Cindy Coats, Gwen Ingram, George Maupin, and Pam Tucker, in particular, have earned my gratitude for keeping our research-based ministry afloat.

Moody Press personnel, particularly editorial director Jim Bell, were gracious in extending the deadline to allow me to complete the manuscript in a manner with which I felt comfortable. Jim was very supportive in the conceptualization and development of this book. Jim Vincent proved to be a patient and helpful editor, offering useful suggestions throughout the manuscript.

My pastor and "boss," Shawn Mitchell of New Venture Christian Fellowship, was a source of encouragement and understanding during this period. He and the entire church staff were quite forgiving and sympathetic as I tried—often with minimal success—to balance my duties at BRG and as executive pastor at New Venture, along with the delivery of this manuscript.

The greatest debt is owed to my wife, Nancy, and my daughter, Samantha, who forfeited their time with me during the writing period. May God abundantly bless them both for their sacrifices toward the completion of this work, and may any success it achieves be shared jointly by them and by God.

PART 1

THE SEARCH FOR SATISFACTION

. . . .

I t's easy to feel confused these days. On the one hand, things seem better than ever. There have been groundbreaking advances in medicine, science, agriculture, international relations, education, and even leisure. On the other hand, when you go to bed at night you may be stumped by two simple questions: "So what was the purpose of today's toils? And why should I get out of bed tomorrow?"

Such questions are not raised when life is undeniably satisfying. Yet millions of Americans struggle with those questions on a daily basis. And they ask themselves, "If things are so good, why do I feel so bad?"

In Part 1 we will explore the foundation of both sides of the dilemma: the good and rewarding aspects of life these days and the foreboding and challenging realities we regularly face. Before we can begin to grapple with our feelings of emptiness, we must have a comprehensive understanding of conditions in America. Let's take a look at the real America of the 1990s.

. . . .

CHAPTER 1
ARE HAPPY DAYS HERE AGAIN?

On the night Harry Truman upset heavily favored Tom Dewey to win the U.S. presidency, the band at his campaign celebration party struck up a spirited rendition of "Happy Days Are Here Again." In 1948, the song was apropos. World War II was over, and Americans were anxious to resume their pursuit of the good life.

For four years, millions had sacrificed family, time, earnings, comforts, and stability. Many had prayed that their God would bless the country's efforts to restore freedom throughout Europe and the rest of the developed world. With the unequivocal defeat of Hitler's challenge to democracy, many concluded that our nation's leaders were right: no nation on the face of the earth could compete with America. In the eyes of millions, America had won more than just a war; the victory "proved" that the lauded American way of life was uniquely blessed and superior. No longer did people need to look to the future as the time when the nation might fulfill its destiny. That moment had arrived.

People were itchy to get on with the new era. And, as during much of twentieth-century America, citizens began to resume the pursuit of "the good life": a life of security and comfort. The search for the good life has continued since then, and some would say the good life is almost here. Certainly things seem to be better than ever; just look at the list of advances beginning on page 12. But if things are so good, why do we often feel so bad?

One of the answers to that question can be found in the 1992 presidential election and another campaign theme song. Just as Harry Truman pulled off a political upset in dumping Dewey, so Bill Clinton surprised many in his march to the White House. Political analysts respected his intellect and zeal, but they viewed him as a long-shot at best. After all, he was vying against other, better-known and more skilled Democratic hopefuls. He defeated his rivals, however, and won the Democratic presidential nomination.

Now he faced a greater challenge: competing against a well-financed, incumbent president. George Bush was, after all, the consummate politician, a seasoned political pro. And his public image was riding high at the time that Clinton and other presidential hopefuls put their campaigns into motion. Just twenty-four months before Election Day, Bush's public approval rating hit the highest point achieved by any president since John Kennedy.

President Bush appeared virtually unbeatable. Thanks to the genius of his military leaders (Joint Chiefs of Staff leader Colin Powell and field commander Norman Schwartzkopf, in particular), the U.S.-led NATO consortium crushed Suddam Hussein and the Iraqi army that had invaded Kuwait. At that point the president's reelection seemed guaranteed.

But things change rapidly in this techno-age, especially public opinion influenced by the latest news reports and speculation; political fortunes can reverse virtually overnight. In President Bush's case, they did, due largely to a changing national economy. After a nasty campaign, a presidential race made interesting mostly by the intrusion of Texas billionaire Ross Perot, Clinton and his entourage savored the sweet spoils of victory at their own party on the evening of November 3, 1992.

Nearly a half century after Truman's upset win, Clinton, the governor of a small state, had been elected the forty-second president of the United States. At his victory celebration, a new theme song played. Once again, the song superbly captured the mood of the nation. The bank of speakers at the Clinton party blared out "Don't Stop Thinking About Tomorrow." The President-elect had seized this Fleetwood Mac tune months earlier as the theme for his election campaign. The song was appropriate because Clinton had focused on the ills of today and described the hopes he had for a better tomorrow.

MORE THAN AN ELECTION

How did Bill Clinton beat the incumbent president? Many said it was the economic recession, plain and simple, that drove President Bush from office in favor of a younger, more progressive doer. Others said the nation had endured more than a decade of Republican leadership that had overseen the rise of economic insolvency, cultural decadence, interpersonal isolation, and conservative politics.

However, Clinton did not defeat Bush (and Perot) because he reflected the political views of the people. In fact, he did not represent the ideology of the electorate. A champion of the *nouveau* liberal perspective, he was voted into office by a public still largely conservative. His victory is attributable to the fact that Americans wanted a real leader, a person who had vision for the future, a vision that provided hope and the promise that the American dream was not really dead, just dormant. (Visionary leadership is one of four elements necessary for us to find satisfaction; see chapter 12.)

George Bush had shown himself to be a caretaker rather than a forceful leader who was in touch with the sweeping changes revolutionizing the globe. During the course of the campaign, Bush habitually made light of the importance of vision, falling back on the derisive expression, "the vision thing." In the end, voters were willing to forgive Clinton his liberal tendencies as long as he delivered a better tomorrow, based on his ability to articulate hope, the potential for personal fulfillment, and a semblance of a plan for making that dream a reality.

Clinton's theme song says all that. "Don't Stop Thinking About Tomorrow" points to a better future, an undying hope. The contrast in Clinton's music and Truman's "Happy Days Are Here Again" reflects more than just the changing musical styles and tastes of a nation. The divergent perspectives of these tunes capture the mood swing of the nation—"Happy Days" focused on the joys of attained goals; "Don't Stop Thinking" focused to the doubter's hope of a better tomorrow.

IS NEWER BETTER?

Interestingly, many observers still believe "happy days" are here. The so-called spin doctors try to place a happy face on

America. They make assertions to the effect that "while the nation may have problems—and what nation doesn't?—those failures pale in comparison to the many successes related to the expectations of the American dream." These cultural therapists argue that when you put everything in context, life is actually pretty good these days.

Are happy days here again? There is a good argument to be made. Ample evidence suggests that the good life is common throughout America. Consider these measures of achievement and lifestyle:

- Two-thirds of all Americans own their homes. And these are not just any homes; these are, on average, the largest homes in the world.

- A college education is now a routine part of growing up for most Americans. Six out of every ten young people attend college for some duration, and the proportion of adults who have earned a college degree has doubled since 1960.

- We have some of the highest household income levels in the world. In fact, Americans have more *discretionary* income than most adults around the world make in total income.

- Despite news stories complaining that unemployment levels are in the 5 to 8 percent range, this means that more than nine out of ten adults who want to participate in the labor force have a job.

- Inflation, which hovered between 15 and 20 percent during the Carter Administration, is under control, currently in the low single-digit range.

- Years ago, the elderly were often living in poverty; currently, only 10 percent of them live below the poverty line. In fact, people in their sixties and beyond control a disproportionate share of the nation's wealth. The median net worth of those age sixty-five and older is 62 percent greater than the net worth of younger adults.[1]

- More than 2 million people get married every year, and most of those marriages endure, producing children who become the pride and joy of their parents. In spite of reports that one of two marriages end in divorce, the fact is only 27 percent of all married people have divorced.[2]

- Our democratic system of government has become the envy and the model for countries around the world. And the system has become increasingly participatory, with the advent of public referenda and initiatives, "town hall" meetings, and óther forms of involvement.

- America is relatively safe from foreign attack, especially with the collapse of the Soviet empire. Not since 1945 has the communist menace been so minor, with the Berlin Wall toppling and the Soviet Union dissolving into the Commonwealth of Independent States. The Cold War has ended.

- Nearly paralyzed by an "energy crisis" less than three decades ago, Americans no longer worry about this condition, as new sources of energy and more efficient uses of those sources have been put into place.

- There are more than 300,000 places of religious worship, where anyone can freely worship the God of his or her choice.

- The entertainment and leisure industries are flourishing, a testimony to people's obsession with relaxation and recreation. We can find various high-quality diversions from the stresses and pressures of daily life. Numerous companies offer us everything from luxury automobiles, such as the homegrown Cadillac and the imported Lexus, Infiniti, and Mercedes, to movie spectacles in theaters and movie rentals for home viewing (generating billions of dollars in revenue). We enjoy recorded music on compact disc and audio cassette, attend sports events in person or watch them on TV, and jet to summer vacations.

- The swift development of computer-driven technologies has made people's lives more efficient and convenient. With personal computers, videotape recorders, cellular telephones, fiber-optic transmission lines, cable television, microwave and satellite communications, and much more, the amount of information available, and the speed at which it is transmitted, have exploded.

- Medical and health care advances are allowing people to live longer, healthier, and more productive lives.

<table>
<tr><td colspan="2" align="center">LIFE IN AMERICA TODAY</td></tr>
<tr><td>ADVANCES</td><td>CHALLENGES</td></tr>
<tr><td>Home ownership</td><td>Racism amid ethnic diversity</td></tr>
<tr><td>College educations</td><td>Weaker Christian commitment</td></tr>
<tr><td>Household income levels</td><td>Anti-Christian sentiment</td></tr>
<tr><td>Low unemployment</td><td>Breakdown of family values</td></tr>
<tr><td>Many enduring marriages</td><td>Selfishness, lack of community</td></tr>
<tr><td>Peace at home</td><td>Global economic competition</td></tr>
<tr><td>Luxury and leisure items</td><td>Devaluing of human life</td></tr>
<tr><td>Medical and health care</td><td></td></tr>
</table>

And the list could go on, in similar fashion, for pages. In many ways, life seems more enjoyable today than it was in the golden days of the fifties that followed the war. Yes, life was simpler then, but we can do so much more now with the social and scientific advances of the late twentieth century. The black-and-white days of "Leave it to Beaver" have given way to the colorful days of high-definition stereo television. Calculators have been superseded by high-speed, powerful personal computers. Toasters and blenders now take second place to more versatile kitchen aids, such as food processors and microwave ovens. Our cars are safer, with air bags and antilock brakes; our hearts beat longer with pacemakers and increasingly successful bypass surgeries; medical research offers a higher cure rate for leukemia; the physically disabled have greater access to buildings and to employment; and we accept the displaced from throughout the world, sharing our goods with refugees from Vietnam, Cambodia, Russia, China, Cuba, and Haiti, many of whom have become naturalized citizens.

In the fifties we began to fight polio and other childhood diseases; today vaccines and booster shots have largely eradicated those diseases. In the fifties we had grocery markets and five-and-ten stores in most towns and villages; today we can shop at specialty stores for electronics, fabrics, home improvement, baby clothes, and books, as well as warehouse-sized discount stores (called "hypermarkets"). Conditions sure seem to be better.

THE AGE OF CONTRADICTIONS

Nonetheless, other conditions in our midst seem to cast clouds on the horizon. Many of those concerns represent contradictions. To name just five:

- Americans have experienced misunderstandings and prejudice as a result of an ethnically changing nature of the country. Every year, the ethnic balance of the population is altered by the increased presence of nonwhite people. Immigration is a major reason. But at the same time that we are inviting nearly a million foreigners to become Americans every year, our communities are beset by deep-seeded racial prejudice and disharmony.

- Though America retains its fantasy of being a "Christian" nation upholding solid morals based on Judeo-Christian values, fewer people read the Bible; fewer attend church on a weekly basis; fewer identify themselves as Christian; and fewer embrace traditional Christian perspectives and lifestyles. Increasingly, as Bible reading, prayer, and evangelism are being outlawed or challenged in public places (such as schools), activities and lifestyles counter to traditional Christianity—such as homosexuality, adultery, and pornography—are being protected by the government.

- At the very time when we maintain that family is a key social institution and must be upheld by people, increasing numbers of adults circumvent marriage through cohabitation, reject sexual purity in favor of premarital promiscuity, deny the absolute nature of marriage in favor of serial marriage, and fault those who stand firm for the refusal to engage in adultery.

- Despite our wealth, America is becoming a dual-class nation: the haves and the have-nots. Economic pressures are undermining our dreams and our relationships. The number of impoverished families continues to climb. Tens of millions of women have re-entered the work force, often against their own desires to help their families make ends meet. Most college students have to take out loans, a financial pressure which hangs over their heads for years. Our studies have shown that even a majority of the affluent feel they never have quite enough money to truly experience "the good life."

- Life itself has been devalued. One evidence is the 1.5 million abortions performed each year; another is the growing public support for euthanasia. The rising suicide rate among both our youngest and oldest people reflects their feelings of lesser importance in American society. Even the widespread ownership of guns reveals how little we value others' lives: there are more guns registered to Americans than there are adults in the entire nation!

On the one hand, we believe that life is good these days. If ever there was a time when Americans had a wealth of opportunities, a universe of knowledge available for the asking, and a wonderland of toys and tools at their disposal, this is it. As Robin Leach, erstwhile host of the hit television show of the eighties, "Lifestyles of the Rich and Famous," regularly asked, "Can it get any better than this?"

On the other hand, many people would answer Leach's question with a resounding, "Yes, it can!" when the query is posed in terms of personal fulfillment and inner peace. Far from crowing about the supremacy of America and the joys of modern living, Americans are entangled in a battle for survival, striving to get through today, somehow, so they can take another crack at making things more fulfilling tomorrow. The sad truth, for most people, is that we are committed to minimizing our pain rather than maximizing our joy.

How we got that way and how we can return to lasting satisfaction and inner peace are the subjects of this book.

NOTES

1. *Statistical Abstract of the United States 1993* (Washington, D. C.: U. S. Department of Commerce, 1994), table 753, p. 477.
2. George Barna, *The Future of the American Family* (Chicago: Moody, 1993), 67–68.

THE SEARCH

1. *What new technological innovations in home, business, and culture affect you personally? What do you like about them? Dislike about them?*

2. *Think of your most cherished dreams for the future that you had five years ago? Have they materialized? How are you adjusting those dreams for the next five years?*

3. *Though we have the education and resources, there seems to be a leadership gap in America. How would you define this gap? What do you think are the reasons for this gap in leadership?*

4. *As we watch the changes in both ethnic and religious composition in the United States, how can we Americans maintain pluralism and tolerance yet stand firm on our own beliefs and unique characteristics?*

5. *Has your own value system been strengthened or weakened by the massive yet subtle changes in values throughout the land? Why?*

POINT OF ACTION

Write a list that shows ways you can resist the "new values" mentioned and maintain the traditional Judeo-Christian values in your daily life.

CHAPTER 2

WHY DO WE FEEL SO BAD?

My marriage is good and that has sustained me through a lot of the tough times," John told me. "But I always feel like there must be more out there than what I'm getting. I look at my colleagues in business and they seem to be doing better than me. Maybe it's just a facade, but they seem more content. I look at my friends and they seem happier. I look at my classmates from college, and they seem to have a better lifestyle.

"I'm not a grass-is-always-greener type of guy, either. But it's kind of like the song by U2, 'I still haven't found what I'm looking for.' The problem is, I don't even know what I'm looking for, and I'm not convinced that if I find it I'll even know it. That's depressing, isn't it?"

John Forrester,[1] thirty-seven and living in northern Texas, is typical of many Americans in this seeming land of plenty. They have the basics—a job, a loving family, good health, and perhaps a savings account—yet something fundamental is missing. As Americans we have far more than ever before, yet in spite of all the benefits and pleasures listed in chapter 1, we recognize that life in America is simply not good enough. We want more of what we have, and we want to possess what we cannot grasp. Millions believe that even future possibilities of hope cannot alleviate the emptiness, disappointment, or hopelessness that we already experience.

Somehow the present does not satisfy the desires of our hearts; so we wistfully and longingly turn to the future. Unlike earlier generations, we do not understand the past very well, and it doesn't teach us much. Against the odds, we rely upon the future for an answer to our quests, straining to catch a peek of a viable society, one that provides the possibility that our dreams may yet be realized. In desperation, we lock onto tomorrow, pretending that it will certainly deliver a justification for living today.

Is Fleetwood Mac right? Is our hope found in only "Thinking About Tomorrow"?

Unless we change our ways, the answer is a saddening yes. For a significant shift in attitudes and behavior has taken place in America. It's more than having sold out to selfishness, the well-chronicled illness of the eighties. And blaming America's cultural demise and social malaise on unambitious Baby Busters (those thirty and under), as some critics do, is an absurdity: they have been the unwilling inheritors of a culture that they neither created nor appreciate. The national fixation with bashing unfashionable groups—Christians, the media, politicians, gays, televangelists, lawyers—merely reflects the latent anger and hostility of Americans toward contemporary life and culture.

THE VOICE OF DISCONTENT

All is not well in utopia. Even though we remain capable of convincing ourselves (and ever-curious foreigners) that we live the king's life, recent studies at our Barna Research Group show that more and more people are plagued by a nagging emptiness that is anchored deep within themselves. It is a crisis of meaning that affects millions of Americans. And because we reap what we sow, it appears that things are likely to get worse before they get better.

America in the nineties is a nation in deep denial. We have figured out ways of compensating for the emptiness and sense of futility that we experience. We do this by dismissing empirical facts. We repress emotional realities. We ignore spiritual truths.

Every community, on either a local or national scale, goes through periods during which it reshapes some of its core values and redefines key behaviors. This is especially true in a dynamic, growing entity such as America. Merely working out the differences involved in maturing as a nation is no big deal. During the nineties, we will increase our population count by more than 25 million people. Our ethnic character is being dramatically redefined. The establishment of a global economy is also reshaping how we perceive work, responsibility, international relations, technology, and politics. Stress and turmoil are natural in the midst of such transitions.

But we're not talking about change that happens in the normal course of national expansion and development. America is beset by a new brand of discontent and uneasiness. It strikes deeper than the ordinary frustrations and disenchantment we have previously recognized and endured, say during the Depression or World War II. The emerging discomfort with life has been building for nearly four decades, although it has only recently begun to be articulated.

The voices of our discontent, represented in this chapter by seven people who have expressed their fears, suggest that the culture we have created is out of control. In spite of all of our knowledge, experience, education, energy, and resources, our nation is essentially without direction. Worse, in those moments when we are strong enough to confront reality, we admit that our cherished American dream and the associated American way of life is now losing its meaning and momentum.

The pain goes even deeper for another reason. We succeeded in creating the society we dreamed of and preached about around the world. It seems that the same dream that motivated us in the past has become the nightmare that paralyzes us today. We thought of having phones without wires to take outside so we could be in constant touch. Now with cellular car phones we cannot escape work and find ourselves busier than ever. The wonder of TV has meant our retreating from neighbors and even family members into isolated worlds of our own.

For decades we prayed that God would grant us our fondest desires. Unfortunately, as C. S. Lewis warned, He did.

THE ALARMING REALITY

"I came out of seminary anxious to save the world. Idealism isn't a bad thing; it can be a powerful motivation that helps you persevere in the face of calamity and trials. But, man, have I had my eyes opened in just twenty years."

David McAllister, age forty-eight, hopes to return to a church as minister one day. But for now he needs a break from the pain that shattered his idealism.

"I pastored a church, a small church, starting as an interim pastor, then becoming the permanent pastor when they asked me to stay and help heal the hurts that were there. I was there for five years," McAllister explains. "By the end, I felt like I was swimming in molasses. People struggle with so much stuff, such deep stuff! I can't help them.

"I was honest with them about it. I told them that I wasn't their solution, only God held the answers to their dilemmas, but that I'd do whatever I could to help them through it. But it was never enough, it was always a minute too late, it was . . . it was just overwhelming. It was hand-to-hand, heart-to-heart, head-to-head combat, twenty-four hours a day.

"I finally had to leave the pastorate. It took me about four years to recover from what I'd been through in ministry. I still feel called to minister, but I have to find a realistic way to do it. People are really hurting."

The pain of his congregation and his own disappointments are due to many negatives now ruling the American condition. As uncomfortable as it may be to address these realities head-on, we must look at the state of our nation.

As you consider the following qualities that define the real America, keep in mind that it is just a sampling. The descriptions may not be pretty, but they are conditions we have to acknowledge and counteract if we are to make progress.

Attitudes

We are a very skeptical and suspicious people. We no longer trust other human beings—often because we know that they probably maintain the same self-absorbed values and goals as we do. We are dubious about product claims, unpersuaded by scientific studies, lacking confidence in the leaders we elected to public office, and judgmental of people who are different from us. People are now deemed guilty until proven innocent, a perverse twist of the justice system upon which this nation was built and one reason why America has more lawyers (in the aggregate, as well as per capita) than any other nation in the world.

Relationships

We live in a nation of more than 260 million people, the third most populated country in the world. We are connected to a global population of almost 6 billion individuals. Yet we are desperately lonely. We cover up that despair by keeping busy—a whirlwind of activity that tires us physically, occupies us mentally, and consumes our resources shamelessly. Our packed schedules prevent us from even having the time to consider whether such a "maximum daily activity" strategy is necessary.

The result of all this is that our personal relationships are becoming more superficial than ever. Families dissolve, friendships move into new phases, work teams are reconfigured—there is less and less permanence in how we interrelate. The dissolution of our relational bonds brings an emotional hollowness that no amount of frenetic activity and mere physical proximity to other people can replace.

Character

We Americans are not often patient people. How do you or your friends react when you choose the "short" line at the grocery checkout line only to find yourself waiting as someone wants an item returned or the clerk asks for a price check? Observe the actions of highway drivers during rush hour or a traffic jam, or listen to the retort of a customer being told that the item they want is out-of-stock.

Oh, we can cite reasons for our impatience: the frantic pace of life, the complexity of our daily existence, and the heightened expectations placed upon us by a growing range of sources. But the result is still the same: America has become a nation of ill-tempered tyrants. We want it all, and we want it now. Perhaps it is the wise man who knows how to pick his fights; but it is the American who decides that all fights are worth picking.

Health

At a time when more than nine of every ten people claim that having excellent health is a high priority in their lives, we find that we are not willing to pay the price for such health. Fewer people are paying attention to the dieting advice they get from doctors, books, television programs, and their bodies. The exercise craze of the eighties has passed. Drug abuse is on the rise again; getting a chemical high has become a higher priority than coping with reality. Alcohol abuse, once common to the adult population, has spread downward to junior high age; in colleges, alcoholic consumption has rebounded in popularity among students. And for some, influenced by sexual passion, sexual contact

OUR DILEMMA

THINGS SHOULD BE SO GOOD. . .

Our attitudes:	Enlightened because of more knowledge
Our relationships:	Better understanding of human interaction
Our character:	Able to give more of ourselves due to progress on many fronts
Our health:	Better due to more discoveries in medicine and nutrition
Our compassion:	More diversity and tolerance
Our wisdom:	Practical application of advances in knowledge
Our technology:	Making life easier and more efficient
Our spirituality:	A new depth due to more scholarship, practice, and experience

. . . YET WE FEEL SO BAD

Our attitudes:	Suspicion and distrust
Our relationships:	Loneliness and surface relationships
Our character:	Impatience
Our health:	Poor diets, substance abuse, sexually transmitted diseases
Our compassion:	Racial intolerance and generational divisions
Our wisdom:	More knowledge but little wise application
Our technology:	More stress
Our spirituality:	Superficial religious activity, cultural idols

with others is no longer considered a health risk, after all, if they wear condoms or are just "smart enough" about their relationships. Sexually transmitted diseases, led by the deadly AIDS virus, continue to invade our population.

Compassion

While we preach brotherhood and tolerance, racial misunderstanding and intolerance are reaching epidemic proportions. Rather than recognize that diversity requires tolerance, we have come to the collective conclusion that diversity requires conformity. Whites, blacks, Hispanics, Asians, and native Americans operate in a sea of mutual wariness and competitiveness. Regional distinctions are suspected rather than celebrated. Some Southerners are still fighting the Civil War against the Yankees, calling northerners uptight, uncivil, and snobbish. Many in the northeast continue to look down upon the rest of the nation as inferior and subservient. Residents of the western states argue that the frontier mentality of progress, exploration, and risk-taking is best and reject all elements of proven tradition. Midwesterners often fall into the trap of self-satisfaction and resist the agents of change and ignore globalism.

Generational schisms have rarely been more overt and better defined. Baby Busters display outright hostility toward the Baby Boomers, claiming that the older generation has abandoned them emotionally, savaged them economically, crippled them politically, and deceived them spiritually. Boomers see Busters as sniveling complainers incapable of rising to the occasion. The older two generations (Builders and Seniors) resent the actions and attitudes of the affluent, powerful Boomers, resulting in a growing number of persons deciding to leave their estates to deserving nonprofit organizations and churches instead of their ungrateful, arrogant children. Boomers, tired of the parochial perspectives and nagging needs of their elders, are often choosing to place their parents and grandparents in institutional care facilities so as not to be personally bothered with, or hampered by, the needs of those elders. And thus the heart of the family is mortally wounded.

Wisdom

We live in a world in which information creates influence and power. There is more raw information available today than ever before, and the mountain of data will continue to grow. But to what avail? Insights into the human experience have not brought a greater level of life satisfaction or community.

The information barrage has led to a nation of people who feel culturally naked, personally disconnected, professionally perplexed, spiritually undernourished, and emotionally uninspired. Although we have the machines and the means to grind out reams of information, we have little grasp of how to humanely interpret that data or to wisely apply the accumulated knowledge represented in the ocean of facts readily accessible.

Technology

Some would argue that the computer makes life easier; that the VCR allows us to control time so we can watch important or entertaining programs to suit our schedule; that microwave ovens, laser printers, and satellite communications enable us to save time; that cable TV knits us into a global village. But most people haven't figured out how to program their VCRs, or master the basic operating system of their computers, or make sense out of the fifty-plus cable channels they already receive. If anything, the same technologies heralded as the means to a more convenient and fuller life have brought on techno-stress. People feel anxiety over being owned by technology, and the fact that the machines have greater capacity than they take advantage of has done little to endear them to the new-age technology.

Spirituality

At the same time that we have broader exposure to a variety of religious faiths, we appear to know less and less about what we believe and why we believe it. America has more religious institutions than any other nation on the planet—more than 300,000 churches, synagogues, and other houses of religious activity. But what difference does it make? We have forfeited our historic ethics and morals to the gods of achievement and comfort. Our moral compasses have been reprogrammed to point to a new north. Our sense of the divine has been compromised so that as a nation we have almost no awe of God or intention of respecting His rules.

We have replaced the presence of God with well-intentioned but superficial religious activity. We have substituted cultural idols for the eternal God. We have swapped the preeminence of the Creator for the centrality and pampering of self. All of these diversions have left us spiritually bankrupt, morally depraved, and ethically uncertain.

Values

The decision-making apparatus of the human being depends largely on the values by which they operate. But even in this realm, Americans have experienced substantial decline. Studies by the Barna Research Group and the Gallup Organization show that Americans today are confused about what is personally important, culturally significant, and morally non-negotiable. They struggle with daily decision making and the policies and lifestyles pursued by the nation because, for the most part, they lack a sound system of values that could serve as the foundation of their activities and pursuits. Americans have ceased to spend their formative years developing the kind of worldview that would help them put information into perspective, leading to defensible and consistent choices.

One immigrant from Hungary described the consequences of Americans' inconsistent values and diminished spirituality during a recent interview with the Barna Research Group. Americans seem "to be so alone," said Andresh Czonka, now a naturalized U. S. citizen living in Illinois.

"Americans are afraid," he continued. "I see the fear in their eyes, I hear it in their voices. They lock their doors. They lie to protect themselves. I feel so bad for the country. But I feel so bad for the individual people; they seem to hurt so much, to be so alone.... My country had problems. But we had an inner strength that is missing here. We had a different group of things we wanted to achieve, different things that we considered important and valuable. I wish this for Americans, to have the inner strength that God can give."

Lacking a consistent value system, most Americans are uncertain about—and even "fear," as Mr. Czonka put it—American policies and what are appropriate lifestyles. Without a sound, consistent set of values, we cannot rationally challenge the decisions made by others because we cannot articulate a reasoned response to the disturbing conclusions of others. Without a stable values system in place, our objections to wrong values lack force and fire; those who pull the strings of power have no need to attend to the emotional ravings of individuals who cannot muster compelling and morally anchored arguments.

VOICES OF FRUSTRATION

Do you sometimes feel overwhelmed by the disorienting and disheartening conditions that have engulfed you? Perhaps you have watched as others around you have agonized over the confusion they feel regarding the meaning of the vast changes now taking place in America today. If you have, you are not alone. That confusion and discomfort is the reigning concern of our culture. It has taken the nation by storm. Only by confronting this debilitating enemy directly can we break its hold over us.

After more than a decade of research among the American people, I have become sensitized to the pain and the anguish caused by our errant decisions. Here are the words of a few of your peers from across America as they describe the emotional and spiritual plague that has overcome our nation. Can you relate to the perspective they represent? Do you hear your own thoughts and words in what they say? Does the frustration of your friends, family, or co-workers resonate with these expressions of anxiety and unclarity?

"No, when you come right down to it, I'm not sure what the point of all this is. I'm not sure why we have to live, or why we should want to live. I'm not suicidal or anything, but then again I couldn't put up much of an argument against someone who was contemplating suicide."

Will Flinn is twenty-four and lives in Bothell, Washington. His cynicism and desire to get by with what he has reflects the lowered expectations of his fellow Baby Busters. "Look," he explains, "I'm going to age in a world where crime, disease, poverty, rotten politics, incompetent government, unethical and insincere religion, environmental decay, and lousy public education are the norm. They're telling me I'm supposed to get excited about waking up every morning to face the daily dose of *this?* And I'm supposed to work hand in hand with the generations of adults who created this mess for me and give them respect?

"I know nobody consciously set out to create this kind of mess. But they did, whether they meant to or not, and now I have to live with it. I am not excited about the future, because it's not a future worth being excited about. I'll never have as many opportunities to get ahead as my parents or grandparents did. Look at their houses, their cars, their vacations, their savings and re-tirement accounts. Man, they've got it nailed. Me? I can't even find a job that pays ten bucks an hour. And I've got a college degree.

"I'm stuck. My generation can't win."

Unlike Flinn, Jesse Malone has finished his working days. The seventy-one-year-old retiree lives in New Jersey and says candidly, "I figure I got about ten more years to live. I'm feelin' good and I take care of myself." And he says New Jersey is a good place to live and "enjoy my days." Still, after seven decades of living in America, he confesses to discontentment and confusion.

"I tell you, I don't understand the world these days. Elec-tronics, relationships, families, money—it's changing too fast and it's so different than anything I ever knew when I was in my prime. Now I'm not saying it's all bad, but you've got to admit, things have gotten a bit crazy these days.

"I think it's all moving too fast. We can't figure it out. It changes overnight. My day wasn't perfect, either, but at least we moved at a reasonable pace. I feel sorry for these young people today because they're just gonna burn themselves out trying to keep up with the world they're frantically creating.

"I keep my distance from all this. Don't need no computers or video players or other new machines. I still read—hey, how many people do that? Everyday, the newspaper, from first page to last page. But people today, they're in too much of a hurry to even follow the daily news and events. We're becoming a superfi-cial society. You can't hold a real conversation with anyone—even if you can get them to slow down enough to grab their ear for a minute!

"I don't know how it's all going to end, but I don't think it's gonna be good."

Californian Sandy Jenkins, age thirty-four, prides herself in her sense of fairness. "I am not a bigot," she says. "I believe we are all equal and were all created to live in harmony and to fulfill some grand design in life. But I simply cannot tolerate the gar-bage that comes out through so many of today's rap songs. These songs preach hatred, violence, sexual abuse, profanity, immorali-ty, a jungle existence. Don't tell me there's a cultural dialectic to be preserved within these songs. They are simply mean-spirited manifestations of the hatred that certain people . . . feel toward the society. I embrace the importance of protest songs, but these diatribes are more sinister than mere protest; they represent a call to hatred and anarchy.

"And I can't tolerate nonsense like [radio talk-show host] Howard Stern. I'm sounding awfully 'far right,' aren't I? I'm not, really. But where is the foundation of decency and righteousness that built this country? Stern has no business being on the public airwaves; his filth is not protected by the Bill of Rights or the Constitution. But the system of justice has been perverted to enable him to use those documents as a fortress to hide behind. . . . We've gone overboard in our desire to be politically correct and sensitive and all-inclusive of weird viewpoints and lifestyles. Somewhere, it's got to stop."

Tanya Jones is only seventeen, but this teenager from New York has been forced to grow up quickly in the city. "It's awful. You can't sleep through the night here, with the sirens and the shouting and the gunshots all the time. I dream of escaping from this place. But I don't know where I'd go. I don't think it's much different anywhere else.

"My daddy left us when I was still little; I was in the third grade. My mom has tried real hard to keep it together, but we've got six kids and she doesn't have much education. She has worked hard all her life and has tried real hard to raise us good. She's done great, keeping food on the table and all of us out of jail. We never been livin' large, or trying to keep up with others. It's been real hard, just makin' ends meet. I love her, but I sure don't want to go through what she's been through.

"It's hard for me, too. A lot of my girlfriends have already had babies. A lot of the boys from school aren't around no more because they're in jail for drugs or for some stupid crime they did. Just about every one of us has been raped or had an abortion or been held up.

"The future? I just want to live long enough to find some peace and rest. To not have to worry about gangs and people breaking down my front door to rob us, and my children being beaten up at school, or livin' in a building with winos and druggies on the floor inside the entry. But I don't think about it much because I know it's just a dream. There's no place like where I want to be, not even in the suburbs. It's just as bad there, but you don't hear about it as much, because then everybody'd be upset and they'd get crazy. I just have to survive as best I can and make the most of my life."

Andresh Czonka, who spoke earlier of the fear he sees in fellow Americans, recalls his hopes on arriving from Hungary and his reality now:

"When I came to this country, I was excited to be an American and to be with Americans. I looked at your country and felt it was the best in the world. And since my childhood I have believed that your country was blessed because of your faith in God and your chasing for the right things in life.

"But now I think differently. I talk to a lot of people when I drive them in my taxi. I am amazed at what I hear. I learn a lot.

"Americans don't have much real faith in God. This surprised me. I thought when the tough times come, Americans make it okay by praying to God and being connected with Him. But this is not the case. Not many people pray. People here think they can do it by themselves. This saddens me, because I am a man of faith. I know I cannot do it except by the grace and power of God."

DON'T TAKE THAT SUICIDE PILL

Perhaps these conversations could all be summarized with a single question: If life is so good, why do I feel so bad? Indeed, the more we analyze the state of our world, the greater the tension that grips us.

There is some heartening news in all of this. Most Americans —regardless of their spiritual, political, economic, family, or professional circumstances—are deeply troubled by the changes for the worse in our country and the lack of purpose in their lives. This recognition that something is amiss lends hope that perhaps we will not continue to repeat the mistakes of the past. Our desire to change present conditions gives hope that we will not pursue the distorted strategies and methods that got us into this disarray.

Most adults are savvy enough to realize that the "good old days" are gone forever. We will not find meaning by returning to the lifestyles of our predecessors. Increasingly, we are recognizing that pursuing the errant paths of the last quarter-century will result only in more dissipation and frustration. There may be a new spirit of adventure emerging that will allow us to be radically redirected. Inner peace and life-fulfillment is possible. However, they will come only after we intelligently and intentionally redefine the thoughts, actions, and beliefs that direct our lives.

THE CHALLENGE

In the chapters that follow, let's explore where we are today in our culture and consider some of the implications of that state of being. And let's not just dwell on the here and now. It will be helpful to reflect on what we might do to make our future merely "sustainable"—a major goal of numerous political and social analysts. Our quest is for substance based on solid values and purposes. We do not simply want to get by; we want to master the possibilities of the day, based on a thorough comprehension of what makes life virtuous and fulfilling.

The primary challenge before us is to identify and restore the sense of purpose that God intended for His creation to have— and from which our sense of fulfillment and joy must come. Be assured that there is reason to have hope and there are rational ways to achieve a modified American dream. It will involve a redefinition of our life goals, the reshaping of our work ethic, a revitalized perspective on faith. Finding the new American dream will require that we return to some traditional viewpoints and behaviors that many people have proudly pronounced to be dead.

Achieving the new vision for a viable America will take deep thought, hard work, and total commitment. The good news is that, with God's blessing, we can reshape that world in such a way that life makes sense and justifies our efforts.

NOTE

1. All names have been changed to protect the individuals' identities. The people and their comments are authentic, however, and are based on interviews conducted by Barna Research.

THE SEARCH

1. *The personal stories throughout this chapter suggest the deep crisis of confidence in our nation. Which of the viewpoints do you identify with and why?*

2. *Surface frustrations and disappointments have been building since World War II due to a major, core reason: "a crisis of meaning," an emptiness anchored deep in the human soul (page 20). How can we regain meaning in our lives?*

3. *We have experienced profound changes in eight areas, including values. Review those eight areas. How does the values area play a role in the other seven?*

4. *One of the eight areas that has undergone change is spirituality. What cultural idols have we substituted for the prominence of God?*

5. *Some of those interviewed say life has no purpose in the midst of material and scientific advancement. What deep needs and problems have the latter advances not been able to solve?*

POINT OF ACTION

There is much division among generations and races, and schisms exist along spiritual and geographical lines across America. Choose an individual from a group other than your own to get to know and love.

PART 2

THE STATE OF THE NATION

A labor negotiator will propose a settlement only after he has gathered all the facts. Similarly, we need to examine the trends that characterize life in America in the mid-nineties before we look for answers. Therefore this section offers a plausible perspective on America—not what it used to be like or what we wish it were like, but what we experience day after day.

In order, we will explore (1) the changes in people's values and attitudes, which influence our assumptions about people, institutions, lifestyles, and beliefs; (2) the American political scene, which merits evaluation simply because the United States is a land where increasing numbers of tasks are being designated as legitimate functions of government leaders and institutions; (3) the role of faith in an increasingly secularized culture; (4) how we accumulate and spend our wealth, operations that reveal the realities of generational conflict over values and other external conditions; and (5) our relationships, by which other people influence our views and behavior.

Finally we will consider the most enduring—and perhaps the most important—social institution we have: the family. In this age of the nouveau family, the fundamental support system for every individual has been revised in ways that sometimes boggle the mind. The changing roles and relationships between husbands and wives, as well as the new threats to children, are having a major impact on our society and personal lives.

CHAPTER 3

A CHANGE OF HEART

Jason Torrey has been working at his profession for close to two decades, ever since graduating from Boston University. When we interviewed him regarding values in America, he shook his head and chuckled. "It blows your mind. You read the newspaper each day and there's something else, some major event happening, that just doesn't make sense. And yet, in a weird way, it's not surprising. You can't really predict it, but you can't really be surprised, either. The values, the morals, the ethics, the convictions we have are just so bizarre."

It is getting harder all the time to discern right from wrong in America. If truth and justice used to be black and white, they are decidedly gray these days. Where we used to respond or make a decision in most circumstances without a second thought, these days we often pause to reflect on the new rules that guide America.

Jason, like most of us, is puzzled by the new world in which Americans live. The source of people's bewilderment is not the confounding arsenal of technology that has so rapidly become indispensable, but the values that are reshaping our world. Those new values have created an environment in which what once was unthinkable has now become the norm.

Consider the task of earning a living. At a time when the median salary among professional baseball players has risen to $1.1 million a year (as of 1993), more than 30 million people are living below the poverty line. And at a time when professional basketball players pull down an average of $1.2 million for playing eighty-two games during the regular season, one in nine Americans is poor.[1]

Our values concerning money and worth seem out of sync. The average salary earned by a chief executive officer (CEO) at an American manufacturing company is 119 times more than the workers in those manufacturing plants earn. And recent reports indicate that the top-dollar man of the year was, again, Disney chairman and CEO Michael Eisner, who earned more than $200 million in 1993—the same year in which the average household income in the U.S. declined for the third straight year.[2] Meanwhile, back in the world of sports, Chris Webber, a highly sought after college basketball player, signed a fifteen-year contract with the Golden State Warriors for nearly $75 million—before he had ever played a single game as a professional.

In contrast, the average annual salary of teachers across the nation was $34,100. The average starting salary of college graduates—the peers of Chris Webber—ranged from $21,600 for social science majors to just under $35,000 among engineering students.[3]

Consider our value system regarding sex, where "safe sex" before marriage is more widely accepted than no sex before marriage. Premarital sex is virtually endorsed by the government, when U.S. Surgeon General Joycelyn Elders and a host of public school administrators warn teens to use condoms and avoid having too many partners in order to reduce the risk of getting AIDS or any of a vast array of sexually transmitted diseases. The surgeon general and other leaders advocate "safe sex" as the means of preventing the spread of social diseases, rather than promoting the only true type of safe sex—no sex, or abstinence. In a nation where most parents express anxiety about their children becoming sexually involved at an early age, the public school system in New Haven, Connecticut, blazed a new trail by making condoms available to ten-year-olds who request them.[4]

Many parents seem to have encountered their own moral dilemmas when raising their children. A majority of parents complain that television and many of today's movies contain too much sex, violence, and profanity. But then we note that the parents themselves are gaining fulfillment through exposure to such media. One week recently, *Billboard* magazine reported that among the ten top-selling videos in the nation, four were produced by *Playboy* or *Penthouse.* Howard Stern, the original "shock jock" whose radio program is filled with sexual innuendo and other brazen language and social commentary, has become one of the most popular radio personalities in the nation. His book, *Private Parts,* quickly rose to number one on the best-seller lists.

Thus adults fight inconsistencies in what they say to their children and what they do in private. Currently, in fact, although we feel the need to protect children from pornography and other forms of sexual perversion, a majority of adults reject the notion of legislation that would prohibit the sale or distribution of pornography.[5]

Business practices have come under fire recently for demonstrating a lack of consistent ethical standards. Harvard Business School instituted a business ethics course in the eighties, and John McArthur, dean of the school, warned graduating students in 1989 not "to go through life focused only on No. 1."[6] The reason people have less confidence in the ethical standards of businesses than they used to is obvious, as convictions among business professionals for insider trading, stock fund manipulation, and such white collar crimes as embezzlement climbed during the eighties.

The punishment for such crimes seems limited. Consider the case of Michael Milken, who made a fortune—reportedly billions of dollars in the eighties—for illegal practices concerning the sale of junk bonds. Eventually charged with financial misconduct, he was found guilty and spent several years in prison and paid one of the largest fines ever exacted from an individual. But after serving a shortened sentence, he was released and allowed to keep millions of the fortune he gained through trader manipulation. Today he is back in mainstream America and has taught a popular course at UCLA in—ironically—business practices.

Even our judicial system has turned family values on its head. Children can now sue their parents for personal freedom from parental rule. One criminal was injured while attempting a robbery and sued the organization he was vandalizing for negligence; he won more than one-quarter of a million dollars from the suit. Another person claimed she lost her psychic powers when injected with dye during a CAT scan and won close to $1 million dollars in damages.[7]

How have we reached such decisions about money, careers, sexuality, business practices, and the law? Most people are oblivious to the fact that the decisions we make are significantly influenced by our values. However, what we say and do is filtered through a grid of personal values that determine who we are and how we handle life.[8]

The values to which we cling are freely chosen, but they are based upon a wide range of influences that enable us to recognize, understand, and process our reality. As a group of "evaluative attitudes," these core beliefs leave a mighty imprint on us—and upon other people, too. Values shape our personality, our moral views and reactions, our theoretical notions of the world, our responses to cultural forces, and even our handling of the mundane affairs of daily life. Our values do more than shape our character; they also provide us with the parameters and perspectives that allow us to express who we are to others.

But as central as our values are to the lives we lead, most people are unable to describe them. In fact, at Barna Research we have found that most adults have spent little time consciously analyzing their values. People's value systems most often evolve in an atmosphere of neglect. The values we embrace tend to be spawned on the basis of our gut-level reactions to the exigencies of the moment, resulting in actions that coincide with a body of poorly conceived convictions.

Typically, we are uncomfortable focusing upon or talking about the values that drive us. "Values aren't something you *think* about," complained one woman, "they're something you act on. If you want to know my values, just watch how I live my life. But I don't stop and think about it, I just do what I do because of who I am and how I perceive the world around me. Studying values is like trying to nail Jell-O® to a tree; you just can't do it, because they weren't made for that purpose."

There is a wisdom in approaching the study of people's values with some caution today. If you ask people to explain the what and why of their values system, little substance rises to the surface. A direct assessment of our values may be useful and healthy, but it is difficult to engage people in a meaningful discussion of the topic, precisely because values are a fluid and amorphous component of our character and activity these days.

Getting a firm grip on our values is difficult today, for reasons we will address in a moment. But we need to persevere in the task of understanding the operating values of our culture if we are to comprehend the current state of the nation and determine how we arrived at our present state. For the values we have used as the guidelines for decision making are at the heart of our cultural chaos and moral confusion.

SEISMIC SHIFT IN VALUES

During the last quarter century, America experienced a major transformation in its values orientation. The shift has, in key ways, been at the heart of the numerous cognitive, emotional, and spiritual transitions that have reshaped America.

Historically, America was a nation whose citizens clung to a group of absolute values as the moral and social foundation of the culture. As the nation developed in adherence to its Judeo-Christian foundation, we accepted a range of biblical precepts as the boundaries of our thoughts, words, and deeds. Even if we did not perfectly conform to those standards, at least we recognized a defined, broadly accepted boundary of propriety. As human beings, we knew that we would not live perfect lives; some of our decisions inevitably would be ill-conceived, and some of our actions ill-chosen. Our collective values system, however, was the one element that enabled us to know when we were going astray and allowed us to reap some degree of personal satisfaction when we were operating in line with those values.

That values system came under attack, however, during the late sixties, a period of societal foment and personal angst. People began to consciously challenge the foundations of the values we had embraced for so long. The outcome was a new way of thinking, which resulted in a new style of life. The consequences of those shifts in thought and action are what we struggle with today.

THE DISCOMFORT OF CHANGING VALUES

But we are struggling not only with the consequences of a values shift, but also with the core issues that make it unsettling to address the question of changed values.

Americans are not a reflective people. We are reactive. We chide those who take time to study options as suffering from "analysis paralysis." We deride people who probe too deeply as being "armchair lawyers," individuals too insecure in themselves or too fearful to make a confident choice. More often than not, Americans pride themselves on rapid response to a condition or challenge. Rarely do we stop to realize that an intelligent and rapid response to a challenge is only possible when we already have in place the values necessary to focus the choices we will make.

Challenging the foundations upon which we make choices causes many people to feel exposed emotionally and cognitively. We generally do not want to consciously consider our values or their implications. Most of us gladly ignore the whole discussion of values, assuming that our values are a "done deal," an issue settled once and for all long ago, and not something we need to address again. Bringing up values creates uneasiness because values pose basic questions about who we are and why we act as we do.

Yet we must examine our values. When we do so, we will recognize that we are in a transitional phase. When you shift from one set of values to another, the fact of the transition is important but also uncomfortable. For most people, change is difficult to endure. But change at the most fundamental levels of one's personality and perspective is a serious matter. As America reforms its basic personality attributes in light of new information and a new understanding of social rules, many individuals are becoming skittish about the ramifications of adopting a new values system.

A second matter of significance is accurately articulating those revised values. To properly identify our current values, we have to deal with basic questions: What values will we now embrace? What values are we choosing to reject? Who makes the decisions of what to accept and reject? Why are we changing from the values that have been held for so long?

We must answer those questions, for a change in values has practical consequences for our behavior and therefore the quality of our lives. So let's examine the ongoing changes.

THE OLD SCHOOL

America has moved out of the era of traditional values. Currently, we feel more comfortable with values that are less anchored in social consensus and global benefit, favoring those that emphasize personal desire and personal benefit. This move is what one analyst calls a jump from orthodoxy to progressivism.[9] It is a switch from a time when there was no question about what we believed and how we would behave in response to major threats and challenges to a period in which there is little predictability because the underlying worldview that once informed our actions has been changed dramatically.

Consider the reliability of our earlier values. We stood firm on several characteristic attitudes:

1. *Money.* Though we did not view money as a virtue in and of itself, we saw money as the primary means of determining the tangible worth of something.
2. *Trust.* We trusted people on the basis of past experience, personal reputation, or an earned position of influence.
3. *Loyalty.* We saw loyalty to people and to organizations as a standard matter of behavior, based upon mutual consideration, depth of character, and consistency of perspective, without regard to personal gain.
4. *Relationships.* Our relationships formed an important cornerstone of society and a valuable component in one's personal stability and development.
5. *The welfare of others.* When faced with a choice between doing that which would benefit the community or that which would only benefit self, we assessed the needs of the community as more important.
6. *Commitment.* A person's word was his or her bond. When a commitment was made, that commitment would be lived up to, even if it meant sacrificing the pleasures or benefits of other opportunities of more recent vintage.
7. *The long-term view.* The dominant perspective was long-term; short-term considerations were valued primarily insofar as they gave a better understanding of how to make better or more worthwhile long-term decisions.
8. *Helping the needy.* We saw excessive blessings as providing an opportunity to help others who were less fortunate. We saw providing tangible assistance to those in need as a major purpose of a democratic government and a free nation.

9. *God at the center.* God was the center of all moral and spiritual truth and the final judge of all matters. Our responsibility was to live in ways that reflected His fundamental principles, handed down to us through the Bible.

10. *Absolute standards.* There were absolutes to be respected and accepted; consensus was not accepted as the proper approach to identifying right and wrong.

The very purpose of life, under the old system, was generally agreed to be the desire to live in harmony with God and His creation, toward achieving a satisfying life on earth, in preparation for eternity with Him apart from this world. Religious faith, particularly one's beliefs about Jesus Christ and how His death and resurrection would impact a person's eternal condition, was a central factor in the development, understanding, and application of values. The Protestant work ethic, as it was called, was a high-profile offshoot of that worldview, extolling the virtues of hard work and the faithfulness of God to bless His people and their efforts.

"WHY DO WE BELIEVE WHAT WE BELIEVE?"

Toward the end of the sixties, however, America was exposed to a frontal assault on all of the values it had cherished for so long. Normally, such a reevaluation of cultural fundamentals results in a healthy debate that enables those who raise the challenge to discover the depth of reflection and meaning inherent within the entrenched system. But in the sixties the generations who stood for the status quo were poorly prepared to defend the traditional values of the nation.

The group that challenged the status quo was the generation we have come to know as the Baby Boomers. In the desire to understand their world more fully and to make better decisions, the Boomers persistently hammered away at the foundations of the prevailing culture.

They asked their parents important questions: "Why do we believe what we believe?" "Why do we behave as we do?" "How did we arrive at the convictions we hold dear?" Unfortunately, the Boomers did not receive clear or satisfactory answers. As a result, many coming-of-age Boomers concluded that the values held by their parents and grandparents were no longer relevant or meaningful in an age of new beginnings and new frontiers.

During that formative period, a cadre of social reformers raised questions and proposed novel answers to some very fundamental realities. Some of the reformers were widely accepted, people such as John and Robert Kennedy, who eloquently and passionately articulated a new way of perceiving the world and personal responsibility. Others struck a different but no less responsive chord with many, as personified by such social and political activists as Abbie Hoffman, Michael Harrington, Herbert Marcuse, Bob Dylan, Betty Friedan, and Malcolm X.

Feeling the freedom to rethink their basic precepts about life, the Boomers energetically created and integrated alternative philosophies and perspectives into their own lives. America was simultaneously waging two bulletless battles: the Cold War with the Soviet empire and the Values War, a revolution of the heart among the people of the nation.

THE FAILURE OF OUR ELDERS

The values revolution would never have occurred if the older generations had been more adept at defending the traditional values that had served America so well for so long. Why were the older generations unsuccessful in persuading the Boomers of the wisdom and utility of the existing values system?

In retrospect, it seems that America had experienced so much of a good thing that its citizens, including parents, had become anesthetized to it. It had been so long since a serious examination of the nation's values had been undertaken, and societal progress had seemed to move forward with such ease and simplicity, that the underlying values of the culture were taken for granted. It took powerful, life-changing events to shake the nation out of its cultural complacency toward the prevailing values set. The murder of three cultural icons (the Kennedy brothers and Martin Luther King), the nation's dubious involvement in the Vietnam conflict, the growing visibility of urban poverty and blight, and, in particular, the sheer boredom and assumed irrelevance of traditional religious activities and their failure to stimulate young people began to raise questions about our purposes and our philosophies.

When pressed to defend their values, older Americans, the gatekeepers of the prevailing values system, gave the impression of simply protecting a hand-me-down structure of values and be-

CHANGES IN VALUES	
TRADITIONAL	**NEW**
Money related to true worth	Time is now true worth
Trust based on reputation	Self-protection and suspicion
Loyalty without personal gain	Loyalty to one's self first
Committed relationships	Relationships of convenience
Benefit community over self	Self first, community second
Your word was your bond	Word shifts with circumstances
Investment in the long-term	Investment in short-term
Wisdom of ages valued	Tradition dismissed
God the center of all matters	Humanity the center of reality
Absolutes governed right and wrong	Relativism governs morality

liefs. To a generation seriously searching for meaning and purpose, statements such as "Because that's the way it is," "That's how we've always done it," "There are some things you just don't question," and "That's the way God ordained it" were inadequate, superficial reactions to important queries.

Older adults proved incapable of mustering zeal or depth in their explanation of their values. When pressed, they became flustered or angered: how dare the younger generation question that which had been sacrosanct for decades. The Boomers were unimpressed by the righteous indignation of their elders. After all, they had been taught, in the very schools their elders had erected, that a strong democracy is one which encourages debate, introspection, and meaningful response. To the Boomers, a system that denied people the opportunity to investigate the moorings of the culture was a culture that had no reason to exist.

OUR NEW VALUES

Jump ahead two decades to the nineties. What you find is the Boomers now responsible for the values that dominate the thinking and the activity of our society. No longer waiting for the caretakers of the culture to step aside, the Boomers have obtained control of the levers of power and authority in America and have conspicuously and persistently moved to craft a society that reflects the values they see as being responsible and helpful.

Just what are those values, and how do they differ from the more traditional perspectives they have replaced? Here are ten elements that typify the nineties' values.

1. *Time over money.* The dominant indicator of the worth of something these days is no longer money, but time. In a fast-lane society, time has emerged as the single resource of which we never have enough, the one which is nonrenewable, the factor for which there is no adequate compensation. Even the machines we develop are largely geared to maximize or multiply our time: VCRs, voice mail, answering machines, personal computers, laser printers, cellular telephones. Attention spans have diminished, media which require oodles of time are less popular (e.g., reading), and even our service-based economy is now built upon gaining access to the time of another person. Money is still important, but it seems more accessible now. We embrace those entities that respect our time and exude efficiency.

2. *Distrust of people.* The entire relational atmosphere in America has shifted so that we feel foolish placing our full trust in other persons. We are now skeptical of the motives and statements of other people, regardless of their track record or our depth of relationship with them. The consequence is a lifelong trail of broken relationships, a sophisticated paranoia about the methods and motives of organizations, and a cynical view toward those who rise to positions of influence or authority. Since we perceive organizations to be doing sub-par work, to have inferior motives, and to have no conscience, we have lost our sense of loyalty to people and to organizations. Instead of demonstrating care and concern for others—a "you-first" attitude—we have moved to a "taking-care-of-number-one" mentality.

3. *Revised ethics.* Living in a period of skepticism, with a news media built on sensational stories and "digging for

dirt," people now believe that the only wise course of action is to question the ethics and the motives of others. Misusing information, or conveying information in a deceptive manner, is no longer deemed automatically wrong. The ends justify the means these days.

4. *Devalued people.* Traditionally, we saw people as an end in themselves; today, we are more likely to view achievements and material possessions as the goals, and people as mere means to those ends. Consequently, relationships remain important, but for a very different set of purposes: personal gain or enjoyment. Relational stability has moved from being a core value to a bonus.

5. *Less concern for the welfare of others.* We now view community service as a luxury rather than a responsibility. With government stepping up its programs, we feel exempted from having to serve other people's basic life needs. We can give money to nonprofit organizations and have them handle such chores. In fact, attitudinal studies show that people give because they want to help others, but the value received is in feeling good about self rather than alleviating the suffering of others. The bottom line decision in any choice between community service and another activity is based upon the relative, personal advantage derived from any of the efforts undertaken.

6. *Distortion of truth.* Honesty has taken on a new meaning these days. A large and growing proportion of the population believe that lying is often necessary; that distorting the truth is OK if it doesn't hurt others; and that bending the rules for personal gain is a common and generally acceptable practice. Gone are the days when you knew that you would be expected to live up to the commitments you made. The idea that we might sacrifice pleasure or personal benefit for the good of others is regarded as unfair and certainly unacceptable.

7. *The short-term view.* These days, it is assumed that you will operate on the basis of short-term gains. With the culture changing quickly, and competition getting more fierce than ever, it is believed that short-term considerations are the most important. The long-term is viewed

as simply the cumulative effect of good short-term activities.

8. *Questioning of traditions.* Americans are unwilling to accept tradition as a valid determinant of lifestyle or perspective. The wisdom of the ages is viewed as the foolishness of this age; everything must be proven valid, over and over, and every tradition must justify its existence anew.

9. *Finding the spiritual truth within.* God has been replaced as the center of moral and spiritual truth. Now, each person is given the task of dictating truth and justice and wisdom according to his or her own principles and perspectives. Rather than accepting responsibility for living in concert with basic biblical standards and admonitions, we now create our own customized ideas of what represents moral sensibility and is ethically appropriate, of what guidelines constitute the means to and the heart of truth.

10. *Consensus over absolute standards.* The concept of absolutes as something to be respected and accepted has been replaced by the notions that consensus and personal preference are the more sane ways of determining right from wrong, good from bad, and the meaningful from the meaningless.

Even our understanding of the purpose of life has undergone a seminal shift. Living in harmony with God and His creation is now seen as mere religious sentiment. Life assumes meaning when you can control the environment and gain some type of temporary emotional fulfillment. Unlike the old days, when most Americans believed in objective, absolute means to fulfillment, the new way of thinking says, "Live for the moment. Grab for all the tangible goods you can acquire." In the process, many Americans conclude they can use whomever or whatever they can to build a world of happiness and comfort for themselves. The work ethic, so deeply rooted in America's faith and lifestyle, has taken a backseat to the play ethic, which extols the virtues of rest and relaxation and has given birth to an astoundingly complex and comprehensive leisure industry.

THE NEW SLATE

The accompanying chart shows several dozen values that have risen and fallen in importance over the past half century. Notice that there are relatively fewer values that can be deemed descriptive of contemporary society. That is because Americans no longer have a consensus concerning values. Instead, the individual values system is the norm; there are fewer commonalities in what Americans deem to be proper for society at large.

The division between traditional and progressive values is obvious. Those who hold a more conservative and traditional point of view regard the values ascribed to the former days as laudable in contrast to the empty and less virtuous values of the current day. Those who accept the prevailing views of the day regard the current roster of values as fitting and commendable.

One middle-aged man from the Southwest whose personal values parallel those of the 1990s rather than those of the 1950s put it this way: "Sure, it's different than it used to be, but so are the life conditions. Some of the old values just aren't possible these days; others are nice, but impractical. You've got to have a values system that works for you, not one that hinders you by always placing you at odds with your world."

This emphasis upon having pragmatic values, rather than timeless values, has changed attitudes and actions in most social and economic areas, from public policy to family relationships and traditions. (See chart on next page.) Even career and employment decisions (including, for management, profit versus employee issues) are affected by the emphasis on pragmatism. The outcome has been largely a population that believes in personal entitlement; a nation that dares not challenge the warped thinking behind "political correctness" lest we be branded anachronistic and insensitive; and a culture in which we cry out that we have been victimized and must be given some means of redress when our desires or expectations have not been met.

THE DANGERS OF TRANSIENT VALUES

Social scientists have observed this phenomenon and drawn similar conclusions. Robert Bellah and his team of researchers spent years creatively investigating the motivations, priorities, and perspectives of Americans. In their ground-breaking research on individualism and commitment in American life, they

DEFINING CHARACTERISTICS: HOW DOMINANT VALUES HAVE SHIFTED, 1950–1995

CHARACTERISTIC	dominant? 1950s	1990s	CHARACTERISTIC	dominant? 1950s	1990s
Overt desire for moral purity	✔		Social harmony	✔	
Belief in redemptive Jesus Christ	✔		Personal integrity	✔	
Bible as guideline	✔		Loyalty	✔	
Maximize pleasure		✔	Commitment to people	✔	
Experiences are key		✔	Fulfillment of responsibilities	✔	
Self-discipline	✔		Diversity of opinion		✔
Servanthood	✔		Value of consensus		✔
Shared purpose	✔		Maximum choice		✔
Community	✔		Personal compassion	✔	
Nationalism	✔	✔	Achieve comfort		✔
Technical knowledge		✔	Adhere to tradition	✔	
Sexual fidelity	✔		Respect for elders	✔	
Convenience		✔	Spiritual wholeness	✔	
Innovation	✔	✔	Equality of people	✔	✔
Excellence	✔	✔	Be in control		✔
Rest/relaxation		✔	Hard work	✔	
Personal security	✔	✔	Importance of family	✔	
World peace	✔	✔	Economic thrift	✔	
Balance in life	✔		Exhibit courage	✔	
Emotional appeal		✔	Personal, powerful loving God	✔	
Protect time		✔	Financial gain	✔	✔
Personal happiness	✔	✔	Humility	✔	
Sacrifice	✔		Self-control	✔	

drew many conclusions about the illusory nature of the heart-beat of the public. One of their determinations, however, was that values are "the incomprehensible, rationally indefensible thing that the individual chooses when he or she has thrown off the last vestige of external influence and reached pure, content-less freedom."[10] The application of such values to everyday living has generally resulted in mere "radical individualism," Bellah said, and he noted that the current wave of self-focused values provides people with little clue as to how to live with purpose and fulfillment.

One of the seductive traps of this new way of life is that we sometimes come to believe that we can validate our values by whether they achieve the outcomes we desired. Such thinking has been fostered by various public education curricula, New Age philosophers, Christian leaders who preach the "prosperity doctrine," and business gurus who confuse values with profits.

Ideally, our values would be a well-conceived, internally consistent series of convictions and beliefs that help us under-stand the world and operate meaningfully within viable bound-aries. But Bellah and company, as well as others, have demonstrated that what we have created in place of proper val-ues is a self-justification system in which we do what we feel like doing at the moment and scurry to find a plausible and popular platitude that will support such behavior. What we have done is replaced values with emotional impulses.

"My parents don't understand the way I think or the way I live," says Rudy, a twenty-year-old from Georgia, who moved to southern California to break into the movie business and who now waits on tables during the day and seeks auditions by night. "Still, every time I do something that doesn't fit with the way they think, but then can show them how it resulted in something that moved me closer to my goals, they can't fight it. If it wasn't right, it wouldn't work."

Rudy is a typical example of an individual who means well, but who acts first and thinks later, analyzing his behavior in light of its consequences. This type of superficial response to en-vironmental stimuli and options often passes for values but be-trays a misunderstanding of the very issue at hand.

Amitai Etzioni, the eminent sociologist, has been deeply troubled by this movement away from standard values. He views America as suffering mightily for its venture into the new values arena. "We need an awakening of values, of caring and commitment," he explained. He is part of a group of scholars and social leaders who front for something known as the Communitarian Movement. Born in 1992, the movement is devoted to restoring venerable rights and related responsibilities to our culture.

"In the 1960s we broke bonds. We got rid of a lot of old ideas and institutions that were racist and sexist and should have been eliminated. But we destroyed the good with the bad, like respect for the family and for community. We were left with a moral vacuum, which people have tried to fill with 'me-ism,' materialism—all kinds of things that don't work." The problem, he says, relates to basic morality. "People became reluctant to make moral judgments, to say something was right or wrong. Everything was considered an individual choice, and all values were seen as equal."[11]

He and his growing contingent of values-sensitive individuals are proposing a restructuring of common values to promote healthy community and lifestyles which support the needs of the nation, not just the individual. "It's time to talk about balancing rights and responsibilities, to bring back the idea of community standards."[12]

"I DIDN'T DO IT"

Etzioni, Bellah, and others all agree on one crucial aspect of moral values: we Americans no longer are willing to accept responsibility for our actions. Not only have we redefined the things that matter most to us, but we have also moved away from accepting responsibility for the consequences of our actions. In an increasing number of instances, we're refusing to admit when the fault is ours—even when the evidence is clear-cut.

This epidemic of finger-pointing has intensified the turbulence in our culture. People want to blame others for their own faults and miscues and to be exonerated of any wrongdoing they personally may have committed. This has generated severe interpersonal conflict between virtually every configuration of people groups: between parents and children, between generations, between consumers and retailers, between political officials and the governed, between the affluent and the poor, between racial groups, and between the police and the public.

Think about the following actions and excuses, so typical of the nineties' reaction to being asked to accept responsibility:

1. Paul Tsongas runs for the presidency in 1992, claiming he is physically fit, but is later discovered to have lied about that claim. His retort is that people would not vote for him if he had come clean, so it is the rotten political system that is to blame.

2. The Menendez brothers murder their parents in California, then boldly claim that it was their parents' own fault.

3. The president of American University is caught making obscene telephone calls from his office, but he argues that he wasn't really to blame since he had been abused as a child.

4. The abysmal late-night talk show hosted by Chevy Chase is mercifully canceled by the Fox network, only to have Chase blame the network for insisting on a particular format.

5. A ten-year-old burned down his parents' house after watching a video that portrayed the same actions. His parents stood by him, criticizing the video as having caused such aberrant behavior in their little darling.

Cultural critics have various terms they use for this recent development. Charles Colson refers to the general loss of heart among Americans, and their lack of remorse over such moral deterioration, as the "death of conscience." Colson, a lawyer who counseled President Richard Nixon and was found guilty for his role in the Watergate fiasco, converted to Christianity in the mid-seventies and today is a lay minister to prisoners worldwide. He attributes the rise of crime in America to the frequent rejection of responsibility and the apathetic attitude of Americans toward accountability for just behavior.[13]

Charles Sykes, an author and journalist, describes America as having become "a society of victims." In his eyes, we have become a nation whose values shift has left us ready "not merely to feel sorry for oneself, but to wield one's resentment as weapons of social advantage and to regard deficiencies as entitlements to society's deference."[14] Sykes' studies have uncovered the new battle cry of the American adult: "It's not my fault."

Perhaps this refusal to accept responsibility for our thoughts, words, and actions should come as no surprise. After all, the values from which we have distanced ourselves, and even the values to which we have gravitated, virtually guarantee that we shirk any blame for what transpires in our midst. When the values we embrace redefine God in ways that are designed to fulfill our needs rather than to clarify truth; when we substitute the unbridled search for pleasure for the quest for righteous character and behavior; when we replace virtues such as hard work, thrift, respect, and courage with compromises such as consensus, sensual satisfaction, and convenience, what other possible outcome might we expect?

ABSOLUTES ARE ANATHEMA

Perhaps the bottom line is what our research first noted in 1991 as being a cornerstone of the cultural demise: the rejection of absolute moral truth. Our most recent studies have found things to be getting worse rather than better. Today, three out of every four adults do not even believe that there is such a thing as absolute moral truth, much less have any shared agreement as to what it might be or how that truth might be determined.[15]

Americans see values as their private domain; there is no sense of having a bedrock of fundamental virtues that are timeless and valid, regardless of the cultural icons and preferences of the day. Values have become one of the hallmarks of individualism in our culture.

As a result, any attempts to identify even a handful of non-negotiable truths for all people in all situations is viewed as intellectually ludicrous, emotionally stifling, and politically incorrect. Sadly, such thinking has even invaded the political process and has begun to undercut the American democracy, as we shall see.

NOTES

1. *Los Angeles Times*, 9 September 1993, C2; (Los Angeles) *Daily News*, 18 October 1993, S2; *Daily News*, 25 September 1993, S2.
2. John Byrne, "That Eye-Popping Executive Pay," *Business Week*, 25 April 1994, 52–58.
3. *Statistical Abstract of the U.S. 1993* (Washington, D.C.: U.S. Bureau of the Census, 1994), tables 245 and 289.

4. Karla Schuster, "Condoms for Fifth Graders?" *USA Weekend,* 28 November 1993, 18.

5. George Barna, *Virtual America* (Ventura, Calif., Regal, 1994), chapter 7.

6. "Harvard School Swaps Money for Principles," *Dallas Morning News,* 1 October 1989, 7H.

7. Charles Colson, "Legality Without Morality," *Jubilee,* March 1993.

8. There are numerous works which have compelling and enlightening discussions about values. Among those that are most readable include Hunter Lewis, *A Question of Values* (San Francisco: HarperCollins, 1990) and Robert Bellah et al., *Habits of the Heart* (New York: Harper & Row, 1985).

9. Though he approaches the topic from a different angle, James Davison Hunter has provided an interesting critique in *Culture Wars* (San Francisco: Basic, 1991).

10. Robert Bellah, *Habits of the Heart,* 75–81.

11. Michael D'Antonio, "Tough Medicine for a Sick America," *Los Angeles Times Magazine,* 22 March 1992, 32–37, 50.

12. Ibid.

13. Chuck Colson, "Where Did Our Conscience Go?" *Focus on the Family,* January 1994, 12–14.

14. Charles Sykes, *A Nation of Victims* (New York: St. Martin's, 1992), 10–11. Sykes argues persuasively that America is increasingly fragmented by the fear-based, self-protective whining that we are being exploited on all fronts. Such complaints, Sykes says, cause people to retreat out of fear and rage, rather than interact with hope, vulnerability, and understanding. Such fear has entered a culture that had once fostered community through shared virtues and values.

15. George Barna, *Virtual America,* chapter 4. The 1991 findings of Barna Research are contained in *What Americans Believe* (Ventura, Calif.: Regal, 1991).

THE SEARCH

1. *If money in any way reflects value, the high salaries of sports stars, entertainers, and CEOs demonstrate that we esteem these individuals above such wage earners as teachers, social workers, ministers, and police officers. Why do you think we are willing to pay celebrities and our heroes so much more than those who can improve our minds and souls?*

2. *Many Americans, like the woman quoted on page 40, are uncomfortable talking about personal values. Why do you think Americans are hesitant to either describe or analyze the shifting values in our culture?*

3. *The values of the previous generation have been radically altered today, especially in the areas of relationships, possessions, and time. Summarize how values in these three areas are different today.*

4. *We no longer accept the wisdom of the ages, or even responsibility for our own actions. What other current factors within the individual and in society will make it difficult to return to traditional values?*

5. *What is wrong with the idea of living out our own personal values system as long as we are sincere, consider others, and don't harm anyone else?*

POINT OF ACTION

Choose one person this week who does not share your values system. In an area where you are living out a set of values, attempt to explain the reasons to him or her.

CHAPTER 4
A SLIDING DEMOCRATIC PROCESS

French statesman Alexis de Tocqueville visited America in 1831 to examine our democracy and determine what made it so durable, productive, and cherished by our citizens. His keen observations were recorded in *Democracy in America*, a classic that remains required reading for students in many government and political science classes. He identified several unique and compelling qualities related to our government. One distinctive was that the people generally felt listened to and genuinely cared for. Another strength was that people felt they could reasonably place their faith in the elected leaders who served for the benefit and welfare of the masses.

If Tocqueville were to return today, he would have to radically revise his analysis. His reflections captured the resilient and optimistic spirit of the Americans he saw. Today, that spirit has been shackled. Americans have little trust in the people they elect to represent them. Surveys measuring the degree of confidence we have in politicians show two firm trends: the levels of confidence in the moral character, job performance, and motivations of elected officials are very low; and those levels are continuing to sink lower with each passing year.

In fairness, we must acknowledge that people's dissatisfaction with the political performance of their leaders and systems is not confined to America. One recent multinational survey showed that of the leaders of the seven major industrialized nations—Italy, France, the United States, Canada, Germany, Great Britain, and Japan—only one of the leaders from those nations had an approval rating above 50 percent in his country.[1] But among the American public a general feeling pervades that politics just isn't working.

A. J. Atkins recalls how special he felt as a nineteen-year-old when Congress lowered the voting age to eighteen. He voted in every election, from local to national. "Now I don't even keep track of when the elections are," he says. "It's an absolute joke. They do what they want as soon as they get into office. You don't hear from them again until it's reelection time, then suddenly they're your best friends and they've been out there doing your bidding. I couldn't be much more cynical about the process."

Another American voter, Donna James, claims "they just don't care, they just don't listen." For several years Donna has had an ongoing battle with government agencies at the local, state, and federal levels. She's upset with her leaders in Mississippi and in Washington, D. C.

"I can't stand it anymore. Now you tell me, what am I paying my taxes for if they can't even work with me to solve my problems? I'm told by my employer that I have to deal through the government, but it's impossible. They lose paperwork, they move slowly, they talk in some kinda doubletalk, they don't care about you as a person."

At times, democratic politics has worked well, as leaders have searched for and facilitated remedies to public problems. In its purest form, politics, through the governmental processes it spawns, is the means by which we resolve societal conflicts and public crises. Every political system has its problems, but when the political machinery is in high gear and running smoothly, the public mood is light and positive.

Too often, however, modern political activity in America degenerates into self-promotion, selfish gain, and public posturing. A bureaucracy intimidates some Americans, enrages others (like Donna), and leaves the rest of us shrugging our shoulders. Although there are individuals whose tireless commitment to true public service courageously defies this distortion of politics, political energy is frequently devoted more to winning elections and defending abstract ideologies than to understanding and addressing the true needs and concerns of the people. Meanwhile, many bureaucrats try to hold onto their positions while offering limited or delayed service. Judging from the way many democratic leaders behave, politics in the nineties is the art of serving self rather than the blessing of serving others.

If Tocqueville were able to inquire about the eroding confidence in the character and motivation of elected officials, some defenders would point to the negative influence of a force that has come to power during the last half of the twentieth century: the news media, especially television. The electronic and print media incessantly bombard us with the latest tales of political skulduggery. The residents of the White House, whoever they may be at any given moment, are constantly challenged by new questions and revelations about past and present behaviors. Confirmation hearings for appointees to federal government posts— individuals who have already been carefully checked out by those promoting the nomination and judged as being "clean"— often result in the unearthing of sordid and seamy secrets that inspire the writers of the daytime TV soap operas to become more bold and creative. And tales of congressional corruption have been trumpeted through investigations and trials that at times have found a leader not guilty; yet the mere repetition of charges has strongly implied that a crime has been committed.

THE LOSS OF DIGNITY

But even defenders of government leaders must agree that during the past two decades a series of crimes and misdemeanors have soured the public on government. The electorate was disgusted in the early seventies when Vice President Spiro Agnew was forced to leave office because he had engaged in illegal financial activities. A couple years later they were shocked, embarrassed, and angered when the president of the United States, Richard Nixon, resigned from office over his role in the Watergate cover-up. Years later, a penitent President Nixon admitted "I let the American people down."[2]

Those events tended to revive belief in Lord Acton's pithy observation: "Power tends to corrupt and absolute power corrupts absolutely."[3] More importantly, though, these events initiated a new era of the media as political watchdog and ushered in a new layer of government: committees and organizations charged with the responsibility of ensuring ethical government.

But instead of prompting self-correction and cathartic relief, Watergate—a story of spying on political enemies, covering your tracks, and telling lies—was a catalyst for increasingly common and more sophisticated acts of dishonesty and subversion. It also introduced the era of microscrutiny, in which the media (and, to a lesser extent, the public) assumed the dual role of character judge and morality police. The heightened sensitivity to the moral and ethical behavior of elected officials produced a curious result. On the one hand, more examples of dubious public service than ever have been uncovered, resulting in the indictment and exposure of numerous representatives of democracy for their acts of moral treason. On the other hand, after a brief period of fascination and frustration, we typically return the rascals to office.

Think of some of the high-profile political representatives whose names have recently been dredged through the mud of suspicion, accusation, and, in some cases, confession or condemnation. Congressman Dan Rostenkowski was stripped of his position as chairman of the House Ways and Means Committee after a federal grand jury indicted him on seventeen felony charges dealing with misusing government funds and accepting kickbacks; as of this writing he has decided to run for reelection and stands a good chance of being reelected. Senators Gary Hart (sexual misbehavior), Joseph Biden (plagiarism), and Alan Cranston (savings and loan scandal) remained on Capitol Hill amid charges and in some cases confessions of wrongdoing.

Meanwhile, Washington, D.C., Mayor Marion Barry (drug abuse) and one-time presidential adviser Clark Clifford (BCCI scandal) have defended themselves in court, and Supreme Court nominee Clarence Thomas had to defend himself against charges of sexual harassment before a Senate committee and a national TV audience before he was finally confirmed as a justice (and deemed innocent of the charges).

The path of suspicion even winds to the White House, where President Clinton has been accused of sexual misconduct and First Lady Hillary Rodham Clinton has had to defend the propriety of her investments.

And many government leaders have been found guilty of wrongdoing. During the eighties seven members of Congress were convicted of crimes ranging from bribery to conspiracy and tax evasion.[4] The list of leaders in the nineties could include numerous congresspersons who abused the congressional banking and postal system; military officers involved in the Navy Tailhook affair; and the literally thousands of state, county, and local officials who have been caught in a variety of dubious or illegal practices.

No wonder that in just the last twenty years we have experienced an anchor-like drop in confidence in all of our political leaders. The proportion of adults who have "a great deal of confidence" in our congresspersons has declined to just 7 percent—that's a 71 percent decline in just two decades![5] Trust in the president varies wildly, from administration to administration and event to event, but in 1993, less than one out of every five people, on average, possessed a great deal of confidence in the chief executive. The stalwart in public confidence, relatively speaking, is the Supreme Court. About one out of every three adults professes to have a great deal of confidence in the highest judicial body.[6]

INSTITUTIONAL INDIGESTION

Americans are not simply expressing a distaste for the individuals whom they have chosen to lead and implement. There is an ever-deepening rejection of the institutions through which these elected and appointed representatives operate. The very system which we originally set up to serve the people is now viewed as a monster with a life—and agenda—of its own.

Take the federal bureaucracy. At the turn of the century, libertarians cried that the government was too massive for the good of the nation. At that time, almost one-quarter of a million people were on the federal payroll. Those activists must be turning in their graves today. The federal government now employs 3 million people. For the first time in history, more people work for the federal government than are employed in our entire manufacturing sector.

The federal government has become a disliked entity not merely because of its size, but more so because of its gross incompetence. The most common concern is the federal budget, which has become a source of jokes for comedians. But the public, which bears the brunt of financing all federal activity, has little to laugh about. Our annual budget for the federal government is nearly $1.5 trillion, most of it funded through our tax dollars.

What makes matters worse is that the hundreds of billions of dollars received by the federal government each year is not enough. Rather than operate through a system funded by the money that is available, government leaders have operated on the basis of deficit spending—a spending strategy that the common person is prevented from practicing. In the last two decades, during which the magnitude of the debt has become front page news on a repeated basis and a major campaign theme for politicians seeking electoral support, the debt has increased more than tenfold, jumping from an outrageous $381 billion in 1970 to an unfathomable $4.3 trillion in 1993. The interest payments alone on this staggering debt load is $120 billion every year. That calls for about $1,200 in taxes per household every year just to maintain the interest payments. The United States may be one of the world's more enviable economies, but it has also become the world's largest debtor nation.

Many citizens have read the tales of the National Aeronautics and Space Administration, the Department of Defense, and other federal agencies spending thousands of dollars for a hammer or a screwdriver. And the citizens' distrust of government is fueled by reports of the perks granted to members of Congress and other political officials: free vacations, home improvements at government expense, lavish meals and parties, free travel, even free parking at airports. The media love to highlight examples of government inefficiency. It's not hard to uncover grist for that mill.

FACTS ABOUT U.S. GOVERNMENT

Taxes equal four months' personal income

Federal debt of $4.3 trillion

18 million federal and state government employees

Confidence in Congress down 71 percent

$1 billion on political campaigns

Interest alone on national debt totals $120 billion each year

Apart from irritation at being represented by a government that is so flabby and out of control, why are Americans so profoundly disgusted at the cost of all of this? Because each one of us is expected to pay his or her "fair share" for the excesses, deceit, and inefficiency. To support the habits of government spenders, the average person spends the first four months of the year earning enough money to cover his or her personal tax liability. In contrast, in 1930 the typical adult devoted one month of wages to covering tax obligations. Most people are not opposed to paying taxes if they feel they are receiving value for that investment. But eight out of ten Americans do not feel that they receive their money's worth from their government.[7]

Many citizens equally resent the government's increasing control of their lives. They regard government as an all-consuming beast driven by an intangible but persistent organizational inertia. And their argument seems strong: even when ideological conservatives have held control of the reigns of the federal government, government regulation has expanded.

If the fruits of regulation were good, such as reduced crime, better public education, safer roads, a healthier environment and reduced poverty, the American people probably would not feel so exploited. But many have discovered that regulations have reduced their options, cost big bucks, and limit their pursuit of the values and lifestyles they desire. Such government is rightly regarded as offensive.

WHERE WENT POLITICAL INTEGRITY?

As the media have reminded us of the importance of virtue and values in our leaders, the absence of integrity in our politics has become acutely apparent. Indeed, the phrase *political integrity* has become an oxymoron.

Contributing to the lack of integrity is the cost of campaigning on the federal level, whether for the U.S. presidency or for the title of senator or representative. Elections are no longer won; they are bought. In 1992, more than $1 billion was spent by candidates seeking election to a federal office—and that only counts the spending *reported* by the candidates. Influence peddlers—political action committees, corporations, lobbyists—spent more than $300 million on those campaigns, for no other reason than to win friends in significant policy-making positions. These friends-of-the-candidate are generally forthright as to their motives for their benevolence. A prime example is convicted banker Charles Keating, who candidly answered a reporter's question as to whether he expected his generous campaign contributions to well-positioned politicians to buy him legislative influence on issues that concerned the banking community: "I certainly hope so."

Sadly, our political system has shifted its focus from governance to self-preservation. That helps to explain why "spin doctors"—the communications consultants and public relations agents who filter and put a positive skew on information for public consumption—are valued members of the political team. But when the people see through the deception, it further undermines the credibility of not only the villain, but of the entire system.

And there's an element of outrage over the deceit inherent in so many levels of the government game. People no longer know what is truth and what is fabrication. For instance, so-called spending cuts are often spending increases dressed up to look like cuts. Consider this explanation of federal budgetary thinking, provided in an editorial from the Mobil Corporation.

> Here's how the government calculates a spending cut. Assume the government is spending $100 million on a program in 1993, and is aiming to reduce future costs of that program. Rather than beginning from the $100 million spending level as its baseline measure, the government calculates how much it would cost in 1994 if the program remained precisely the same—with spending increases based upon inflation, growth in services, and other elements that would otherwise automatically go into effect factored in. On that basis the government figures 1994 costs would be $105 million. Then, in its new budget plan, it allocates $102 million to the program. Like magic, an actual increase of $2 million becomes a $3 million "spending cut." A business or household that operated on such accounting principles would go under in no time.[8]

Capitol Hill veterans have a storehouse of examples of budgetary excesses and deceptions. One of the most common is for the savings realized by cutting back in one area of spending to be quietly plowed into another program area—the infamous "carve-and-spend" philosophy most recently championed by the Clinton administration. As one White House aide explained, "We carve money from one department or program, make the public announcement of the savings, then apply those moneys to other programs we promised to develop."[9] The multitude of crafty strategies for fooling the taxpayers has done much to erode the public trust in leaders and the system.

POPULISM OR ELITISM?

One explanation for the slide in integrity among our leaders is the shift from being a democracy governed by a relative handful of elites to a democracy in which the public demands greater input into the decision-making process.

During the first two centuries of America's history, a relatively restricted number of individuals managed the political process (e.g., policy development and implementation, electoral authority, and campaign parameters) and worked both behind the scenes and in the public eye to establish community standards. People were welcome to vote for whomever they pleased, but the "old boy network" reigned regardless. Once the votes were counted, all that really changed was the identity of the political party that held the upper hand during a given period. The seasoned political pros from each of the parties jointly shared the decision-making apparatus and guided the unfolding of the aggregate governance process in spite of election results and public mandates.

During the sixties, however, the basic assumptions about the political process were radically challenged—and eventually altered. As the issue of equality exploded onto the scene and arrested the center stage, the distribution of political power was undermined in new ways. The decade of turbulence established the politics of segmentation, in which every splinter group, advocacy agency, and demographic subgroup arose to seek its equitable measure of recognition, resources, and influence.

Suddenly, the politically disenfranchised and powerless were players to be taken seriously. The range was awesome: women, blacks, homosexuals, the physically handicapped, veterans, Hispanics, singles, evangelicals, fundamentalists, Jews, children, senior citizens, and many others—all gained access to the reigns of power and began to exercise their newfound strength in unforeseeable ways. This began the era of what *Megatrends* author John Naisbitt has termed "the era of participatory democracy."

THE SHRINKING POWER PIE

This recasting of the basic rules of the game, however, created a debilitating development. Each of the groups ushered into the political arena obtained relatively little influence for itself. Instead, the power pie was sliced into a myriad of tiny slivers, each recognizable but inconsequential by itself. The cumulative effect of this decentralization of power was the stalling of the political machinery.

When the handful of elites ruled the roost, one thing was guaranteed: they would stumble forward deliberately and predictably, even if it was only their own limited and self-satisfying agenda they were pursuing. Their actions were a direct outgrowth of the values and philosophies they had created and cherished. Many people complained that the goals of these barbarous officials were not in tune with the will and heart of the people they were called to serve. Those complaints fell upon deaf ears. But change did occur as the power players did what was necessary to maintain peace, progress, and personal political prominence.

As unsatisfying as the old style was, at least there was predictable movement. In contrast, modern politics is paralyzed because we have so many players, each with only a small power base, and is thus cumulatively undermined by the absence of consensus regarding values and ultimate ends. The elites, who used to rule the roost, receive little deference these days. But in their place we have yet to establish a smooth process for mediating the conflicts that inevitably erupt in a system characterized by differences rather than similarities.

Unlike the decades in which politics produced solutions, the politics of the nineties mostly produces friction and frustration. That can be attributed partially to a political world crippled by various ethnic and social voting groups that replaced a largely homogeneous population. Beyond segmentation realities, though, we suffer from a heightened emphasis upon immediate gratification and short-term goals rather than on building for a better future and meeting long-term goals. Further, we are restrained by the ascendance of special interests rather than an agreement to work for the common good.

THE RAVAGES OF RELATIVISM

Once again, we also encounter the ravages of relativism intruding in the process. Under the elite system, whether the values that sustained policy decisions and political decisions were representative of the public mood was irrelevant. What mattered was that there were clear, if sometimes warped, values that permitted decisions consistent with those values to run their course through the political labyrinth. You pretty much knew what you were getting and what you could (or couldn't) do about it if you didn't like the results.

Under the new populist system, however, there is no overriding agreement on goals, values, methods, or purposes. The consequence for those engaged in political and governmental affairs is moral, ideological, and policy gridlock. In fact, what we have tagged "participatory politics" in the nineties has become the politics of complaint more than the politics of productive involvement. People provide more verbal input than ever in the form of ideas and complaints but are less active in productive ways, such as voting. Since the early seventies, only half of the voting age population has actually cast a ballot in the presidential elections; other elections typically draw fewer than one out of every four registered voters to the polls, while many of the statewide initiatives and referenda are decided by small minorities of voters.

That is not to say that the ways of elitist democracy were perfect, or even preferable to what we have on our hands today. No, during the first two hundred years of the republic we experienced a good share of corruption, poor judgment, inept performance, public deceit, and idled progress. The values systems underlying political efforts were sometimes errant; the operations designed to implement policies sometimes ill-advised. Millions of Americans were disenchanted with politics then, as now. Small thinking and special interest maneuvering have been evident all along.

The issue, however, is the manner in which Americans have understood and handled those conditions. In the current environment, we speak of the virtues of pluralism but demonstrate little tolerance for those whose interests and methods conflict with our own. Without the equivalent of an old boy network to make the tough decisions on our behalf (i.e., cutting deals and making compromises that conform to the participants' unique view of a better future), we are left to our own devices to develop suitable substitutes for those individualistic efforts.

LACKING THE TOOLS

The problem is not that the American people are incapable of making government and politics work. The problem is that we simply don't have the tools to play the game at the level required. The basic democratic model could certainly be adapted to modern needs to create an adaptive, smoothly functioning and innovative system of governance. The barrier is that the people, who now hold a larger stake in the process itself, are limited by the resources available for deployment. Consider just three of those limits.

- *Americans are poorly informed about the substance of issues.* Media coverage tends to provide a lowest-common-denominator perspective on policy matters. The nineties have ushered in the era of the sound bite, where we gain much of our insight from a few choice words edited for television, void of their full context. Lacking a deeper understanding of the details and the nuances of critical issues, most people are incapable of deducing how to respond appropriately to the myriad of policy options clamoring for attention and resolution.

- *Most adults have a very restricted range of policy and governance interests.* People who focus on tax issues often ignore foreign policy matters. Those who enjoy reflecting on social welfare matters may well nod off during interaction related to commerce regulation. Thus, even though people have opinions on a range of subjects, their depth of knowledge and interest in those policy and governance arenas is appallingly thin.

- *We are so busy with other lifestyle and career pursuits that relatively few people really understand the implications of what they claim they want.* In a fast-paced, competitive society in which we're busy looking out for our own best interests, few stop to ponder the longer-term or society-wide ramifications of having certain personal desires or interests met.

The frightening truth is that Americans continue to clamor for responsibility and authority without having sufficient levels of trust, comprehension, and involvement. At the same time that many Americans are demanding a greater voice in the process of change and governance, they are largely complacent regarding many aspects of political decision making and fail to take advantage of the opportunities that currently exist to provide input.

WHEN OPINION POLLS LIE

Clearly one reason we feel so bad about our times is the lack of good government. Sadly, even the public opinion polls, the so-called voice of the people, can contribute to poor government. You can't pick up a newspaper or listen to an evening newscast without hearing about the results of some survey. George Gallup, the father of public opinion research, was fond of noting that such research was healthy for the nation because it enabled government officials to remain in touch with the feelings of the people they represent. His view was that surveys brought back the value of the town meeting in the political process. In Gallup's view,

> the newspapers and the radio [and television] conduct the debate on national issues, presenting both information and argument on both sides, just as the townsfolk did in person in the old town meeting. And finally, through the process of sampling referendum, the people, having heard the debate on both sides of every issue, can express their will. After 150 years, we return to the town meeting. This time, the whole nation is within the doors.[10]

Gallup believed that "in a democratic society, the views of the majority must be regarded as the ultimate tribunal for social and political issues." An advocate of the people, Gallup and the army of public opinion researchers who have capitalized on his innovations have strenuously argued that opinion polls would be among the tools that would help shape and inform the political process.

Undeniably, good research can be a breath of fresh air in the smoke-filled rooms of the political deal-makers. Survey results have been one of the most effective means of alerting elected leaders and career bureaucrats to the needs and the preferences of the American people. The extensive attention given to poll results has even had the effect of awakening the American people to some issues about which they would otherwise have remained ignorant.

Unfortunately, public opinion polls are used for more than keeping in touch with the heart of the people. They can become tools of manipulation, especially by the many elected leaders who base their decisions not on what's best for the people in light of a comprehensive philosophy of life but on what's best for the reelection prospects of a politician. Armed with polling data that estimate the direction and intensity of people's opinions on the subject, many politicians will avoid the hard road of legislating in ways that conflict with people's desires, even though the policies supported may be best for the long-term security of the nation. Instead, some will use polling statistics as their motivation and justification for pandering to public desires, even though those leanings may have discernible long-term, negative consequences.

Reliance upon public opinion surveys may well be one of the reasons that political ideology is so confusing these days. The old labels of *liberal, moderate,* and *conservative* have less meaning today than at any time in the last fifty years. Political candidates no longer think through a coherent worldview that helps them to organize information, analyze conditions, and arrive at a reasoned, logical conclusion. The traditional approach—to vote your conscience—has been largely replaced by the admonition to vote your constituency's current whims as determined by the latest survey. Thus, we have officials voted in as "conservatives" who support increased spending, extended government regulation, and new government programs. We have "liberals" who support aggressive military action overseas and reduced government spending. This inability to gauge a candidate's true ideological bent has been one more of the reasons for discomfort by an electorate baffled by political proceedings these days.

One of the most unfortunate consequences of the fascination with and increasing reliance upon polls is that they can be so easily manipulated. The danger is not only that survey results will be skewed—through improperly worded questions, improper sampling techniques, biased data interpretation, and a myriad of other distorting factors—but that people's opinions themselves are swayed by what they perceive to be the preferences and opinions of a majority of other people.

Is using opinion polls as a major decision-making influence —one way to measure the will of the public—really harmful? Sometimes it is. The public at-large rarely studies the issues carefully and generally has no philosophy of policy making or governance to act as a decision-making filter. Its opinions are based on a handful of sound bites screened and promoted by a biased media and often have little depth.

Research professionals have provided ample evidence that many of the reactions treated as solidified public opinion are not truly reflective of what people would state if they were even slightly better informed about the issues being measured. Typically their stated opinions are coarsely formed ideas and still-in-process thoughts that would never have been expressed publicly had it not been for the intrusive research process itself. When these "phantom opinions" are used as a basis for shaping public policy, it can be detrimental to the well-being of the nation.

THE NEW POLITICAL ARENA

The end of the twentieth century has introduced an entirely new political arena. It is an arena in which people want more influence in decision making, but have a limited appetite for the details of most policy and issue debates. Those whom they have chosen to represent them in government positions use every tool available to assess people's opinions, attitudes and reactions, but often abuse such insights in the quest to justify their reactions to political opportunities.

It is an arena in which the distinctions between ideology and pragmaticism are blurred, and a time when people's confidence in both the system and those involved in the system is eroding rapidly. Although technology has given the average person access to greater input, the complexity of the issues, processes, and human motives behind the legislative and governmental processes have dampened the direct correlation between an individual's input and political output.

It is a time when people have every right to feel disoriented and ask, "If things are so good, why do I feel so bad?"

NOTES

1. "The G7 Summit," *Time*, 5 July 1993, 13.
2. "The Rise and Fall and Rise of Nixon," *Newsweek*, 2 May 1994, 79. President Nixon made the comment during a 1977 television interview with David Frost.

3. *Bartlett's Familiar Quotations*, 16th ed., 521:5.

4. Elaine S. Povich, "Capitol Offenses," *Chicago Tribune*, 5 June 1994, 4:4

5. These data are from tracking studies conducted by the National Opinion Research Center, Chicago, as reported in the November/December 1993 issue of *The American Enterprise*.

6. Ibid.

7. *OmniPoll*, 1-94, a report published by the Barna Research Group.

8. "The Numbers Game," *Newsweek*, 11 October 1993, 7.

9. Frank Greve, "Administration Exaggerating Savings," Knight-Ridder Tribune News Wire, 27 November 1993.

10. David W. Moore, *The Super Pollsters* (New York: Four Walls Eight Windows, 1992), 58.

THE SEARCH

1. What are some of the key reasons that we are losing confidence in our political leaders?

2. The budget and number of employees in the federal government continues to escalate. Why are they not able to more effectively solve the nation's problems?

3. We have moved from governance to self-preservation (page 66). Why is this the case and what effect does and will this have on our democratic process?

4. How have the political methods of many special interest groups radically changed our democratic system? (See pages 67–69). If minorities are better represented, how can the politics of fragmentation have negative consequences for the average American?

5. Public opinion polls help alert leaders concerning the views of the American people. What ways are polls used that might be detrimental to the governing process?

POINT OF ACTION

Find out who your elected representatives are on all levels of government and let them know your views on key issues.

CHAPTER 5
NEW FAITH
FOR A
NEW AGE

Kids ask the strangest questions. Take four-year-old Anna Fay. Her mother, who we'll call Judith, was an avowed atheist and determined to raise her child as an atheist, too. Until Anna's grandmother died, that is. The question of death puzzled Anna, so she quizzed her mommy about why people die and what happens to them after they die. Addressing those innocent but deep questions was like dodging "metaphysical shrapnel," Judith recalled. "It forced us to reexamine our own beliefs and to consider, between improvised answers, the potential effects of those beliefs on her."

But Anna wasn't content to learn only about death. She raised probing questions about life, too. Her mother struggled with those inquiries. "You never really understand how handy the story of Adam and Eve is until, barely grasping the matter yourself, you've explained evolution to a four-year-old and been rewarded with 'But how did the first person get born?'"[1]

In another part of the country the birth of Tara Wold would send her parents, Ray and Phyllis, into a faith search of their own. But it wasn't because of Tara's questions about meaning and purpose in life. Tara was just one day old when it struck her parents that they'd better start focusing on some of the more eternal questions of life.

"We were sitting there in the hospital talking about what it was going to be like raising her in the next twenty years. Suddenly, we realized we were going to have to explain a lot of real basic stuff about life to her—and then we kinda stared at each other in a panic and realized we didn't have any idea what we believed about most of this stuff! We started to rethink a lot of our views and life philosophy at that point, knowing that the day's coming when Tara will be asking some tough questions. We want to be ready. Not just for her, but for all of us. It's been a frustrating, but a valuable learning time for Ray and me."[2]

Warren Billingsley comes at spiritual matters from a different angle. He is not a Johnny-come-lately when it comes to religious matters; he has always been keenly aware of the spiritual dimension and a student of religious factors. He majored in religion and philosophy at a secular university. Immediately afterward, he enrolled in a theological seminary and spent three years enjoying his studies before graduating with honors. Then he assumed the role of pastor of a small Protestant church in the Midwest. After four years of frustration, he moved into an associate pastor role at a larger church in a metropolitan setting. He became even more disillusioned and left the full-time ministry.

Today, Warren sells insurance and makes a handsome living. But he freely admits to being deeply troubled by his faith journey. "I had such high expectations of sharing my spiritual knowledge and passion with others. When they weren't into it, it really depressed me. Then I moved to the city to try to focus my efforts on discipling individuals and small groups of people. But even then, I was let down by people's superficial emphasis on God and faith." The disappointments of his ministry greatly impacted his personal spiritual development after he left church work. "I guess I was more influenced by them than they were by me. These days I attend churches off and on, and I regularly read the Bible, but it's almost out of habit. This is one of those desert periods for me—and it's gone on for a long time. But I know that faith is a critical dimension of a full life, and I am looking forward to reclaiming the spiritual thirst and excitement that made my twenties such a wonderful time in my life."

The experiences of Beth McBride could fill a book in themselves. Born into a devout Catholic family, she departed from Catholicism when she left for college. After four years of sorority parties and good times, she tried Eastern religions as a means of "self-expression and inner peace." After her first failed marriage (there have been three so far), she sought solace in fundamental Christianity. For several years she toed the line at a traditional, highly regimented church of about seventy people before acknowledging her own anxiety over the black-and-white nature of that church's teachings. She was disillusioned, but not shattered. "Life goes on," she explained.

After some spiritual drifting, she wound up meeting regularly with a small group of people who adhere to what some would consider New Age spirituality. "I never gave up on the spiritual side," she proclaimed proudly. "My quest was to find meaning and truth that worked for me. I still have friends from all of my past associations and religious experiments, but now I feel that I'm on target for me." She meets with her group every week at a local restaurant, where they talk for hours, sharing stories and experiences and relating them to an eclectic mixture of religious views. They explain things through such concepts as karma, reincarnation, meditation, prayer, nature worship, and self-awareness. They are serious about gaining insights into the spiritual realm; they constantly read and dissect religious classics by a broad range of authors. In the past year alone, they have read and discussed works by M. Scott Peck, Carl Sagan, Carlos Castaneda, Thomas Merton, Louise Hay, Emmett Fox, John Bradshaw, and Marilyn Ferguson. "I am getting more in touch with myself and my inner being all the time. I am at peace with the cosmos."

THE SEARCH FOR SOUL

America in the mid-nineties is a nation desperately searching for meaning and purpose in life. Millions crave the type of inner peace and spiritual security that the major religions all promise to their followers. The problem is that the majority of Americans, in spite of having been part of various religious groups throughout their lives, have been left empty by their faith experiences. Still driven to satisfy that inner longing, their search continues.

Most Americans identify themselves as "Christian." However, the very term has lost its original meaning. In the modern context, to be a Christian in America is virtually synonymous with being American; it is seen as a birthright to be labeled a Christian. Two out of three adults these days still consider the

United States to be "a Christian nation." And four out of five adults still consider themselves to be Christian, even though most of them confess that they do not have a relationship of any real depth with God, with Jesus Christ, or even with a church.[3]

Americans have seemingly developed a comfort with Christianity. Long ago Christianity ceased to be a source of healthy challenge to one's morals, ethics, goals, lifestyle, or worldview. Mounting evidence suggests that our religious beliefs are less focused today on the transcendent and more focused upon the mundane. And that is why most Americans—and many Christians—feel so bad when it comes to their daily personal lives. They are unable to focus on God's care and recognize His involvement in their world.

CHRISTIANITY, AMERICAN STYLE

Consequently, American Christianity, like population demographics, has come to be viewed as a hierarchical quality, not unlike age, educational achievement, or household income. To many people, the Christian world can be divided into levels of Christian commitment, with all of the people in the top four levels being spiritually equal in God's eyes, and only the fifth level, that is, non-Christians, being distinct in His eyes. In this hierarchy, the more devoted one is to the Christian faith, the higher on the continuum he or she stands. Here is how the continuum looks:

Level 1: Raving religious zealots. These are the fundamentalists and evangelicals. They study the Bible, constantly attend church, give away large portions of their money to church work, and even talk about their faith most of the time—sometimes with people they don't even know. They take the Bible at face value and perceive personal spiritual growth to be a cornerstone in their lives.

Level 2: Born-again Christians. These followers of Christ are also driven to know and serve God, but they are not quite as aggressive about their faith as Level 1 Christians. Their primary thrust is to have a personal relationship with Jesus Christ. They, too, are generally involved in the life of their church and have very strong feelings about Jesus Christ and the importance of Christianity in one's life.

Level 3: Run-of-the-mill Christians. Typical Americans, these people were raised with regular exposure to a church and still frequently attend one. They believe in God, own a Bible, and give money to their church, but they are less intensively committed to religious growth and activity. They do not have (nor understand) a "personal relationship" with Christ.

Level 4: Cultural Christians. A growing sector of the population, these people have a nominal faith in Christ and a loose connection to a church. More than anything, cultural Christians have inherited their Christian perspective and moorings, but they do not take matters of faith too seriously. Easter and Christmas are good times of the year to check in with the church and see that things are going along as always. Being American pretty much makes them Christians, they figure, so as long as the nation is in God's favor, so are they.

Level 5: Nonbelievers. These people may believe in something, but it is not the historical Christianity upon which America was built. This group ranges from adherents to other faiths (such as Judaism, Buddhism, Islam) to people who do not believe that there is a higher power or universal life force (i.e., atheists).

These days, the shape of the curve is still changing. Some church historians claim that America was formerly dominated by people in the top two levels of the continuum. Today, we estimate that the evangelical/fundamentalist strata contains roughly 10 percent of the population; the born again group, excluding those in the top level, constitutes another 25 percent or so. Levels three and four comprise about 50 percent of all adults. The remaining 15 percent are the folks who maintain atheistic or non-Christian beliefs.

DIVERSE DENOMINATIONALISM

Apart from the spiritual perspectives of people, most Americans freely associate with some type of religious institution or organization. And when it comes to examining the religious institutions on the horizon, the landscape is littered with options from which Americans may choose. Most religious organizations define God as impersonal and distant or a loving God one can know without having to come to Jesus Christ.

But Americans who choose genuine Christianity will find a faith calling for a personal relationship with God through His Son, Jesus. There are two primary paths that Christians may pursue. The Catholic Church remains the religious monolith in America, the religious choice of an estimated 50 million adults. The alternative is the Protestant brand of Christianity, which has seen its most prolific expansion and development in the United States. There are more than two hundred Protestant denominations in America, offering a spectrum of worship styles and belief systems. Altogether, Protestantism claims more than half of all adults in this country, totaling an estimated 110 million adults. The range of involvement in Protestant churches varies widely, from the large Southern Baptist Convention, a loose federation of about 38,000 churches and some 15 million members, down to tiny denominations such as the Schwenkfelder Church (five churches, cumulatively attended by less than 3,000 people).

Other religious movements exist in America. There are numerous New Age sects, none of which has blossomed into a full-blown movement on its own, but which collectively encompass several million followers. Mormonism (formally known as the Church of Jesus Christ of the Latter-Day Saints) has continued to attract millions of people—the latest count is above four million members. What is not as widely known, however, is that the Mormon faith also loses huge numbers of people every year, a pattern which has caused the once-striking growth of that church to level off. Eastern religions have a toehold (Buddhism and Hinduism are the largest), while the Islamic faith remains relatively small but growing in size.

Judaism is the faith that has the most disproportionate cultural influence given the number of adherents it has (an estimated 2 percent of the population). It is estimated that there are more than three hundred other "minor" faith groups that have a discernible following nationwide. Certainly, America is not a nation lacking religious alternatives for the people.

A CHRISTIAN BEGINNING

America has been called a Christian nation because its first settlers were believers in Jesus Christ who came to escape religious persecution. The pilgrims who first arrived in New England were seeking freedom to practice their religion. America was thought of as the land where they could escape the oppressive rule of the British monarchy and worship independent of the king's influence and regulations. In many ways, the religious quest of the settlers was an extension of the Reformation, in which people rejected the corruption of the Roman Catholic church and sought to return to the basic tenet of Scripture, rule by God alone.

In creating the boundaries of the nation, the authors of America's Constitution were greatly influenced by the scholarship of Samuel Rutherford. He was a fiery Presbyterian minister from Scotland whose book *Lex, Rex* was banned and publicly burned in the British Isles. A central theme of his writing was that no person, whether he be the king or another recognized leader, had authority superior to God. Rutherford's views were not appreciated by George III, but they resonated with the religious views of most of the early settlers. Another prime influencer was William Blackstone, a British jurist whose book on English law became an indispensable manual for the colonists as they struggled to identify a workable set of guidelines for their fledgling nation.

The ideas of these seminal thinkers lived on through the efforts of men such as John Witherspoon and James Madison. Ultimately, the Constitution reflected the fundamental principles espoused by Rutherford and Blackstone, namely that America was a nation that believed in a supreme Creator who remains active in people's lives; that the Bible is the highest authority; that government must be evaluated in light of Scriptural principles and standards; and that God created all people as equals, and though we are all fallen creatures, we possess specific, inalienable rights.[4]

America has probably never been a nation in which a majority of its citizens had a personal relationship with Jesus Christ through which they relied upon Him, and Him alone, as their source of eternal salvation. However, historical documents make clear that Christian values and principles permeated the culture of early America. For close to two centuries, it was understood that the Bible was the final authority against which all legislation, public policy, and social reform were to be measured. Even those people who had doubts about Christianity generally accepted its teachings as the core philosophy on which the nation was governed.

THE HUMANIST INFLUENCE

As time passed, however, the religious heritage of the nation became less of a guiding influence on matters of public policy and lifestyle. By the time the Civil War ended in 1865, America's Christian foundations had been substantially challenged and persistently replaced by humanist thought and behavior. Darwin's theory of evolution gained widespread favor. The commercial success of J. D. Rockefeller, J. P. Morgan, Andrew Carnegie, and others fueled the latent desire of Americans to prosper materially. Rampant lawlessness, excessive drinking, and self-determination went a long way toward undermining the Puritan ethic that had once been so ingrained in America's culture.

The intervening century, from the Civil War to the Values Revolution of the 1960s, saw the Christian church in America undergo countless tests. From slavery to prohibition, women's rights to two world wars, the Depression to prostitution, there were enough issues of foment to keep the clergy and those committed to the church constantly on guard. After a surge in church planting, the Christian churches of America entered a period of stagnation during the early part of this century, followed by a brief resurgence after the Second World War, and then a precipitous decline from 1960 onward.

CHURCH VERSUS STATE

Perhaps the most significant development during that period was the acceptance of the notion that America needed to be freed *from* religion, rather than freed *for* unlimited religious independence. Led by an activist and antireligious Supreme Court in the early twentieth century, the doctrine of separation of church and state was reinterpreted to mean that America was to be a land in which the rule of the state is supreme and the church but a seen-but-not-heard-from party. Supreme Court Chief Justice Charles Hughes made this abundantly clear in 1907 when he proclaimed the perspective of his court: "The Constitution is what the judges say it is."[5] Since that time, more and more justices have ruled that the Christian faith shall not receive the same freedoms the creators of the Constitution originally intended and that are routinely granted by the Court to other lifestyle activities and philosophies.

DECLINE OF ATHEISM

In spite of the legal and political roadblocks constructed to the affirmation of Christianity, one religious response that never caught on in the U.S. has been atheism. Madeleine Murray O'Hair and others have energetically beaten the drum for atheism, but this perspective has never caught fire. Its high point has been the catchy phrase attributed to German philosopher Friedrich Nietzsche: "God is dead" (although someone has said that God has already responded by saying: "Nietzsche is dead"). Today, we estimate that only about 6 of every 100 adults is an avowed atheist.[6]

Why hasn't atheism grown during periods of stress, travail, family turmoil, political confusion, and ideological turbulence? There are two explanations one might offer, one theological and the other normative.

From a factual standpoint, atheism has sputtered largely because it is a life view that eliminates purpose and hope from life. By erasing God from the picture, atheism leaves only the bleak possibility that what we experience from day to day is all there is to life. As wicked, selfish, and ignorant as we are, this is a frightening prospect. It abdicates moral and ethical foundations to the whim of humans and destroys all hope that there is a force that controls the world in a knowing and loving manner.

Many atheists have confessed that theirs is a depressing, sometimes empty life. They experience isolation from being outside the mainstream worldview and the absence of a coherent community based on shared, meaningful values. They struggle to explain even the most basic realities, such as creation, death, human nature, and the purpose of life. Indeed, the atheistic worldview is one which is based primarily on negating the beliefs of others, rather than positing a coherent and convincing worldview of its own.

THE DEMISE OF CHRISTIAN INSTITUTIONS

However, although Nietzsche's claim of God's demise was unfounded, one could certainly argue that many Christian churches, denominations, and other religious bodies are all but dead.

One reason is that the church, including evangelicals, has largely capitulated to the culture. Many in the church have not spoken persuasively on behalf of godly values, choosing instead to isolate themselves from "worldly" culture or to oppose changes with simple arguments that ignore social and intellectual objections. Those who have engaged the cultural leaders, whether by protest, letter writing, or other forms of confrontation, have done so with insensitivity or aggressive tactics that distort their message. Their behavior has not always been gracious or humble. As *Newsweek* wrote of some Christian institutions, they "often seem more concerned with group grievances than individual behavior."[7]

The last quarter century, in particular, has witnessed the deterioration of the image of the Christian church in America. Confidence in the institutional church has dropped to all-time lows; currently, less than one out of every four adults maintains a great deal of confidence in organized religions.[8] The proportion of people who believe that religion is having a rising influence on society are outnumbered by those who believe its influence is declining by nearly a six to one margin.[9] The proportion who believe that Christianity has all the answers to leading a successful life has dropped to less than two out of every five people.[10] And most adults do not believe that Christian churches are sensitive to the needs of people—whether we examine the needs of people, overall, or the needs of specific people groups (e.g., single parents, blacks, men, young adults, the affluent).[11]

Decades of perceived indifference to the masses has created a crisis of confidence for denominations as well as for local churches. Our research has consistently found that people have little appreciation for, or loyalty to, denominations. Most Americans haven't the slightest idea why America is home to twenty-one different Baptist denominations, or why there are seemingly constant splits, mergers, divisions, and alliances within most of the major denominational groups.

In fact, we discovered that the public image of most Christian denominations is dangerously low—and falling. Recently, the highest rated of the six major denominations we tested had just three out of every ten adults who held a very favorable impression of that denomination. Other major denominations had a very favorable image among less than one out of every ten adults! The substantial proportion of people who had no image at all of these large denominations is a testimony to the perceived irrelevance of these church groups to a growing segment of the population.[12]

Most adults are not highly convinced of the pertinence of Christianity to their lives,[13] and this is reflected in a continuing decline in membership in Protestant churches; since 1970 seven of the nine largest Protestant denominations have had membership losses. Most of the numerical growth that occurs within churches (close to 80 percent) is growth attributable to people transferring their membership from one church to another or via natural increase (birth, adoption, marriage), rather than through the conversion of new people to the Christian faith.

Churches are also struggling with a new trend in church attendance and loyalty, that of having "multiple church homes." Currently, about one of every seven adults has two or more churches which he or she regularly attends; the historical pattern of selecting a single church and sticking with it over time is falling by the wayside as people conclude that one church is incapable of meeting their plethora of needs, and that there are no apparent benefits to making a lasting, singular commitment to one church.[14]

THE LOSS OF PERSONAL RELIGIOSITY

As religious faith, one source of solace during tough times, appears to be dwindling by denominational measures, it also appears to be losing in terms of personal spiritual depth. Over the last four years, activities that relate to personal spiritual development have gradually eroded. There has been a decline in church attendance, Bible reading, involvement in small groups (e.g., Bible studies, fellowship groups, and prayer groups), evangelism, and offering voluntary assistance to the church in its ministry endeavors. Other measures of involvement, such as attending Sunday school and engaging in prayer, appear to have plateaued.[15]

The reasons for this decline in spiritual involvement run the gamut from changed lifestyles that preclude regular church involvement (millions of Americans now work on Sundays, a practice which used to be outlawed but has been overruled by the desire to have a seven-day-a-week economy) to negative personal experiences that have driven people out of the church; to alternatives that seem more attractive or meaningful (e.g., replacing church time with family time, leaving Christianity in favor of self-realization practices, and watching TV); to simply giving in to complacency and apathy regarding religious aspirations.

RELIGIOUS ATTITUDES AND PRACTICE

TRENDS RELATED TO CONFIDENCE IN THE INSTITUTIONAL CHURCH	TRENDS RELATED TO PERSONAL BELIEF AND PRACTICE
Fewer have a great deal of confidence	Nearly half believe Jesus made mistakes
More believe influence is declining	Most don't know all Ten Commandments
Fewer think it has all the answers for successful living	Most don't know who preached the Sermon on the Mount
Most don't believe it's sensitive to people's needs	Most don't understand Christ's sacrificial death
Less loyalty to denominations	Most don't understand the Bible's claims
Protestant churches not relevant to daily life	Most have never read the entire Bible
Less benefits in a single church commitment	

All of these explanations have been made possible, however, by beliefs that have recently gained credence. Former churchgoers and never-attenders articulate these viewpoints well. We'll let Jeff Brown, a fictitious former church man, list them:

- "Religion is a private matter. What you believe, how you pursue those beliefs and relationships, and what one's faith looks like is nobody else's business."

- "The costs of religious involvement outweigh the benefits and value received." According to Jeff and others, the goal is to get at least as much back as you invest in the process. He claims the scale is unbalanced these days, with people being asked to give more of their personal resources, including time, money, and their physical presence, than they can expect to be returned in other ways via the church's ministry to them.

- "Religious insights are nice, but they don't help in my day-to-day needs." Although churches might preach and teach on matters of eternal importance, Jeff and his friends think churches offer little practical help regarding daily issues and struggles such as family, finances, career, relationships, values, and self-esteem.

- "I can have a full and satisfying spiritual experience apart from a community of believers." Jeff and his friends in-

creasingly question the concepts that churches have traditionally relied upon to connote value in the corporate pursuit of God and His character. In an era of staunch
individualism, and a time when people are less willing to
accept a series of beliefs promoted by any given church,
many now choose to encounter God without seeking or receiving the benefits of participating in the life of a nearby
congregation.

BRING ON THE HERETICS

Contributing to the negative attitudes toward organized religion in general and Christianity in particular are the distorters
of the gospel, ranging from faith healers and preachers of a
health and wealth gospel to outright charlatans seeking money
from the gullible. Among the false doctrines being promoted in
books, radio programs, and even nationally via Christian television stations are: the deification of man; a reinterpretation of the
Trinity; support for reincarnation; belief that whatever God's followers want, He is obligated to provide; and the rejection of
physical sickness as anything more than Satanic trickery.

Some preachers and churches reject the literal interpretation of Jesus' words in Scripture and exalt personal emotional or
mystical experiences above biblical principles and standards.[16]

To counter false teaching, modern apologists such as
Charles Colson and Josh McDowell have lifted the pen to clarify
the truth in positive fashion as C. S. Lewis and Francis Schaeffer
did earlier in the twentieth century.

But in the end, the people have emerged from the battle of
truths with a greater degree of confusion than clarity. To millions of Americans, the theological debates and ecclesiological
debates have been little more than a performance of dueling dei-
ties. Theologically untrained and poorly informed, many Americans make an emotional decision as to who is right: "I hear all
the complaining about Ken Copeland, but he sure seems happy
and sincere," was the bottom-line response of a woman from Ala-
bama who regularly attends a Southern Baptist church in addition to sending money to the controversial televangelist from
Oklahoma.

In fact, to many people, the efforts to root out theological
charlatans has been counterproductive. "I'm sick and tired of
hearing them debate this religious point and that. None of us

really knows for sure what God meant when He gave men the Bible, so how we can we be so high and mighty as to tear down another Christian who is just trying to do his best to teach others?" The man who said this, a laborer in his fifties, told Barna Research that he was indignant over the Bible battles that have embroiled so many church leaders. "It's like those Southern Baptists, always fighting about who's right and who's wrong. Can't they find points of agreement and stick to that? We'll all find out who was right when we meet the Maker anyway. It's enough to turn you off to churches or religion altogether." As for so many others we have interviewed, the denominational and intrachurch infighting has had a more profound effect on people's religious thinking than has the substance of the debates themselves.

To most people, then, while many of the newer strains of doctrinal appeal or theological positioning is odd, it seems more important to protect the right to pursue such bizarre theologies than to correct off-center thinking. The strength of the New Age philosophies has come from people's openness to experimentation with religion, combined with the upbeat, optimistic, and results-oriented tenor of these unusual spiritual pursuits.

TWENTY-FIRST-CENTURY SYNCRETISM

Meanwhile, among the general population, Bible illiteracy and misconceptions about Jesus make most Americans vulnerable to false teaching as they continue their search for truth about God and a meaningful faith. Findings of the *Barna Report* during a series of surveys from 1991–94 reveal these unorthodox realities maintained by Americans:

- Nearly half of all Americans believe that Jesus made mistakes during His earthly ministry.

- Most people did not know that the Sermon on the Mount was preached by Jesus Christ. Nearly as many as named Jesus as the preacher of that famed message believed that Billy Graham was the one who delivered those words.

- Most people believe that the Ten Commandments are valid for today, but less than four out of ten adults can correctly recall just four of those ten commandments.

- Most Americans have no understanding of the role or person of the Holy Spirit, or of the ramifications of asserting that the Bible contains no error and can be taken literally.

- While most people claim that they have made a personal commitment to Christ that is still important in their life today, surprisingly few (about one-third) also believe that their eternal status is fully dependent upon God's grace and the death and resurrection of Jesus on behalf of a sinful human race.

- A majority of Americans have never read the entire Bible, from cover to cover. Most adults cannot name the titles of the first four books, or the Gospels, contained in the New Testament. Most people do not recognize the book of Jonah as being part of the Bible.[17]

The conclusion that must be reached is that most Christians seem to have a modest grasp, at best, of the basic foundations of their faith. Under such conditions of ignorance and apathy (the "I don't know and I don't care" response to biblical authenticity), it is easy to understand why cults, errant teaching, and diminished spiritual fervor take root.

The practical outcome has been for America to be a nation in which syncretism is in full blossom. Syncretism is the condition in which people pick and choose the elements they approve of from different, irreconcilable faith systems and then piece those elements together in a unique, idiosyncratic, customized faith system. The prevailing concern of people is no longer "Is my faith pure and true?" The dominant concern today is "Does my faith make me feel good and help me understand the world in a way I find reassuring and personally beneficial?"

An allegedly Christian woman profiled in a weekly newspaper was extolling her brand of "Christianity." Diane believes in a variety of divine entities and that she can channel her thoughts and energy directly from them, that there is reincarnation, and that she can communicate with unborn children. She also says she can heal people from incurable diseases—she says she healed herself of ulcerative colitis—and that there is divine truth which we can know through our senses if we chase it doggedly enough.

When the interviewer questioned whether her claims were truly in line with classical Christianity, she was offended. "I am very deeply Christian." Diane's explanation of her faith positions is that she has matured beyond her Catholic upbringing to embrace a form of Christianity that now "encompasses many faiths and pathways to fulfillment."[18]

The largest study of people's religious affiliations ever conducted in America confirmed that many of those who are not orthodox Christians nevertheless associate themselves with Christian churches or denominations. The study by Kosmin and Lachman, in which 113,000 adults were interviewed, found that less than one-tenth of 1 percent of all adults labeled themselves "New Age."[19]

The researchers noted that most of those who have accepted New Age beliefs and practices do not describe themselves as followers of the New Age movement. "Many who have had a spiritual experience beyond the confines of traditional definitions of religion in the groups in which they were raised would, if asked directly, admit to New Age beliefs. However, they maintain their traditional religious identification [otherwise]. Thus, a Methodist with some New Age beliefs or views likely [is] identified as a Methodist in our survey."[20]

Several Barna Research studies confirm that leaning toward New Age philosophy. One of every five adults reported their primary deity as something described by "the total realization of all human potential" or "a state of higher consciousness a person may achieve."[21]

ANOTHER GOSPEL

Some argue that the answer to these non-Christian philosophies is to clearly proclaim the gospel of Jesus Christ, crucified and resurrected for the sins of every person. Evangelism can work. However, our research suggests that many of these lay evangelists are sharing something other than a purely biblical message about faith, salvation, and godly living.

Large proportions of these lay evangelists—more than one-quarter of them—spread beliefs which suggest that salvation can be earned, regardless of one's beliefs about or relationship with Jesus Christ; that all religious faiths basically teach the same lessons, insinuating that the identity and doctrine of the religious group to which the religious seeker attaches himself or herself doesn't matter much; that Satan does not really exist, but is a symbol of evil; or that Jesus was not perfect.[22]

Thus, we can start to see the chain reaction stemming from the faulty faith perspectives maintained by the most zealous of Christians. The faith being delivered to those who are searching for spiritual truth sometimes is Christianity, but many times it is a paganized form of that faith. Although it is difficult to criticize the intentions and the heart from which such efforts at proselytizing come, the content of the conversations that ensue underscores the loss of orthodoxy among many believers.

A CONTEXT FOR COMPROMISE

More than simple unorthodoxy is contributing to people feeling uncertain about religious faith as a solution to their personal problems. At the same time, Americans have found temporary but alluring satisfaction in new pleasures and pursuits. Other lifestyles and ideologies have offered people a greater sense of comfort, security, and sophistication than has been accessible through the Christian faith.

Along with the pursuit of pleasure, those unable to accept a religious message are turning to humanism and materialism. In fact, secularism, sometimes termed secular humanism, has become a serious challenge to traditional Christian doctrine. The basis of this movement has been that religious faith is merely a mystical crutch that helps the uneducated masses cope with life and helps to keep order among the people.

Humanists place their faith in that which has been discovered through the mind and resourcefulness of humankind. They revere advances and breakthroughs in areas such as the natural sciences; they worship the expansion of education and the enlightenment it is supposed to deliver. Rather than point to God as the omnipotent and omniscient source of all the wonders of our reality, humanists have a logical explanation for everything, leaving God out of the picture. Those things that cannot be explained by anything other than a superior being's touch are described as being inexplicable at the moment, to be explained when the appropriate technologies and foundational discoveries have been made. Through the humanist's lens, human history unfolds according to our ability to understand it, rather than God's desire to reveal it.

The rise of materialism also has undercut Christianity's role as the moral, ethical, and spiritual centerpiece of the American character and lifestyle. America has been a leader in the materialistic fever that has challenged the rest of the world. In our rapid economic ascension during the last four decades, people have become increasingly convinced that their needs and desires can be best satisfied by acquiring possessions that satiate their lusts.

The practical effect of this perspective is that it places our hopes on what we can achieve through our own abilities and cleverness. God is left in the dust, an intangible and unpredictable dispenser of gifts to His creation.

NO LEADERSHIP, NO REVIVAL

Yet another reason Americans question the power of Christianity to change their lives is the leadership crisis that has appeared within the church. Strong leadership is imperative within the local church, where the quality of the teaching, worship, and outreach must be carefully directed by one who is inspired by and in touch with God and His Word. Professional educators have studied the learning process and discovered that the most effective form of instruction is behavioral modeling. Indeed, churches that prosper spiritually are those where the leaders are demonstrating true Christianity through their lives, as well as through their words.

Unfortunately, unbelievers and followers alike are struggling with modern Christian leadership practices in three areas, according to Barna Research findings. The first area is personal morality. The moral failure of so many Christian leaders has received national exposure. The tales of Jimmy Swaggart and Jim Bakker are near legendary. The misconduct of evangelists such as Peter Popoff have brought ridicule on the house of God. Media exposés of high-profile church leaders such as Larry Lea, Robert Tilton, and Benny Hinn have shaken people's confidence in Christianity.

Meanwhile, those attending (and sometimes friends of those attending) local churches learn about senior ministers, youth pastors, or other Christian workers who have resigned because of some moral or ethical failure. Activities range from misuse of funds and deceit to marital infidelity and even child molestation.

The second weakness in Christian leadership has been the snare of politics. Many Christian leaders have been bitten by the political bug and have paid a price for it. More importantly, the Christian faith has often suffered for the unwise political maneuverings of high-profile leaders. Pat Robertson, Jesse Jackson, and Jerry Falwell are just three obvious, national examples of the ravages politics plays on the faith community. Even individuals like the highly esteemed evangelist Billy Graham have understood that intensive and extensive involvement in political decision making can have some debilitating effects. The Reverend Billy Graham has reportedly said that his well-publicized meetings with presidents and other leading statesmen may have taken some people's focus off of God and led to a misunderstanding about the supremacy of God's purposes in the political arena.

The most devastating leadership problem faced by the church, however, is the lack of qualified and gifted leaders to guide the church. Studies have shown that few of today's pastors believe they have been gifted by God as leaders; that few say they were adequately prepared by their university and seminary educations to lead people; that only a handful have identified a vision for the future they feel called, by God, to pursue in tandem with their church; and that most of them find their mastery and their enjoyment of leadership lacking. There is, after all, a substantial gap between preaching God's Word and leading God's people. Although the two are clearly related, they are not interchangeable.[23]

FACING THE FUTURE

In spite of all these problems that tend to muffle the message and distract the listener, most Americans retain a faith focus: we still desire to have a spiritual edge to our lives. Often we are complacent in our pursuit of spiritual truth and personal character, yet most Americans believe that personal religious development remains vitally important in their lives.

The challenge that faces us is how to address people's desire for spiritual truth. In an age when counterfeit spirituality can look, sound, and feel like the real thing, facilitating healthy Christianity is a difficult assignment.

Nothing underscores the difficulty of the challenge more than the thirst for spiritual authenticity exhibited by the Baby Bust generation. These young adults have been raised to explore all of their options—and they are doing just that. Brought up during the information explosion of the eighties and nineties, they are now aware of the myriad of religious groups and philosophies that are open to them.

The Busters are the first generation in America's history that has not assumed that Christianity would be the starting point for their spiritual journey. They are not so much interested in religion—i.e., institutional forms, organized activities, routinized doctrine, and theology—as they are in real spiritual meaning and experience. They are actively searching for faith systems that can positively and profitably inform their own worldview and lifestyles. It seems that the directions that the Busters pursue may tip the scales toward understanding the faith patterns and preferences for America in the decades to come.[24]

NOTES

1. Roy Rivenburg, "No Need For God?" *Los Angeles Times*, 10 June, 1993, E5.

2. The Wolds, Warren Billingsley, and Beth McBride are actual people interviewed by the Barna Research Group; their names have been changed.

3. George Barna, *What Americans Believe* (Ventura, Calif.: Regal, 1991), 77–79; and the *OmniPoll*, 2–92, research conducted by the Barna Research Group.

4. John Whitehead, *The Second American Revolution* (Elgin, Ill.: Cook, 1982), 28–32.

5. Quoted in Robert Bork, *The Tempting of America* (New York: Touchstone, 1990), 17.

6. *OmniPoll*, 2–94, a survey of 1,000 adults, conducted in July 1994 by the Barna Research Group, Glendale, Calif.; this parallels the results we have tracked for more than a decade, in which 4 to 7 percent of the public typically describe themselves as atheist.

7. Howard Fineman, "The Virtuecrats," *Newsweek*, 13 June 1994, 32.

8. "Confidence in Institutions," *The American Enterprise*, November/December 1993, 94–95; displaying data collected by the National Opinion Research Center, from 1973 through 1993.

9. The Gallup Organization, "Religion in America," 1993.

10. Ibid.

11. George Barna, *America Renews Its Search for God* (Ventura, Calif., Regal, 1992), 64–68.

12. Ibid., 60–64.

13. George Barna, *What Americans Believe* (Ventura, Calif.: Regal, 1991), 182–90.

14. These data come from various sources: denominational statistical reports; *The Yearbook of American and Canadian Churches*, published annually by Abingdon Press; Barry Kosmin and Seymour Lachman, *One Nation Under God* (New York, Harmony, 1993); research conducted by the Glenmary

Research Center, in Decatur, Ga.; and various surveys conducted by the Barna Research Group and The Gallup Organization.

15. George Barna, *Virtual America* (Ventura, Calif.: Regal, 1994), chapter 3.

16. Hank Hanegraaff, *Christianity in Crisis* (Eugene, Ore.: Harvest, 1993), chapter 4; and Michael Horton, ed., *The Agony of Deceit* (Chicago: Moody, 1990), chapters 2, 5, and Appendix C. In addition to Hanegraaff and Horton, Dave Hunt and R. C. Sproul have identified and refuted aspects of cultic or nonbiblical teaching.

17. These findings are all derived from a series of national public opinion studies conducted by the Barna Research Group from July 1991 through July 1994. Each of the seven studies included interviews with random samples of between 1,000 and 1,520 adults. Many of the specific statistics have been reported in the Barna Report series, published annually since 1991 by Regal Books; and in the video series produced by Word, Inc., featuring George Barna, entitled "Ministry in a Changing Culture."

18. Lance Ritchlin, "Christian Channeler Looks to Angels for Wisdom," *Metropolitan Accent*, 2–8 June 1993, 3.

19. Barry Kosmin and Seymour Lachman, *One Nation Under God* (New York: Harmony, 1993), 17.

20. Ibid., 300.

21. Barna, *Virtual America*, chapter 7.

22. These statistics are drawn from the seven national public opinion studies (*OmniPoll*) conducted by the Barna Research Group from July 1991 through July, 1994.

23. George Barna, *Today's Pastors* (Ventura, Calif.: Regal, 1993), chapter 7. Also see Darius Salter, *What Really Matters in Ministry* (Grand Rapids, Mich.: Baker, 1990).

24. George Barna, *Baby Busters* (Chicago: Northfield, 1994), chapter 9. Other insights derived from conversations with Rev. Dieter Zander, currently serving at Willow Creek Community Church, Barrington, Ill., and formerly a pastor to Busters at New Song Community Church in Covina, Calif.

THE SEARCH

1. The Wolds and Beth McBride are examples of those seeking answers in organized religion today. What inner needs are not being met by organized religion? In what ways do Americans attempt to compensate for the emptiness in their lives?

2. Briefly describe the five levels of commitment within American Christianity. Some wonder why, if we are a "Christian nation," such serious trouble exists? How would you respond?

3. What were some of the reasons that Christian values reigned during the early years of our nation? How did this change in the last century and particularly from 1960 onward?

4. The chapter outlines the shift away from biblical faith in terms of ignorance, heresy, syncretism, personal reinterpretation, and human centeredness. How can a person acquire and live out a biblically centered worldview.

5. Christian leaders have engaged in questionable behaviors in three areas: personal morality, political maneuverings, and being poorly qualified (or lacking in confidence) to lead church congregations. Which of these three failings do you think is most damaging?

POINT OF ACTION

Make a list of three goals this month to either place you in the top level of Christian commitment or help you grow further in this top level.

CHAPTER 6
SUCCESS
AND WEALTH
REVISITED

A fter thirty years with IBM, Jim Reed felt secure. Though his salary as a financial analyst wasn't spectacular, he had great benefits, steady annual pay raises, and the hope of life-time employment. But when the computer giant affection-ately known as "Big Blue" laid off tens of thousands in 1992 and 1993, his seniority mattered little. He now works out of his home as a landscaper; he gets by, though he could not help his youngest son return to college for a senior year.[1]

An IBM co-worker, David Shahbazian, was told by his supervisors that he was a "surplus" employee when he was released. He and his father, brother, sister, uncle, and one cousin had collectively served ninety-one years with IBM, but that family loyalty to the company couldn't save David's job.

"I never missed a day; I believed in the [IBM culture]. I placed on IBM a higher trust."[2]

Shahbazian and Reed are like thousands of workers who have found job security to be a mirage in the nineties. Corporate heavyweights such as IBM, Sears, and General Electric have been reducing their work force—"downsizing," they call it. Almost half the 8,000 businesses that are part of the American Management Association reduced their staffs in 1993, part of a downsizing trend that continued throughout 1994.

The cause is not merely the economic downturn of the early nineties, but a total switch in how American companies manage costs, regard competition, and view their employees. American television sets are manufactured in Mexico; fashion design stays in the U.S., but cloth weaving takes place in Asia where cheap labor is plentiful; and better technology and cheaper labor has caused U.S. makers to fall behind Japan and other importers of most consumer electronics and heavy metals, including steel.[3]

The global village predicted by Marshall McLuhan and others three decades ago has arrived. America has become part of a global economy, and management, more intent on cutting costs and retaining or increasing (and in many cases restoring) profits, will cut workers from the payroll, even people who have been with the company for decades. In the early nineties a Time/CNN poll found that 53 percent of Americans believe job insecurity will be part of their lives for many working years.[4] The net result of all these factors is that the old definitions of, and means to, wealth have been rewritten, throwing the staid world of finance into chaos. Lifestyles are being challenged and redefined by new patterns of wealth distribution. The government's role in the economy and in the regulation of businesses and individual lives has become convoluted and controversial. The business sector is experiencing a reshaping of its focus, image, place in the emerging world order, and the standards it applies as it works toward reaching its goals.

A quick look at the national economy can tell you a lot about what's happening these days. During the past decade, we have sustained unprecedented changes: the types of jobs that are increasing and decreasing in number and in significance; new levels of personal, corporate, and government debt; an infrastructure that continues to deteriorate; a volatile stock market; growing levels of poverty and economic hopelessness; and new standards and expectations for those striving to earn a living and do an acceptable job.

For the average American—if there is such an animal—wealth and economic standing have become confusing to understand and to master.

THE NEW HAVES

Here's a classic example of a "things are good but I'm feeling so bad" development: The U.S. economy expanded substantially in the last quarter century, yet the buying power of the American household dwindled. Between 1970 and 1991 the gross domestic product (GDP), which measures the market value of all goods and services produced in the U.S., increased by 68 percent. Meanwhile, the cost of goods, as measured by the consumer price index, increased by 251 percent. During that same time period, the median household income increased by only 4.6 percent. In fact, the median household income has actually been declining for several years.[5]

The net worth of Americans has also been declining over the past decade. Most of us are losing ground economically, and although we can't always quote the statistics to prove it, we are keenly aware that it's getting harder and harder to make ends meet.

Increasingly, America is becoming a nation of haves and have-nots. Wealth is being accumulated by an ever-smaller pool of people, while a growing segment of the population is struggling just to retain whatever level of economic stability they might have possessed. These days, 1 percent of our nation's households control 33 percent of the total wealth, with the number of millionaires continuing to escalate. We currently have more than 1 million millionaires in America—although a million dollars isn't the same outlandish sum it used to represent. After making adjustments for inflation, $1,000,000 in 1948 was the equivalent of just $185,000 in 1990.[6] But poverty, the other end of the spectrum, has proven to be a stubborn reality. After a period in which fewer individuals were living below the poverty line established by the government, the trend line has begun inching upward again. In 1960, 22.2 percent of the population was poor. That was sliced in half by 1978 (11.4 percent), but has been increasing in recent years, hovering at almost 15 percent in the early nineties.[7] These statistics equate to more than 35 million poor people, including some 14 million impoverished children.

Poverty also is related to race and ethnicity. Living in poverty is much more prolific among nonwhites than among whites: almost one-third of the black and Hispanic households live below the poverty threshold. Almost half of all black children in the U.S. grow up in poverty.

As bleak as these figures are, they may actually *understate* the true degree of poverty that exists in America. Although the levels change with economic shifts, a recent release from the Department of Commerce indicated that a single individual was deemed to be living in poverty only if he or she was making under $7,144. A household with two persons under the age of sixty-five was considered impoverished if the persons comprising the household jointly earned less than $9,138. A family of four was deemed to be poor if family members had an aggregate income of less than $14,336.[8] Given the cost of living, and the fact that a large share of our poor individuals and families live in cities (where the cost of living is higher), the official government statistics may be missing millions of others who are not able to make ends meet.

OUR RESPONSES TO HAVING LESS
Mind Games

Financial hardships have taken a toll on our psyche too. Not only do people tell us that worrying about money and finances is their top source of anxiety and frustration, but we have found that people also spend inordinate amounts of their free time simply trying to figure out how to best spend their money. The typical American now spends 9 percent of his or her nonworking, nonsleeping time gathering information about products, according to studies. That represents almost 950 hours per year per family—the equivalent of nearly six full weeks of each year spent just collecting information about the products we might purchase.[9]

Going into Debt

More and more, people's response to tough economic times and unworkable family finances is to declare bankruptcy. These days, close to 1 million individuals declare bankruptcy *every year*. Bankruptcy is becoming so common that the process is losing its stigma; it is even being promoted by some as a "strategic" response to financial ills.

Bankruptcy has become an option for many because of the extreme amount of debt incurred. Although it is commonplace for people to criticize the government for its outrageous spending practices, millions of Americans are doing no better, though their levels of debt are on a smaller scale. In 1992, the most recent year for which statistics were available, individuals and families had assumed huge levels of debt. Mortgage debt exceeded $4 trillion; consumer installment loans (such as lines of credit) represented another $741 billion; credit card debt was an additional $258 billion. In total, the 96 million households in our country had formal debts of more than $5 trillion, or almost $52,000 of debt per household. During 1993 many homeowners refinanced their mortgages under lower interest rates, reducing debt, and more became active savers. Yet every month tens of thousands of families still buckle under the pressure of their debt payments, and mortgage and finance companies continue to push home equity loans as a tax-deductible "saving," encouraging Americans to once again add to debt load.

Withholding Inheritances

One way older adults have responded to having less—and to their children's differing values—is to leave their estates to persons and organizations outside the family. We are finding in our research that a growing proportion of the population reports that they will pass their wealth to people or organizations not part of the family. A larger proportion than ever of that wealth is being left to nonprofit organizations and to needy individuals rather than to the children and immediate families of those who have accumulated the wealth.[10] Why the change in estate planning? "I love my children dearly," was the way in one woman put it, "but I just don't agree with their values or the way they have chosen to live. It's not my place to tell them how to live, but I don't have to leave them my money and possessions of value, either. I'll give it to charities that are promoting things I believe in."

Another frequent reason given for the change in inheritance patterns is that the older generation believes many of the potential recipients of their proceeds, typically the Baby Boomers, are already wealthy enough. The older generation wants their estates to be the means of accomplishing a positive difference in people's lives, not simply a means of excess, and they are arranging their wills and trusts in ways they believe will ensure this result.

CHANGING EXPECTATIONS

In the past, about 80 percent of the wealth associated with Boomers has come from gifts and inheritances, but that is expected to change.[11] The expectation of inheriting wealth from older generations—and then learning that those assets will instead go to another party—has become a major source of intra-family animosity. Recent studies have noted that many Boomers have been counting on obtaining the residual wealth from their parents. When they do not receive much in cash and goods or, worse yet, discover that they are excluded altogether, they are crushed—financially as well as emotionally.

The Baby Busters, our youngest adults, have all but given up on the inheritance route. We learned that most of them believe their parents, whose selfishness and unbridled spending patterns are legendary, will squander everything they own before death, and the Busters therefore assume that they are totally left to fend for themselves.

WOMEN AT WORK

One of the key reasons why many households have been able to maintain some semblance of economic parity during the recent hard times has been the return of women to the labor force. These days, three out of every five women hold some type of paying job, many of those either part-time positions or service-oriented businesses run from the home. Women represent almost half of the labor force. In fact, in a major break from the profile of the past, only about one out of every ten women is married, has children, and does not work.

The explosive growth of women in the workplace during the last quarter-century has taken its toll on the fairer sex, though. Several recent surveys have shown that women who have been in the labor force are more likely to question the wisdom of becoming wage earners. A majority of women now say that as soon as they can, they hope to exit the work force and restore a more traditional balance to their lives and to focus more on family issues and needs. The effects on family life of two wage earners is chronicled in detail in chapter 8.

Women, both married and single, have not found work to be satisfying or fair, despite predictions of fulfillment by many feminists. Women still get paid less than a man does for the same job, an estimated seventy-two cents for every dollar that a man would receive for performing the same function. Though women have made some serious strides in the workplace (about 40 percent of all managers, executives, and administrators are female) there remains a "glass ceiling"—an invisible, unfathomable wall separating the top echelons of the company from those below—

women have not been able to break through. Today, less than 2 percent of all Fortune 1000 corporations have a female chief executive.

Many women have also found that even having babies has failed to keep them out of the labor force. That is partly so because of the deteriorating economic climate in America, as more women now say that they "have to work" to maintain their family's financial stability than say they work because they want to.

But another major motivation to continue at work even after bearing a child has been the encouragement and support of employers. AT&T, for instance, found that the average cost of giving a new parent up to one year of unpaid parental leave was 32 percent of an employee's annual salary, a figure that paled in comparison to the investment needed to replace the new parent, which AT&T found to be 150 percent of that parent's salary. AT&T has been a supporter of the new parental leave law because it may mean the new mother will be able to return to work later, much to the company's benefit. Under its own parental leave policy, AT&T found 60 percent of its new parents returned to work within three months, and all but 10 percent returned to work within six months.[12]

Recent studies show that more than six of every ten women who have children under the age of two are in the labor force (at least part-time). For millions of those women, though, working outside the home means they are caught between the proverbial "rock and hard place." They take a job because they want to help their family, and that requires money. But the act of working undermines their very purpose, since their family time suffers and the cost of child care consumes a substantial proportion of their take-home earnings. Americans will spend more than $16 billion on child care services in 1994.

REENGINEERING CORPORATE AMERICA

The economic difficulties at the end of this century have not bewildered only individuals; businesses also have found the nineties to present major challenges. Corporate management has responded to those challenges by becoming chameleons. Businesses change their complexion when such a change will protect or enhance their existence. The most recent survival tactics and corporate buzzwords have to do with a practice known as "reengineering." The term alludes to the need to redesign the busi-

THE "SCHIZOPHRENIA" IN AMERICAN BUSINESS

Invest in the future	Keep the numbers up today
Take risks	Not at the expense of the business
Do everything now better	Add new projects, better communication
Know all the details	Delegate to others
Commit to precise plans	Be flexible and able to change
Be a leader	Cooperate, listen well
Work hard, long hours	Stay physically fit

Source: Adapted from Rosabeth Moss Kanter, *When Giants Learn to Dance.*

ness, from the top down, to account for the numerous and profound changes that have reshaped the business environment in America. It addresses everything from the size of staff, the titles, and the relationships between the organization and its customers down to corporate personality and repositioning in the marketplace.

Some of the most common transformations and strategies employed include downsizing, TQM (Total Quality Management, which includes employees in the evaluation and strategies to improve customer service and product quality), employee training and education, comprehensive computerization, and restructuring to allow for greater flexibility and communications.

Why such a radical response to the new environment? Professor Rosabeth Kanter of Harvard captured the heartbeat of the need in the early portion of her best-selling management book, *When Giants Learn to Dance.* The conflicting demands produced by the new economic realities put managers in a no-win situation, she said, and their often contradictory behavior is a natural result. Here is how she described the charge to business leaders.

- Think strategically and invest in the future—but keep the numbers up today.

- Be entrepreneurial and take risks—but don't cost the business anything by failing.

- Continue to do everything you're doing even better—and spend more time communicating with employees, serving on teams, and launching new projects.

- Know every detail of your business—but delegate more responsibility to others.

- Become passionately dedicated to "visions" and fanatically committed to carrying them out—but be flexible, responsive, and able to change directions quickly.

- Speak up, be a leader, set the direction—but be participative, listen well, cooperate.

- Throw yourself wholeheartedly into the entrepreneurial game and the long hours it takes—and stay physically fit.

- Get lean and mean through restructuring—while being a great company to work for and offering employee-centered policies, such as job security.[13]

The result for many businesses has been a schizophrenia that has all but paralyzed them. Being pushed and pulled in so many incompatible directions has left many committed business leaders and capable employees exhausted, confused and financially ragged.

NEW CONFIGURATIONS

Corporate America has had a make-over. Today, we find that the real vitality in the business sector comes not from the major corporations whose stories fill the pages of *Fortune* and *Time*, but from small businesses—those operations that employ fifty or fewer people. They are quicker to adapt to cultural changes, have lower overhead and thus can be profitable with less volume, fill niches that large corporations often find unattractive, and provide some of the missing relational benefits that may not be valued in a larger corporation.

During the past five years, the federal government informs us that all of the net job growth in America has been among small businesses. Large companies have lost millions of jobs, while midsize firms have also experienced an erosion of their occupational base.

Why have large organizations been hit the worst by the economic downturn and the cultural transitions of the nineties? The list of reasons varies from company to company, but a group of barriers are common to most. In addition to the global competition mentioned at the beginning of the chapter, we can add the following factors:

- replacement of middle management personnel with technology (e.g., computers with sophisticated software)
- replacement of skilled or blue collar workers with technology (e.g., robots)
- inability to comply with increased government regulations
- organizational ranks overloaded with highly paid, often-unnecessary senior management personnel
- corporate cultures that resist change
- inefficiencies attributable to the inability to decentralize functions
- inability to respond quickly to marketing attacks by smaller, aggressive competitors
- intrusive boards of directors, who increasingly meddle in the day-to-day affairs of the company's operations and insist upon short-term profits even at the expense of long-term prospects
- a fragmented market in which customer loyalty is an anachronism.

PRODUCTIVITY PERILS

In addition to the structural turmoil noted above, the many corporations in America face a more insidious villain: excessive debt.

If you thought the uncontrolled spending of the federal government was bad, realize that businesses are in debt to the tune of over $5 trillion today. To put that in perspective, the cumulative debt load of American businesses exceeds that of our federal government and individuals *combined!* Some debt is necessary for proper capitalization; this is known as leverage. But a company that is highly leveraged is in trouble. And in today's global economy, it is hard to be competitive when creditors are breathing down your neck.

The situation would be manageable if there were some hope that productivity levels would skyrocket in the coming years. The recent record has been less than encouraging: of the eight largest industrialized nations of the world, the increased productivity of America has been dead last for the last two decades.[14] There are two primary reasons to worry about the competitive edge of America: the quality of the emerging labor pool and the move toward a service-based economy.

The labor problem is not related to a shortage of able workers, but to a paucity of industrious workers. In our research, numerous employers, from large and small companies alike, bemoaned the fact that the Baby Bust generation represents the future of the business sector. "If they are what I'm going to have to rely on to make a living in the future, I might as well sell out today and get what I can. The next generation is just not a hardworking, future-looking group. They want a lot of participation in decision making but they just don't produce."

The words of this fifty-eight-year-old executive in a large corporation were echoed by many of his peers around the nation. The Busters, saddled with their pessimistic outlook on the future, a lack of appreciation for education, and generally less ambition to achieve than held by preceding generations, have sucked much of the energy and enthusiasm out of the marketplace with their lack of gusto for making a place in history for themselves.[15]

A recent University of Michigan study concluded that the Boomers were a breakthrough generation in their willingness to jump from company to company in their passion to ascend the corporate ladder. But the Baby Busters who follow them, the report asserted, will have an even deeper effect. They will change careers six to twelve times, on average, during their work years—not just switching from company to company, but from industry to industry. This will leave a devastating mark on our economy: (1) less employment stability; (2) less continuity for businesses trying to operate effectively; (3) a diminished personal sense of accomplishment, which will affect self-esteem and relationships; (4) lower income levels, since the individuals will be starting over each time they jump industries; and (5) severely minimized expertise established within industries, due to the constant moving and need for people to start anew with each transition.

EXTERNAL INFLUENCES ON BUSINESS

Businesses are increasingly troubled by external intrusion from the government and from lawyers. Keeping these wolves at bay has, in itself, hindered the ability of many businesses to remain competitive or even afloat.

Today, it costs businesses nearly 5 percent of their revenues to comply with the myriad of federal regulations that our legislators create. The process has become so detailed that in 1938 a manual of governmental rules pertaining to business operation, the *Code of Federal Regulations,* was issued to present in organized form the many parameters and restrictions placed on businesses. That initial printing saw a codebook that was an amazing 18,000 pages in length. A cry of "foul" rose from the private sector as they waded through the jungle of provisions and legal gobbledygook required to keep Uncle Sam off their backs.

But it turns out that the 1938 version was just a dress rehearsal compared to the scope of today's federal regulations. The size of the law compendium tripled by 1970, to 54,000 pages. It then doubled again by 1987, filling 110,000 pages with fine-print, nonsequiturs, and legal minutiae that absolutely boggles the mind and numbs the heart.

Naturally, there must be enforcers to make the publication of this compendium of policies and trivia worth producing. And the legal profession has risen to the occasion. Between 1967 and 1983, the number of lawyers graduated from our law schools increased seven times faster than did the population of the nation. No nation in the world has close to the number of attorneys that argue for a living in America. In fact, we produce more lawyers *each year* than exist in the entire nation of Japan![16]

And these individuals are making a difference. The cost of regulations and lawsuits each year drives many companies either out of business or to new locations overseas. Piper Aircraft, for example, now pays more for product liability insurance than it pays to manufacture some of the airplanes it sells. Pharmaceutical companies paid an average of $72,000 in 1984 for $100 million of liability insurance. Just two years later, the coverage equation had changed: it suddenly cost $1.8 million per year for just $15 million of coverage.[17]

The record-setting number of lawsuits have clogged the court with cases—tens of thousands more than judges and juries can hope to hear in any given year. Though some of the lawsuits are justified, most of the suits, like bankruptcy, become an immoral but strategic response to a situation. Since our existing legal system does not require that a case be initiated only if there is sufficient merit, there are literally hundreds of thousands of frivolous suits pending court action. Innocent people suffer because they have no means of protecting themselves from human avarice. Robert Samuelson, a *Newsweek* columnist and self-described "lawyer-basher," succinctly summarized the crisis created by unethical legal action:

> The social costs transcend actual litigation. The protracted nature of legal disputes exacts an enormous psychological toll on people, regardless of who wins. The rising threat of suits feeds mistrust and inspires more elaborate contracts. There's more precautionary behavior: defensive medicine is practiced; new products are withheld if they might somehow provoke a suit. All this requires more lawyers. The biggest—and least visible—cost may be all the talent that is drained into an essentially unproductive occupation.[18]

Overall, between the aggregate cost of lawsuits and changed procedures resulting from government regulation, businesses waste an additional $300 billion every year in their efforts to remain afloat and, hopefully, earn a profit. It's getting tougher all the time.[19]

FROM GOODS TO SERVICE

A less tangible but no less important consideration is that the very foundation of the U.S. economy is shifting. When America began, we were a nation whose economy was based on agriculture. Over time, we shifted to a manufacturing-based economy, in which wealth and monetary rewards were a function of the goods we produced for both domestic and international consumption. Presently we are moving deeper and deeper into being a service-based economy. The fastest growing occupations in the country are service-oriented; many of the fastest growing industries are services. By some accounts, we are already service-based: three-quarters of all jobs are service-oriented or associated with a service-based organization.[20]

This move has far-reaching consequences, some of which are already being felt. For instance, a service-driven economy does not produce anything tangible. Consequently, its stability is in question. It also requires a different type of labor force, with different skills and abilities. Today, that means that many adults have to be retrained in order to understand the new tools and foci of a services-driven firm. Perhaps most important, a economy founded on services is one that pays less in wages than does one driven by the production of durable goods. That helps explain why household incomes have not continued to grow as in the past.

Economic analyst Louis Rukeyser notes that some economists expect a growing service economy to "produce a period of slower economic growth, declining productivity and stagnant wages.... Since some service occupations pay worse than many manufacturing or construction jobs, critics have charged that the continuing shift of jobs to the service sector could help drag down consumer incomes." Rukeyser then noted that "seven of the ten occupations expected to produce the most jobs—sales-workers, waiters, janitors, clerks, nurses' aides, receptionists, and secretaries—are all service jobs that pay less than the average weekly wage."[21]

Between now and the close of the decade, more than 90 percent of all new jobs are projected to occur in the service sector. This new emphasis in our economy has one key benefit: A new wave of small businesses is rising, featuring one-person entrepreneurial firms that could not compete in an industrial-centered economy. In an environment in which "knowledge workers" (e.g., computer technicians and business consultants) are highly valued, such entrepreneurs can create viable places for themselves by assisting downsized corporations. Simultaneously, others who wish to provide valued services, ranging from physical care to home security, or from gourmet cooking to bookkeeping, have the freedom and operate in an appropriate business climate for making a decent living without any corporate ties.

THE DREAM DESTROYED

Pieced together, the changes that are reshaping the American economic situation cast giant shadows of discouragement throughout the land. What was once the mightiest economic force on the face of the planet stands as a still strong but also befuddled and uncertain economic presence. The United States' place as the leading economic force has been tarnished, if not replaced.

For individual citizens, though, the sad reality is that the American dream has vanished. When young adults dream about their future, they do so with severe limitations on their hopes and dreams. Older adults, those who had been working for years to achieve their dreams, have been rudely awakened by the ravages of an economy gone haywire and a nation whose values have fostered such a collapse.

Even those who have achieved wealth and prosperity have encountered an unexpected crisis: the recognition that riches often fail to bring happiness or fulfillment. Data from our studies, confirmed by Gallup research, show that the people who are most affluent are not necessarily the most content. Individuals whose lives are committed to a significant cause or purpose other than personal comfort, individual achievement, or the accumulation of wealth typically achieve higher levels of personal contentment, satisfaction with life, and fulfillment with their life's work.

In the midst of such bad news about the American economy, many look to personal relationships to meet their needs for contentment and satisfaction. Even there many are failing to connect, as we shall see.

NOTES

1. "White Collar Wasteland," *U.S. News & World Report*, 28 June 1993, 49.
2. Ibid., 45.
3. George J. Church, "Jobs in an Age of Insecurity," *Time*, 22 November 1993, 36.
4. Ibid., 35.
5. Data from U.S. Bureau of the Census, *The Statistical Abstract of the United States 1993*, (Washington, D.C.: U.S. Government Printing Office, 1993), tables 690, 712, 756. The statistics quoted are in "constant dollars," which is the mathematical reinterpretation of the statistics to adjust for inflation.
6. Louis Rukeyser, *Business Almanac* (New York: Simon & Schuster, 1991), 107.
7. *Statistical Abstract of the United States 1991* (Washington, D.C.: U.S. Department of Commerce), table 735. In 1991 the federal government set the poverty line at $6,932 in annual earnings for a single person; $8,865 for a two-person household; and $13,924 for a four-person household.

8. *Poverty in the United States* (Washington, D. C.: U. S. Department of Commerce, 1993), vii.

9. "Tomorrow in Brief," *The Futurist*, January 1993, 15.

10. Barna Research Group, "The Eye of the Donor," a report published in 1994, pages 1–4.

11. (Los Angeles) *Daily News*, 4 October 1993, B4.

12. "The Feds Focus on Parenting Policies," *Business Week*, 28 June 1993, 82.

13. Rosabeth Moss Kanter, *When Giants Learn to Dance* (New York: Simon & Schuster, 1989), 20–21.

14. Rukeyser, 5.

15. George Barna, *Baby Busters* (Chicago: Northfield, 1994), chapter 7.

16. John Silber, *Straight Shooting*, (New York: Harper Perennial, 1990), 216.

17. Ibid., 228.

18. Robert Samuelson, "I Am a Lawyer Basher," *Newsweek*, 27 April 1992, 62.

19. Silber, 234.

20. Rukeyser, 5.

21. Ibid, 183.

THE SEARCH

1. *The U.S. economy has expanded substantially in the last quarter century, yet economic growth recently has stalled. What factors are working to impede economic growth, thus affecting your wallet, your job, and your family?*

2. *The author describes how an era of massive wealth transition greatly affects the near economic future, including relationships. How are relationships being affected among the four generations: Seniors, Builders, Boomers, and Busters (see pages 105–106)?*

3. *The chart and listing by Professor Kanter (pages 108–109) describe the conflicting messages businesses hear today regarding risks, teamwork, flexibility, caution, bottom line, etc. How do such messages fit in with the changes in corporate America?*

4. *America is quickly losing its competitive edge in productivity. How does the emerging labor pool and service-based economy work against us (review pages 110–111)?*

5. *According to a University of Michigan study, many Baby Busters are frequently changing jobs. What do you think are the positive and negative effects upon the person and the business when an employee changes jobs on a regular basis? What are the implications for the general economy?*

POINT OF ACTION

Examine your present job or home situation and list three concrete ways you can improve productivity in the next month.

CHAPTER 7
DISCONNECTED RELATIONSHIPS

R andy considered himself the black sheep of the family. Older brother Tom was a highly regarded radio personality; his sister Suzie was married to a successful lawyer and enjoyed life in a prestigious section of New York City. In contrast, Randy was the least vocal of the three and had withdrawn from family life. After college he drifted for several years.

Randy married but the marriage failed; within three years his wife left him. He began drinking heavily and eventually found himself homeless. It wasn't until Tom and their father made a concerted effort that they finally located Randy and helped him get his life back together.

"My life wasn't worth a buck," Randy recalls. "Two years ago I spent my days searching out scraps of food to eat and warm doorways to sleep in. I misjudged my family. I thought they didn't care. But they did. They proved that. What they went through to find me and restore me is amazing. Yeah, maybe I don't have Suzie's money or Tom's fame, but I am who I am, and that's enough. They love me and they're standing by me. They're helping me pull my act together, and I'm determined to make them proud of me again."

Randy paused to collect his composure as his eyes moistened. "My family pulled me out of the gutter and is bringing me back. I would be helpless without their belief in me and their willingness to put their own lives on hold for a while to support my needs."

WE NEED EACH OTHER

Many will agree that after our health, our relationships are most important to us. Relationships can turn lives around. They often instill meaning and purpose in life. Most people recognize that living in isolation is unhealthy. We need other people to cope with the complexities and pressures of daily life.

Likewise, relationships are the glue that holds society together. The deeper the bonds run within a society, the more capable that society is of handling the stresses and strains borne from the challenges of the day.

Our Emotional Needs

The driving force behind much of what we do is the desire to satisfy deep emotional needs. The way in which we develop intimate relationships reflects our intense need for full love: acceptance, support, understanding, patience, reward, touch, and esteem. Though some psychologists claim that most humans have only dysfunctional relationships, few would deny that we are largely driven by our relational needs, no matter how we behave in order to fulfill those needs.

Our Social Needs

Sociologists approach the study of Americans from a different angle but reach a similar conclusion. On the basis of examining the social interaction of people, sociologists have concluded that we are inherently social creatures and have an inner craving to be linked to the lives of other people. Sociologists note that a culture can remain strong only if there is healthy interaction between divergent social segments and cultural subgroups. Interpersonal connections typically dictate how well a society fares in the face of competition and changing conditions.

Our Spiritual Makeup

Christian theologians assert that people's quest for lifelong relationships is a consequence of the way in which God made people. The Bible relates the story of a Creator who wants to be in relationship with His chief creation at the same time that human beings themselves have a deep need to be included in the life of significant others. Further, a clear calling of the church, those individuals whom God calls to reflect His character, is to facilitate meaningful community among all people, based on a common belief in God and His principles.

Though they approach the quest for relationships from different viewpoints, the psychologist, the sociologist, and the theologian agree on one thing: people need each other. Yet despite our innate need for meaningful relationships, most Americans experience little fulfillment in their existing roster of relationships. Even those who are committed to developing lasting, synergistic relationships with a range of people have found that society has set up numerous roadblocks in the journey to deep, fulfilling relationships.

PEOPLE WANT PEOPLE

Real friendships are at a premium in America. Everybody wants them; seemingly few know how to achieve them. Consider some of the research findings from our recent surveys:

- Most adults admit that they want to have a greater number of deep friendships.
- A large proportion of adults describe themselves as "feeling all alone" or "lonely."
- The process of identifying potential friends is a mystery to many. Places that formerly served as the spawning grounds for new relationships—jobs, neighborhoods, community social clubs, even churches—are no longer a pertinent or effective means of finding other like-minded people.
- One of people's highest-rated desires for the future is to have "many close, personal friends" on whom they can rely; less than one-fourth of all adults believe they have achieved this goal.
- Suicide, which has increased in recent years, is often attributed to feeling alienated from the world and from individuals.

Why do we continually strive, perhaps against the odds, to locate people whom we might incorporate into our circle of intimates? Because most of us have at some point in our life known the blessing and joy of having close, reliable friends and want to experience an even greater dose of such stability and exhilaration in the days ahead. Again, the research clearly shows that people who have successful marriages, those who have good friendships in place, and people who receive tremendous pleasure and support from their involvement with extended family are most likely to rank personal relationships as contributing to the greatest measure of fulfillment in life. Those who lack such relationships generally desire them and are anxiously seeking the means to reap relational benefits.

LONELY IN AMERICA

But what we want and what we have are often two different matters. Although most Americans want close friendships, loneliness pervades our culture. In fact, the more time passes, the more loneliness seems to be a distinctive attribute of the national experience.

"Americans are perhaps the loneliest people on earth today," George Gallup recently told church leaders. The national pollster believes Americans suffer from personal isolationism. After reviewing multinational studies by his Gallup Organization, the eminent researcher concluded that millions of Americans have intense feelings of loneliness and feel separated from humanity.

Loneliness takes its toll. Psychologists claim that loneliness evolves in five progressive stages. The first stage is *confusion*. The individual cannot understand why he or she is experiencing loneliness. Next comes *isolation*, in which the individual feels personally insignificant and wholly out of touch with the rest of the world. This overwhelming sense of disconnectedness is followed by *feelings of hostility and anger*, as resentment toward one's condition builds and consumes. This anger is often directed at others, as well, especially those who seem popular and emotionally fulfilled. Once the anger burns out, *depression* takes over, leaving the person in a state of mental and emotional despair. The situation seems hopeless, made even more severe by increasing self-doubts about personal worth. This depression is not unlike the depths of despair experienced by the person who mourns the loss of a loved one, but in this case the one who died is, in an emotional sense, the self.

Finally, loneliness can lead to *exhaustion*. The person may feel completely worn out—mentally, emotionally, spiritually and even physically—as a result of having run the gamut of emotion turbulence.[1]

LONELINESS IS A BY-PRODUCT

We can trace the spread of loneliness to ten primary factors. The more of these conditions that are present in a person's life, the more deeply entrenched in loneliness the individual may become—and the more difficult it will be for him to shed separation and emotional distress to achieve fulfilling relationships.

Time Perspectives

Like a snowball rolling down a steep hill, the pace of life in America has moved at an ever-increasing rate of speed. One reason for the quickened pace is the widespread acceptance of the philosophy "more is better." In the realm of relationships this equates to knowing more and more people, as if the mere acquaintance with numerous people would meet the deeper emotional needs of the person.

Simultaneous to this emphasis on numbers of friendships is an increase in the options available to a person in a given day. Thus, although we know that connecting on an emotional level is important, we are tantalized by the prospect of meeting yet other sensual needs through the accessibility to a vast array of events, experiences, and challenges.

The result is a fast-paced, experience-driven, multiple-option world, where personal values pale beside the possibility of exposure to the latest, the biggest, the fastest, the most prestigious, the best, or the most expensive.

The blur of activity we call the nineties has engendered a society in which the participants face a critical paradox: they want meaningful friendships but not at the expense of the full panoply of experiences and opportunities. Our clever solution? Relationships based on "quality time." In a culture in which there are more experiences to be had and not enough time to include them all, people have persuaded themselves that they still can get the maximum benefits out of a relationship by substituting intensity for the minutes and hours usually needed to establish a solid relationship. The underlying assumption is that you can have the best of both worlds: lots of meaningful friendships and lots of experiences.

Many Americans have concluded that significant relationships can be had through one of two strategies: either high intensity encounters or high commitment encounters. High intensity relationships are those characterized by brief, relatively infrequent bursts of interaction, known as "quality time" relationships. The assumption is that because both people are fully focused on each other during the short time allotted to the encounter, the intensity of that mutual concern will compensate for any deficiencies that might result from being short-changed as to time. High commitment relationships, on the other hand, are those built upon the belief that a friendship grows deep only when both parties invest serious amounts of time in the development of trust, understanding, and mutual appreciation.

Americans currently think that people must size up the potential of a relationship and make a choice; friendships are seen as an "either/or" proposition, equally likely to be fulfilling if they are based upon quality time or quantity time. The majority conclude that with time being limited, "quality" time is better than no time at all. So they forgo commitment.

One immediate consequence of this choice has been loneliness. There are no studies on record which suggest that deep, lasting, meaningful, fulfilling relationships are created and nurtured simply through quality time encounters. The hit-and-run strategy for intimacy on the basis of quality time is doomed to failure. Yet, because we see life through a flawed hierarchy of priorities, we continue to pursue substantive relationships through means bound to facilitate superficiality.

Individualism

When philosopher and critic Alexis de Tocqueville journeyed from France to America in the 1800s to see what were the unique strengths of the growing, independent nation, one of his chief conclusions was that America progressed because its people were allowed the freedom to think creatively, to pursue their dreams, and to develop a unique persona. He was impressed by the responsible individualism that facilitated such diversity of thought and activity.

Individualism has its strengths, but Tocqueville would see something different today—individualism that has degenerated into a pastiche of mere selfishness. A crucial factor in the productive individualism he observed was people's willingness to be responsible, ever-mindful of community obligations and cultural parameters. In our friendships, however, we have perverted individualism to become disconnected from the communal good, often evaluating potential friendships in light of the ability to receive without having to give. Too often, it seems, we regard others as tools rather than partners, as things to be exploited rather than people to be satisfied.

Like every human community, America has always had its difficulties working out relational boundaries and processes. During the early years of the United States, the frontier mentality gave birth to more than its fair share of egomaniacs and selfish boors. However, the cultural traditions of that day also enabled people to develop a network of friends based on being family, neighbors, and community members. Today, those base line opportunities are absent and nothing has arisen to replace them in the patchwork of relational opportunities. The result of the relentless pursuit of individualism, whether it is based on ego, selfishness, or more laudable purposes, is alienation and isolation.

Failed Communication

Never before has there been so much transmission of information and so little true communication. Innovative communications methods and machinery have been developed and embraced in the past decade, yet the human beings for whom those tools have been developed have increasingly lost touch with the art of personal communication.

Dialogue has been largely replaced by monologue. In peer relations, parenting, prayer, and political debate, little time and effort is devoted to listening; the lion's share of communication resources are committed to divulging our version of the picture. Studies have consistently indicated that as America matures, its people are becoming less and less capable of sustaining a meaningful conversation in which both parties' needs and concerns are substantively addressed. That bodes poorly for the future of relationships, which deepen largely through mutual understanding and appreciation.

Our research has noted that many lonely individuals are so desperate to form meaningful liaisons with other people that they seemingly cannot contain themselves when a likely prospect for a friendship comes along. Rather than pursue the relationship at a reasonable pace and strive to achieve balance in the development of both sides of the relationship, they charge ahead, bent on telling the other person what's important and forgetting to absorb the ideas, feelings, and information offered (and important to) the potential friend.

Millions of Americans have lost the art of listening, processing the information gleaned, and responding in an appropriate manner. Our survey findings suggest that the inability to respond appropriately is due at times to focusing on personal needs rather than the needs of the other party. But many times we have found, the difficulty in bonding is often associated with people's inability to articulate care, concern, understanding, and commitment.

Privacy

Relationships require that people be available for interaction. Yet with the stresses and pace of life accelerating in recent years, millions of people have found their home to be less a place

TENSIONS THAT LIMIT OUR RELATIONSHIPS	
CULTURAL INFLUENCES	**DEEPER PERSONAL NEEDS**
Need for experiences, opportunities	Need for friends
Settling for quality time	Wanting quantity time
High-intensity encounters	High-commitment encounters
Traditional individualism	Seeking community
Our point of view first	True dialogue
Need for privacy	Need for deep interaction
Benefits of technology	Retain personal touch
Past family dysfunction	Need for openness, vulnerability
Convenient shared activities	Self-sacrificing, long-term relationships
Media-distorted viewpoints	Realistic commitment

for interaction with friends and neighbors than a retreat center where they can get away from the strains and tensions of the moment and be entertained and physically recharged for the next day's battles. One outgrowth of this lifestyle of retreat is that we have reduced the chances for building friendships. Once we pull into the driveway, rush through the front door, and throw on the security locks, we protect ourselves from physical danger and time depletion—but also from the personal interaction that may lead to satisfying relationships.

Currently, America is entering a period in which the desire to assure privacy is growing. We fear that the government will gain too much information and pry away rights. We fear that businesses will discover too much about our income levels and buying patterns and annoy us with telemarketing and incessant advertising. We fear that employers will learn things about our past or our hopes for the future and impair our ability to get ahead in our careers and in life. We fear that those activities we do in secrecy will become known and taint our reputations or our ability to enjoy life.

This quest for privacy has also led to a separation from others. We protect our time at all costs and now use technology to help do so. VCRs perform a time-shifting function, allowing us to tape programs or rent movies and watch when we desire. Answering machines and voice mail systems permit us to interact without having to personally get involved. Cellular telephones enable people to make connections on-the-run. Time efficiency has come to mean that we can accomplish more and experience more, but not that we have more time for people. Social experts predict a growth in "cocooning"—that burrowing into one's home where comfort and entertainment replace contact with people outside the immediate family.

Technology

America has been on the leading edge of developing and embracing new global technologies. Virtually every industry in our economy has been significantly transformed in the last twenty years by new forms of technology. That technology has also thwarted personal relationships. Consider what happens when we spend the day interacting with machines instead of people. On the job, at least, we used to expect people to talk to and work with other people. Now, with computers networked to each other, people often complete their day's work without leaving their PCs. The trend nationwide is for large companies to be decentralizing, sending people back home so they can work from there, letting them "talk" by electronic mail and send reports by computer modems and fax machines. Working out of their homes, these employees can interact with colleagues and supervisors for days without actually seeing them.

America also is a transient workplace, where one out of every six households changes location each year to take advantage of new opportunities in the national marketplace. That constant uprooting, driven by technological change, tends to negate the personal relationships people forge. New studies also show that increasing numbers of adults, aware that they are likely to move again in the near future, refuse to devote themselves to making new relationships because they expect those emotional ties to be lost in the next career move.

Family Background

Millions of Americans indicate that they are wary of moving into deep relationships because they had ventured into emotional vulnerability in their family and been burned. Since most people believe the family is the safest arena in which to build significant relationships, those who have been hurt or whose expectations have been unmet in their family involvement are reluctant to risk further discouragement or pain in relationships with nonfamily individuals.

Fear of Commitment

A large percentage of adults in our nation fear making commitments that will come back to haunt them. In much the same manner that Baby Busters have turned to cohabitation as an insurance policy against divorce, many adults are cautious of attempting to build deep relationships with people because they fear making themselves vulnerable to emotional hurt.

The fear of relational commitment is not solely based upon the potential of being emotionally exploited or injured. Many people are skeptical of relationships as they witness the newspapers recounting, on a daily basis, lawsuits in which husbands and wives, lovers, companies and employees, governments and taxpayers, retailers and customers, go to battle over some amazingly petty disagreements. What seems to frighten a large proportion of adults is the possibility that anything they say, or do, might be used against them at some later date—perhaps even out of context.

Many people, especially women, also fear the possibility of suffering some type of abuse. One study we conducted indicated that one out of every five adults has endured some type of serious emotional, physical, or sexual abuse in the past, and that almost half of all adults personally know someone who has been significantly impacted by such abuse.[2] A majority of all Americans, sensitive to crime, say that they now plan their daily schedules in ways intended to minimize the possibility of being victimized by crime. Likewise, a majority of Americans retain a level of skepticism about the motives of other people and alter the interaction that would have come about naturally had they not been fearful of being exploited.

Dominance

One of the trends we noted a few years ago was a deepened drive to control all aspects of one's time and resources. That drive impacted people's willingness to allow themselves to get into a relationship in which both parties were seen as equal. Because we are skeptical of the underlying motives of others, we tend to seek dominance in relationships (at least initially). Because we feel it would be inappropriate to immediately trust others, it is difficult to get to a point where both individuals feel comfortable with the other.

Convenience

In a culture bred on taking advantage of experiences and opportunities, making time for friendships has assumed a lower place of priority. We are happy to make the most of those serendipitous moments when we find ourselves with others whom we enjoy, but going out of our way to schedule times together and to coordinate such encounters overwhelms many individuals.

Taking advantage of the emotional benefits of relationships is one thing, but acting as the activities coordinator is another matter altogether. Because people's schedules are so packed with activities, trying to find times when connections can be made conveniently can be a chore in itself. The hardship of trying to bring together a group of people is exemplified by the changing pattern of personal athletic participation. Over the past two decades, the pattern has been for individual sports to grow in popularity while team sports have remained stable or on the decline. The reason has less to do with people's enjoyment of group sports —indeed, from a spectator's perspective, attendance at team sports events has skyrocketed—than with the agony of trying to get a group of ten or more people together at the same place, at the same time, for the same purpose.

Media Perspectives

A final factor restricting relationships of the nineties is the mass media. Television, movies, magazines, books, and newspapers have changed our views and behavior regarding relationships by distorting the nature of modern relationships. Movies and TV programs, in particular, often depict relationships as greed-driven, sex-based, heartless incidents of interaction. The nightly news programs and the news magazines pounce on "human interest" stories in which the ugly side of human personalities is exposed. Portraying these relationships as commonplace has helped to twist our notion of what we must expect if we get involved in the lives of other people.

ALIENATION

As pervasive as loneliness is, our relationships suffer from more than isolation. There is also alienation. From generation to generation, from race to race, Americans do not really know one another. Indeed, they are estranged from one another.

Many believed race relations had improved during the past three decades, with the passage of government policies such as the Civil Rights Act of 1965 and Affirmative Action, designed to promote racial equality. We have seen more television shows featuring black families, beginning with the highly rated "The Cosby Show." Hispanics, Asians, and African-Americans have held more visible positions in government and commerce.

Yet our government policies have not changed people's hearts and attitudes. Our surveys have found that prejudice remains widespread, and more than three-fourths of all adults say they *expect* massive race-based riots and violence to rock the nation before the end of this decade. The evidence of racism is unavoidable. Whites stick with whites, and "people of color" tend to associate with people from their own ethnic groups. Rarely do the races mingle in true friendship. Though they will gather temporarily for matters of business and commerce, those are relationships of convenience, superficial acquaintances that extend no deeper. The segregated housing of Chicago's South Side, Los Angeles' Korea Town and San Francisco's touristy but separated Chinatown testifies that segregation is still practiced, sometimes subtly, sometimes not.

The fears and prejudices of America's different ethnic groups exploded into the living rooms of America (via television) on April 29, 1992, when blacks and Hispanics rioted after an all-white jury found four Los Angeles police officers not guilty of using excessive force in the beating of motorist Rodney King. The officers were white; King was black. Many rioters said their rage was against a judicial system biased against minorities. Some said the police department was racist. Interestingly, Hispanics angry at the largely white police force also participated in the rioting. And blacks attacked not only white-owned businesses and motorists, but also Korean merchants, charging them with unfair pricing and a distrust of black customers. Koreans hired their own kind, but rarely had African-Americans as employees, black protesters said.

Afterward, a police sergeant in North Richmond, California, said the riots were not an isolated pocket of frustration about race relations. "Our cities are not a powder keg waiting to explode, but they're like a slow fuse burning all the time. Daily there are race crimes: shootings, beatings and violence. L.A.'s flame just got higher. People noticed. But believe me, it's ongoing everywhere."[3]

Such isolation among the races shows itself in racial epithets and even physical attacks, as occurred on college campuses in the early nineties in dorms and between fraternities. It shows in the segregated neighborhoods and even at summer picnics and city festivals, when members of races mingle rarely, and typically only by accident. They arrive in separate vehicles and depart to separate neighborhoods. This separation feeds the estrangement among the races.

Americans say they are open to befriending people of other races, but few actually have done so—and there is little evidence that they will in the future. The widespread racism in America is yet another relational blockade based on fear—fear of those who are different. As America becomes more and more heterogeneous through immigration and high birth rates among noncaucasians, we face a rising potential for increased racial and ethnic misunderstanding.

Alienation also is spreading among the generations. Seniors regard the Baby Boomers as selfish and unappreciative; Baby Boomers at times resent having to help the elderly (even their parents) with lodging or medical care; and Baby Busters think both previous generations have bungled the world and left them with fewer jobs and options. As one Buster, a twenty-year-old college student, argued, Boomers are "swiping the inheritance from us. Can we get ahead in the world today? Not unless they'll let us take a meaningful part in the proceedings. Instead they're freezing us out. . . . [Boomers] claim we don't have the drive and the ability to get ahead in a global world. [It's] easy to complain when you never had to take on the same challenge."[4]

In the previous chapter we saw that alienation also exists between different classes. The middle class envies the upper class, the so-called haves. Meanwhile, the lower class resents both the middle and upper classes as having more than they. And in the next chapter we will see that the estrangement exists even in our families. Divorce is only one form of estrangement between men and women. Husbands and wives live separated lives, and their children can be ignored even in a whole—i.e., a "not divorced" —family unit. And as noted in chapter 2, relationships are fractured even among different geographical segments. Rifts continue between those in the South and North, with their origins tracing back to the Civil War. People of the West and Midwest are victims of stereotyping and themselves tend to generalize when interacting with those who live in other regions of America.

NO WONDER WE'RE LONELY

With relationships disconnected on so many levels—race, social, family, and location—no wonder Americans feel lonely and isolated. Until we can establish some modicum of trust in the human capacity to connect emotionally and develop a higher level of confidence in people's desire to love others as they wish to be loved, the chances are good that we will remain a nation divided by our differences rather than one driven together by our common needs.

The division in relationships even extends to parents and children. As we will see in the next chapter, this division within our families is also a threat to the stability of our culture.

NOTES

1. Much fascinating research has been conducted on relationships and alienation. The five-step flow of responses to loneliness alluded to here is from the work of Daniel Kiley, a professor at UCLA, and is initially expounded in his book *Living Together, Feeling Alone* (New York: Prentice-Hall, 1989).

2. Barna Research Group 1993 study. Cited in *Ministry Currents* July–September 1993, 11–13, a newsletter published by the Barna Research Group.

3. David H. Hackworth, "This Was No Riot, It Was a Revolt," *Newsweek*, 25 May 1992, 33.

4. George Barna, *Baby Busters* (Chicago: Northfield, 1994), 41.

THE SEARCH

1. *This chapter gives ten reasons for loneliness, which makes satisfying friendships less likely. Name five reasons why maintaining satisfying friendships is more difficult than ever.*

2. *How can the church fill the void in terms of both friendship needs and meaningful relationships in general?*

3. *Within the ten reasons for loneliness and unfulfilling friendships are several personal fears. What major fears do we have about establishing close relationships?*

4. *Technology can alienate and depersonalize humans. Two other external influences that can adversely affect meaningful relationships are our family background and media perspectives. Which of those two has had the stronger negative impact on your developing relationships? How has it affected them?*

5. *What are some of the negative results emanating from a lack of close relationships in our society?*

POINT OF ACTION

Make a commitment to do one of the following three things this month: (1) develop a new friendship; (2) take an existing friendship and strengthen it; (3) attempt to understand and reach out to a person you dislike.

CHAPTER 8

THE FAILING FAMILY

Researchers don't agree on a lot of things. They question each other's findings and even when they come to the same results, they sometimes argue as to the cause. Coffee drinkers who switched to decaffeinated coffee after being told by researchers that "decaf" is less likely to cause cancer than regular coffee were left in uncertainty recently when another finding argued that decaffeinated brew contributed to higher cholesterol levels and increased the risk of heart disease by 10 percent.[1]

But social researchers hold aloft a vast array of studies —from cultural macroanalyses to community values surveys—and nod their heads in agreement on one point: the family plays a central role in the development and stability of a nation and its culture. At the same time, historians studying numerous societies in the modern era have not found one society that has thrived without durable, cohesive, "traditional" families. Throughout modern history, leaders and analysts alike have acknowledged that the basic building block of a stable society is its families. The traditional family—one in which people living together are related by birth, adoption, or marriage—is at the foundation of a strong nation.

It is this long-term, panoramic perspective that makes the current state of the family in America so disturbing. Almost every measure available to us indicates that the stability and strength of the traditional family in the U.S. is on the decline. Despite America's history of strong, cohesive families, today's parents and children are challenged by unique stresses. Can they handle the pressures of the present day while remaining consistent with normative moral values and behaviors?

Many who analyze American society consistently express concern about the deterioration of the traditional family—and with good reason. The heart of this concern is not that old forms have been replaced with new forms. Such anxiety exists because the old forms are being replaced with no forms. The substitutes being proposed and experimented with are only weak stand-ins that show little promise of helping people make sense of life, endure its hardships, and enjoy its pleasures.

The weakening of the family system in America raises serious questions as to how we, as a growing nation of 260 million people, will individually and collectively summon the emotional, economic, and spiritual depth to survive the blizzard of changes that is reshaping the world around us.

A NEW DEFINITION

During the last three decades, the American people have questioned virtually every foundation of family life, including the very definition of family. The fact that we have raised the question in this book of "what is family?" demonstrates just how thoroughly the undercurrent of change has been shaking the family structure.

Without much fanfare, we have shifted from a nation in which "family" meant a group of people related to each other by marriage, birth, or adoption to a country that now defines family as all those people we deeply care about and who deeply care about us. Today, two out of every three adults embrace this latter definition, giving rise to the "nouveau," or alternative, family mind-set.[2]

Most Americans still accept individuals who are married, or those who are married and have children, as constituting a family unit. That consensus is not likely to change. What is significant, however, is that most adults have come to believe that the traditional definition of family is too limited in scope. Consequently, we have moved beyond the concise, time-honored framework to a more encompassing definition of family.

"I don't think that God really meant that a family is made up only of people who said something in a church ceremony or who were the products of a marriage relationship." The views of this middle-aged woman from Indiana reflect a common perspective. "A family is supposed to be a circle of love. If the people who we have called family don't really have that kind of love, then they're not really a family." Like so many people from her generation, the woman who said this is not opposed to rewriting the rules that describe the nature of family.

"Our country would be much better off if we could look at family as the group of people who really know each other and care about each other. Family is about being there for each other. It's not supposed to be a rigid legal or religious thing."

Her views are echoed, in different words, by many people across the nation. The idea of having rigid and consistent boundaries for the family is denounced as archaic and legalistic. In this age of freedom of choice, we believe that one of our inalienable rights is to decide for ourselves who is and is not part of our family. Because we tend to think that there is no set of guidelines for the establishment and development of family, we argue that the boundaries can shift from time to time, as long as people's desires are addressed. We downplay the biblical and traditional perspectives on family relationships and behaviors.

"We're so tied to our historical politics and a kind of parochial spirituality that a lot of times we dismiss opportunities to allow adults to find deeper and more proper self-expression through different forms of relationship." The speaker, a professor at a liberal arts college located in the Midwest, reflects the thinking of many who believe the earlier guidelines are confining and irrelevant in an age of change. "It would be far superior to sanction new forms of marriage and parenting and family than to resist modern realities and cling to old ways which no longer work. We ought to free the family to be what it must become: the sum of love relationships expressed in whatever forms that love must take. Defending old traditions and standards which no longer fit our culture makes little sense."

What counts in the minds of a majority of American adults is the existence of an emotional connection between individuals. If two people work for the same company and have lunch together once a week, and if they share a deep interest in and concern for each other, most Americans would now claim that theirs is more than a friendship. Today, they are a family. Two individuals who are "lovers" would be considered by most people to be family, whether they plan to marry each other or not. The apparent or stated presence of a sincere emotional bond is enough to qualify people as family. A wedding or public ceremony is simply a formality. These days, family is not thought of as bringing people into compliance with a legal or spiritual standard. Family reflects an emotional acknowledgment and attachment of people to each other. Many advocates of the new definition are influenced by the lifestyle and philosophical transformations of the past three decades.

IS THERE A COST?

This new definition has been called convenient and unrestrictive. But it also is a way to destabilize traditional families. The new concept renders family little more than a temporary, fluid set of relationships, created and dismantled at the personal convenience or emotional whim of the individual. No longer shackled by the constraints of commitment and responsibility, nor accountable for decisions of the past and obligations to the future (such as children or financial liabilities), family has become yet another conduit to bliss and personal gain. The rewarding aspect of this new definition, for many people, is that when the relationship ceases to supply the desired outcomes, the deal is off. The once-significant relationship ceases to be family and is relegated instead to the category of friendship or acquaintance (or "former lover"). No guilt, no legalities, no self-deprecation—just instant freedom to pursue the next "meaningful" relationship.

The nouveau family, however, comes with a lofty price tag. Such relationships are less valuable and powerful because they are not bound by cultural expectation and personal consent to be enduring, predictable, reliable, and secure. Thus, the standards by which we measure the value and validity of family have dramatically changed. In making the trade-off of permanence for convenience, we tend to favor relationships that come easily rather than those that require effort. We have tacitly decided that new relationships are more exciting and appealing than long-term relationships. For many, family has become a tool to be used to further our personal desires, rather than something to be nourished as a social building block from which we gain stability, true identity, and character.

Consequently, even when people enter into traditional family circumstances, there is little promise of the continuity of the family bonds. If too many pressures are exerted on the family members, the emotional balance may be ruptured, resulting in the reconfiguration of the family to merely a set of acquaintances. Without a moral philosophy or standard that upholds the sanctity and permanence of marriage, or the significance of family unity, there is no enduring reason to maintain such commitments in the face of challenges, hardships, or crises. The result is often divorce.

The reduction of family to a reflection of the day's feelings about the safeness of, and connection with, one or more people has opened the door to all kinds of revolving family ensembles. The nuclear family has been replaced by a relational network that constantly redefines itself. Homosexual couples, precluded by law and by social custom from marrying each other, are now accepted by millions of Americans as legitimate families, even if the homosexual partners are not legally married. People who cohabit need not wait for common-law marital status in the eyes of most people, since a couple's feelings about, and commitment to, each other are what now determine their family standing.

NEW VIEWS ABOUT MARRIAGE

Interestingly, this new perspective on the meaning of family may be one way to anticipate the potential hardship or even failure in the relationships that matter most to us. Our research discovered that most adults want to get married; most adults believe that God intended marriage to be a lasting, permanent relationship between a man and a woman; most adults want their own marriage to last a lifetime; and most married adults find that their relationship with their spouse is the most satisfying relationship in which they are involved. More than 2 million people get married every year, and even a majority of divorced adults eventually remarry.[3] If marriage were such a despicable, unsustainable, and antiquated institution, the people who have experienced it at its worst would not be so likely to give it a second chance.

A Self-fulfilling Prophecy

However, we also find that fear of marital failure is becoming a self-fulfilling prophecy. A majority of young adults today say that people who get married should expect their marriages to dissolve in the not-too-distant future; many tell us it is "virtually impossible" these days to have a marriage that lasts until death dissolves the partnership. Since marriage is based on a commitment, we have learned that many individuals, preparing themselves for what they assume is the inevitable collapse of their marriage, hold back emotionally in the marriage relationship so as to reduce the sting of a split in later years. The very act of withholding full commitment to the relationship, however, virtually condemns the marriage to failure from the start.

Joan Vickers, in her mid-twenties, reflects the thinking of many young adults about marriage these days. "I grew up in a home where my parents always fought, but once they stepped outside the house, they were all smiles and laughs for the neighbors to see. My generation is simply more honest. We don't want our marriages to break up, but we're facing up to the fact that it's just so hard anymore to have a real working marriage. . . . Just about everyone I know who has been married for any period of time has gone through real intense problems in their marriage, or has already gotten divorced. I think it's just about inevitable."

Though divorce is not "just about inevitable," as Joan claims, it has become an increasingly common and accepted part of the family landscape. One of every four living Americans who has ever been married has also experienced divorce in his or her own marriage. That is less than the one in two figure incorrectly cited in news reports,[4] yet it does represent loss and rejection among 25 percent of adults (and their children) and a sense of uncertainty for many who enter into marriage.

People are less shocked by divorce than they used to be. In fact, marital disasters are so common that the social stigma which once accompanied the dissolution of a marriage is now barely grounds for pause. As one respondent told us in a survey we conducted concerning family matters, "Divorce is part of marriage. You can just about expect that at some point the marriage will break down and divorce is the only reasonable course of action."

No-fault Divorce

The floodgates for divorce were opened in 1970 with the enactment of the no-fault divorce law in California. For the first time, protracted, ugly legal battles over who was to blame for the broken marriage were no longer necessary. Other states jumped on the bandwagon during a time in our nation's history when experimentation was fashionable and traditions and absolute values were out of vogue. Granting people the maximum range of rights while holding them minimally responsible for their actions was the order of the day. The determination to make family a comfortable and satisfying experience remained at the heart of family law.

WHAT BABY BUSTERS EXPECT
A Desire for Enduring Marriages

The newest twist on the family scene is the distaste of today's young adults for the infidelity and marital indecisiveness of their elders. Our research among the Baby Bust generation (those born between 1965 and 1983) suggests that that generation prefers a return to a more traditional and enduring form of marriage and family. Busters sense the value of long-term, dependable relationships based on mutual commitment and nurtured through a promise to work through the difficulties. Almost 80 percent would marry if the right person came along or are already married; 85 percent believe God intends marriage to last a lifetime. Only 11 percent regard marriage as an outdated institution.[5]

This perspective among young adults is not altogether unexpected. Busters represent the first generation in which a majority may grow up in a home torn apart by divorce. Given the emotional ravages of divorce, which are felt most keenly by the children, the Busters' rejection of the Boomer pattern of disposal marriages is not surprising. And, as a more practical and relational generation than the Baby Boomers, today's under-thirty crowd views marriage and family as valid and viable, even in a culture changing as rapidly and profoundly as ours.[6]

Busters, as a generation, have been more widely scarred by the effects of growing up in a family divided by divorce than was any prior generation. The national sample of Busters to whom we spoke frequently made reference to their intention to protect their own kids from the suffering they experienced at the hands of their parents' divorce or mutual disrespect. Although the developing generation has yet to clarify and solidify its fundamental values system, it has been deeply affected by the harsh realities of a broken family.

Fear of Their Own Expectations

An obstacle to such a turnaround, however, is the fear harbored by Busters of not being able to live up to their own expectations. Our interviews among Busters discovered that they have been horrified by the family models created by the Boomers. Most Busters boldly state that they want to create marriages unlike those of their parents and to treat their own children with greater love and respect than they feel they were given by their own world-distracted parents.

"I know that the one hurt the most was me." Gene, twenty-three and a college graduate, watched his parents divorce when he was in junior high school. He lived with his mother until age eighteen; then he left for good. "Yeah, they were the ones who divorced, they were the ones who yelled and screamed, they were the ones who found out about the other sleeping around and bad-mouthing the other. But I was the one who stayed up crying nights, worrying about what would happen to me if my parents left or why the only adults I knew and loved couldn't agree on enough to give the relationship a real try.

"It affected everything in my life: my school work, my friendships, my dating, even my ability to relax and sleep soundly.

CHANGES IN THE FAMILY	
TRADITIONAL CONCEPTS AND BEHAVIOR	NEW CONCEPTS AND BEHAVIOR
Family is related by marriage or birth	Family is a group of caring people
Permanent relationships	Relationships based on mutual self-interest
Divorce not an option	Divorce made easy
No sex or cohabitation before marriage	Living together before marriage
Husband works; wife at home	Dual careers; daycare
Children in wedlock	Single-woman childbearing
Family members share meaningful activities	Members pursue own activities

How do you sleep soundly when your family is being torn to shreds?

"I don't know what I'll be doing ten or twenty years from now, but I can promise you that I will never treat my kids that way. I will never abuse my wife the way that my mom was emotionally savaged, or allow my wife to strip me of my sense of worth the way that my mom undercut my dad. Living that way is the worst kind of abuse imaginable, and I don't want to be associated with it anymore."

Gene is typical of his generation. Disgusted by the widespread marital infidelity of the Boomer generation, Baby Busters reject adultery as a valid reaction to an unfulfilling marriage. They intend to take marriage and family responsibilities more seriously. How they respond when the pressure is on remains to be seen—especially in light of the redefinition of family boundaries.

THE HOPE—AND FAILURE—OF LIVING TOGETHER

Given the life-views and basic assumptions of the current generation of young adults, it is not surprising to see them search for means of protecting themselves against marital disaster. The most widely embraced protection plan has been to test a potential partnership by living with that person. Cohabitation before marriage has become increasingly popular during the past two decades; indeed, the National Center for Health Statistics reported that during a recent five-year stretch, the incidence of cohabitation among people aged eighteen to twenty-four increased by almost 2000 percent![7]

The evidence shows that men and women living together prior to marriage often is a precursor to divorce. People who cohabit prior to getting married actually have an 82 percent greater likelihood of experiencing a divorce than do people who do not live together prior to their wedding vows.[8] The reason, apparently, relates to commitment. If a couple feel the need to test the depth of their compatibility before making a decision, the chances are good that they do not have what it takes to endure the tough times that every marriage inevitably confronts.

A different, but no less frightening, commentary on the dangers of cohabitation came from the Justice Department in 1992. It released a study showing that not only is domestic violence exploding in America, but women who cohabit are 56 times more likely to be beaten by their partners than are women who are married.

Unfortunately, whether out of ignorance of such facts or out of the stubborn belief that they can beat the odds, most young adults have paid no heed to the facts on the outcomes of cohabitation.

NEW RULES, NEW ROLES
Women in the Workplace

The family has also been greatly affected by transitions in the roles of men and women. In the traditional scenario, the man worked outside the home during the day, earning the money on which the family lived. The woman stayed at home and had children, assuming the primary responsibility for managing the home and raising the kids in concert with the perspectives and values she and her husband shared.

Such family arrangements are often greeted with nostalgic sighs. "Those were the good old days, but that's not realistic today," working parents often explain. Whereas in the fifties more than two out of every three households used to fit the scenario described above, just one of every four households matches those criteria today.[9] More commonly, we now have both the husband and wife working outside the home. In six out of ten households, both individuals hold paying jobs. The proportion is even higher among households in which there are children under the age of eighteen.[10]

The emergence of the working woman has been studied in detail. This new role for women assumed great prominence in the late sixties, when the cries for the liberation of women from the drudgery of housework and the purported unfairness of single-handedly carrying the child-raising responsibilities were loudly proclaimed. Now, after a quarter century of experience in the marketplace, with women striving to gain and handle equality in all realms of occupational experience, the jury is still out as to whether the mass employment of women has resulted in the liberation or the subjugation of women.

Some recent research suggests that nearly three of every four employed women have evaluated the realities of leaving the home for the workplace and have concluded that a woman is more likely to gain fulfillment by being a full-time mother.

"I got sucked into the view that women should be part of the corporate jungle, that unless we were battling alongside men for prominence in the marketplace, both the world and women would suffer for our absence." A mother of three kids, ranging from ages five to fifteen, Lorraine laughs at what she now considers her arrogance and naïveté of ten years earlier. "Let me tell you, after a decade in the trenches, worming my way up that ladder, I'm not sure the ladder is worth worrying about. I'd give just about anything to go back to the way it used to be. It's not that full-time parenting is easier than working at a career, but I find that I'm spread so thin that I just can't do my best at anything anymore."

Like many women, Lorraine must work in order to supplement the family income. If holding down a job once was a statement of independence by women, today it is also an act of financial necessity. Three decades of rising costs of living and persistent inflation have reduced the ability of the typical male to provide for the needs of his family at a level of comfort. Consider this reality: a dollar spent these days would have purchased the equivalent of $3.61 worth of items based on 1970 economics.[11] As we continue to lose ground economically, many women have joined the work force to help meet the family needs.

As a manager at a Fortune 500 company during the past seven years, Lorraine has weathered the working-woman storm well. "Frankly, I had to reassess my life in the last couple of years and I came to a conclusion that surprised me. In the end, being a more traditional kind of woman—a mother, a wife, a volunteer—those things are more important to me than whether or not I get a promotion or help my company meet its annual goals." More women are coming to the same conclusion: being a mother is more important than anything she accomplishes outside the home.

The Economy and the Family

In chapter 6 we discussed the pressures a struggling American economy has placed on families. We noted that two-income families are beginning to dominate; three of every five women hold some type of paying job, many of those either part-time positions or service-oriented businesses run from the home. Clearly, some women must work in order to help pay for the basics of food and children's clothing.

It would be difficult to reverse the patterns that now dominate our society. Our views on lifestyle and economics have been dramatically—and perhaps permanently—altered. The departure of most women from the home in favor of the workplace, regardless of the motives, has shifted the dominant responsibility of child care away from the nuclear family to a burgeoning group of professional child care providers. This new profession has grown into a $20 billion industry and has raised numerous questions as to how the replacement of mother care with other care has affected the well-being of our children.

How Fathers and Mothers Respond

Few parents are satisfied with the shift in gender roles. Husbands seem as dissatisfied as wives about mom having to work outside the home. Our research among men who are married to working women finds that a significant proportion of the men feel emotionally abandoned. A large share of fathers are disappointed that their wives cannot devote more time to the needs of the family. Although Americans do not like to think of "going backwards"—i.e., returning to lifestyles and viewpoints popular in the past—millions of husbands would be quite pleased to have their wives return to traditional family duties on a full-time basis.

For their part, a majority of American women who hold down paying jobs feel overwhelmed by the weight of responsibility they now shoulder. In the transition from housewife and mother to employee, few of them shed the primary accountability for the nurturing of their children and the maintenance of the home. Instead, they added a new series of pressing duties to what was already a difficult portfolio of tasks. Many women are proud of their ability to compete in the marketplace and recognize that their lifestyle dreams and expectations demand that they remain on the job, yet they indicate that being a full-time mother and homemaker would not seem as limiting as it once appeared. However, few women expect to be leaving the workplace in the foreseeable future, citing the expenses of larger house payments, car loans, school tuition, health care bills, and a host of other economic challenges.

Having Children

Our perceptions on family and gender roles have also changed concerning childbearing. These days three out of every ten children are born to a single mother. And the percentage of single women having children continues to rise, despite all the public squawking about the importance of two-parent families and the widespread view among adults that a two-parent family provides a superior environment to a single-parent raising a child. In fact, among white women, a newborn delivered today is ten times more likely to have an unwed mother than was the case in 1960. Giving birth as a white, single mother has grown fastest among those who are well-educated and affluent, indicating that the social stigma of illegitimacy may be gone.[12]

THE OLDER SINGLE MOTHER

One impetus for having children without having a complete parenting team is a seemingly inexorable maternal urge that has affected many single women. "Why should I wait until I'm past my prime to have a child?" asked one unmarried woman in her early thirties. "Who knows when I'm going to meet the right man? In the meantime, I'm going to have a child and be a great parent."

Isn't it going to be extremely difficult to play all of the adult family roles simultaneously: parent, breadwinner, homemaker? "Just because it's tough doesn't mean it's impossible," the woman explained. "I want this really bad. I can't afford to wait until I'm in my forties, and I can't afford to marry the wrong guy, just to have children. This way, I can have it all."

In fact, a higher proportion of the single women bearing children these days are older than the norm. A practice traditionally reserved for teenage girls who became pregnant against their own desires, giving birth out-of-wedlock is now more common among the Baby Boom women who deferred family in favor of career and other lifestyle pursuits. As the aging process has caught up with them, they have chosen to reverse the traditional route. They are opting for a child first, then marriage (hopefully) later.

Many unwed mothers gained confidence in their ability to pull off this strategy by noting the huge number of single moms already in the work force. Although the economic hardships of being a divorced mother have not escaped most unwed moms, they point out that there is a major distinction between the two types of women. "Divorced women who get custody of the children have been thrown into a new economic situation without warning and are unprepared for the problems and needs they'll have to deal with. I'm different," explained an unwed mother-to-be, "because I've prepared and planned for this type of existence. I have help lined up, my job is secure and pays well, my housing situation permits me to care for a child without losing my space and my privacy."

Hollywood may also have played a role in the perceived feasibility of being an unwed mother. Many women who star in movies and television shows have chosen to go the unmarried mother route over the last five years. Celebrities such as actresses Jessica Lange, Susan Sarandon, and Sherilyn Fenn have received publicity for their decision to enter motherhood without a committed male partner. True to their art form, they have put a very positive public spin on their decision and its consequences. And so do the celebrity-focused publications such as *People, Us, Premiere,* and the *National Enquirer,* and the plethora of television shows that track the lifestyles of entertainers.

Some analysts have pointed out that as the majority population of the U.S.—white Anglo-Saxons—follows the lead of the black population, where almost two-thirds of children are raised by single mothers, the same outcomes are likely, namely, poverty, emotional duress, health problems, and child abuse. Studies have linked the economic and emotional pressures of being an unwed mother to such disturbing patterns of behavior. To date, those warnings have fallen upon deaf ears.

The threat to the American family extends beyond parents to our children as well. As we will see, the outcome has been children who are forced to grow up too soon, little adults deprived of childhood and play. This too is a reason we sometimes feel so bad. But there is hope.

NOTES

1. "Heart Disease Worries? Watch the Decaf," *Science News* 140:11 (14 September 1991), 165.
2. This remarkable shift in perspective is drawn from primary research by the Barna Research Group conducted in 1992 and 1993. These findings are described in greater detail in chapter 2 of *The Future of the American Family* (Chicago: Moody, 1993).

3. The condition of marriage in America can be better understood by examining the hard data, rather than the errant cries of the mass media. Helpful sources include *Faithful Attraction*, by Andrew Greeley (New York: Tor, 1991), and *The Future of the American Family*, by George Barna (Chicago: Moody, 1993), chapter 3.

4. George Barna, *The Future of the American Dream*, 67–68.

5 George Barna, *Baby Busters* (Chicago: Northfield, 1994), 118–19.

6. This information is drawn from studies conducted among Baby Busters and originally reported in *Baby Busters*, by George Barna.

7. These data were provided by the National Center for Health Statistics, Washington, D.C.

8. This is based on data from the National Center for Health Statistics and the U.S. Bureau of the Census.

9. This is based on data from the U.S. Bureau of the Census, reported in *Statistical Abstract of the United States, 1993* and in *Historical Statistics: Colonial Times to 1970*.

10. These figures are released by the U.S. Bureau of Labor Statistics.

11. *Statistical Abstract of the United States* (Washington, D.C.: U. S. Department of Commerce, 1993), table 755.

12. *The Index of Leading Cultural Indicators*, by William Bennett (New York: Simon & Schuster, 1994), 46–48.

THE SEARCH

1. In what ways, if any, has your definition or perception of what constitutes a family changed during recent years? What caused the change?

2. How (and why) do you think that families may become a means to personal ends rather than ends in themselves?

3. Instead of living together unmarried (cohabitation) and no-fault divorce, what are some effective ways of promoting satisfying, long-term marriages?

4. Research is discovering recent dissatisfaction with two-career families. Why has women's attraction to the workplace decreased recently?

5. What tradeoffs could be employed to make it possible for the mother to stay home with the children if she and her husband so desired?

POINT OF ACTION

Make a list of things you will do with your immediate family in the next month that will involve spending quantity time as well quality time together.

CHAPTER 9

OH, TO BE
A CHILD
AGAIN

In chapter 2 we met Tanya Jones, seventeen, of New York, who described the shootings, robberies, and fights in her neighborhood, and the pregnancies of her teenaged girl-friends. She has been forced to grow up fast.

"I read a lot of books, and I learn a lot," Tanya told us. "I read about how city kids lose their childhood earlier than others. I'm like that. I've been an adult since I was about seven or eight, helping my mother with the younger kids, working for small money to help out, worrying about staying clear of pimps and dealers."

ADULTS BEFORE THEIR TIME

Children don't have to live in the inner city to learn to grow up fast. In the nineties in America, many children are being forced to be adults before their time. We adults seem to have lost our appreciation for the importance of allowing children to be children. Increasingly, we push our youth to become little adults, adopting the language, clothing, food, work habits, and entertainment preferences of their elders. Children are even beginning to encounter some of the same stresses as their elders.

Playing to Win

There was a time when being a child meant innocence, freedom from a highly scheduled day, and activities that could be categorized as "child's play," pure and simple. Children could blow bubbles, find tadpoles in a neighborhood pond or creek, run through sprinklers on a hot summer's day, or play games with mom or dad. Today most children in suburbia and our central cities can never find watering holes with tadpoles, have replaced sprinklers with trips to water parks, and play alone at such computer games as Nintendo's "Mario Brothers." None of those activities are bad, but they are generally more frenetic, more isolating, and less educational than the relaxing games of yesterday's youth.

Even truly fun sports such as baseball and hide-and-seek are being replaced by the high competition and must-win settings of Little League and high school sports. The height of this must-win mania may have been reached in 1993 when the coach of the Libertyville High School football team north of Chicago staged a faked shooting to motivate his players. A supposed fan of the opposing team shot the coach with blanks, and the coach hit the floor groaning from his "wounds." Most of the players were shocked and frightened, and they lost a key play-off game after the incident. The coach later apologized, saying he was only trying to help the team.

Pressures Children Face

That coach wanted his teenaged charges to play just like adults, and he used tactics to make them as intense as any professional players. The emphasis on creating mature kids as quickly as possible comes from all directions, starting as early as age three. Consider the cumulative effect of these realities:

- Preschool attendance has become a virtual expectation. Suburban youngsters who enter kindergarten unable to recite the alphabet, read simple books, and do basic addition are now deemed "slow" in some areas of the country.
- Many under-age children are working. The Labor Department reports that the incidence of under-age youth holding paying jobs illegally has more than quadrupled in the last five years.

- The incidence of children viewing R-rated movies with their parents has skyrocketed. More than 10 million kids who are supposedly protected from viewing such films by the ratings system see one or more of these movies each year. Parents seem to believe their "mature" young children should be exposed to adult themes early in life. So children learn about sex, homosexuality, rape, torture, and sadism much earlier in life than did their parents. Watching such movies has forced them to consider adult dangers and aberrations earlier than they would otherwise. The exposure to such movies, in general, has proliferated with the accessibility of VCRs and cable TV. A significant share of the viewing choices of children are not monitored by their parents.

- Guns, knives and other weapons are becoming commonplace in our junior high schools and high schools. On any given school day, it is estimated that more than 2.8 million students—one of every ten teenagers—are packing more than a lunch on their way to school.[1] Some city school districts have begun to install metal detectors to ferret out guns and knives children may bring to school. Those caught with weapons often explain that they had to protect themselves against possible gang attacks.

- Sexual promiscuity has run rampant in the last two decades. The Centers for Disease Control report that nearly three out of four high school seniors have had sexual intercourse before they graduate, and a majority of all high school students (grades 9 through 12) have had such experience.

- Safe sex doesn't always work as planned. The number of unmarried teenagers who have become pregnant has just about doubled in the last twenty years. Forty percent of those pregnancies end in abortion. Every year a half million single teenaged girls give birth to their first child. Whether by abortion or childbirth, these teenage girls surrender their childhood. Raising a child by oneself or having an abortion takes its emotional, physical, and financial toil; the loss for the girl is much more than her virginity. With the loss of innocence goes many lost opportunities.

- Teenagers are responsible for buying more of the family purchases. They directly spend more than $80 billion per year and influence the spending of another $100 billion annually. Most of the money they spend is given to them by parents for family purchases. In fact, almost 40 percent of today's teens are responsible for the weekly grocery shopping for their families. In addition, substantial proportions are charged with buying other major household items on behalf of the family, including television sets, stereo equipment, kitchen appliances, and magazine subscriptions.

- "Latchkey children," those children who return home after school with key in hand and an empty house waiting, are growing in numbers. Despite a public outcry over the dangers of having latchkey children, more than four out of every ten families with kids under seventeen leave those kids on their own at least once a week. Between the end of school and dinner time, children who are teen-aged or younger are left home alone; they are in charge of the house, without any supervision.

The results are quite clear. The National Academy of Sciences tells us that one of every six children suffers from some type of mental or emotional disorder, including depression, anorexia, and chronic drug abuse. The youth suicide rate has tripled since 1960, while the number of suicide attempts continues to escalate, reaching a record high every year. Academic achievement is declining, leaving millions of high school graduates incapable of reading and doing basic mathematics. Sexually transmitted diseases plague millions of youngsters.

CHILDREN OF CRIME

Street gangs, violent and anti-authoritarian, continue to flourish, primarily as a form of family for many kids who missed the attention they needed. Serious crime has grown rapidly among our young people, reaching epidemic proportions in our major cities.

And children are learning sad lessons about justice and right and wrong when in America less than 10 percent of all crimes committed result in the imprisonment of the criminal.

Children are also being taught that crime can gain a person glory. A large group of high school guys in southern California, many of whom were athletes and campus leaders, became media celebrities for holding a competition to see how many young girls each of them could seduce or overpower in a selfish, vicious game of sexual conquest. They called themselves the Spur Posse and received lots of coverage on the TV tabloid shows as well as national television news. In the late eighties children observed adults siding with subway vigilante Bernhard Goetz, who killed four young thugs on the New York City subway system. Many praised Goetz as a "hero" and a "defender of justice" before he was found guilty of murder.

Some blame juvenile delinquency and sophisticated, even cold, children on a criminal justice process that does not work. And it does not: the punishments meted out, when there are such punishments, frequently do not fit the crime. The threat of penalty does not seem to act as a deterrent. We do not have a sufficient number of law enforcement officials to uphold the laws that exist. And even those criminals who are apprehended and wind up serving time in prison generally come back to inflict further injury on people and society. Nine out of ten of today's prisoners are violent or repeat offenders; two-thirds of all prisoners released from state prisons have been found to commit a felony or serious misdemeanor within three years of their release.[2]

Children seeing such "justice" wonder not only about right and wrong but, like their parents, live in fear that they may be victims of crime.

THE IMPACT OF FAMILY BREAKDOWN

However, most experts attribute the fear, cynicism, and lost innocence of our children to something more basic: the breakdown of the family through divorce or neglect by parents. "There is a mountain of scientific evidence showing that when families disintegrate, children often end up with intellectual, physical and emotional scars that persist for life," explains Karl Zinsmeister, a Research Fellow at the American Enterprise Institute. "We talk about the drug crisis, the education crisis, and the problems of teen pregnancy and juvenile crime. But all these ills trace back to one major source: broken families."[3]

Broken families extend beyond families torn by divorce. Families in which one parent is not showing respect and love to

HOW CHILDREN ARE PUSHED TO BECOME ADULTS

Highly competive sports	Teenage pregnancy
Pre-school attendance pressure	More purchasing power and opportunities
Under-age children working	Latchkey children (parents not at home)
Massive doses of sex, violence in media	Juvenile crime
Lethal weapons in schools	Divorce or neglect by parents
Sexual promiscuity	Direct pressure to "grow up" from adults

the offspring also fracture family ties. Alcoholism and abuse are two major culprits, with reports of abuse ranging from verbal and physical to sexual continuing to climb. Even neglect of children has its consequences, family authorities say. All these actions reflect society's growing devaluing of children.

Some analysts warn that the failure to address these matters with swift and deep responses will permit the continued degradation of life for our children. "If we fail to come to terms with the relationship between family structure and declining child well-being, then it will be increasingly difficult to improve children's life prospects, no matter how many new programs the federal government funds. Nor will we be able to make progress in bettering school performance or reducing crime or improving the quality of the nation's future work force." These sentiments were expressed by Barbara Dafoe Whitehead, author of the now-famous article that ran in *Atlantic Monthly* pertaining to family values and the family crisis in America: "Dan Quayle Was Right."[4] Like most researchers who study family issues, her work concludes that families have lost their sense of purpose and that our children, more than anyone, are suffering the consequences.

THE LOSS OF FAMILY TRADITIONS

The 1992 Barna Research Group study of family behavior uncovered a mammoth shift in intrafamily activities. One of the most significant transitions has been the abandonment of family traditions. Those repetitive, predictable activities between parent and child that served as a mechanism allowing kids to ease into adulthood and maximize the enjoyment of youth have been lost. Traditions as varied as eating meals together, praying as a family, playing games together, attending church as a family, taking extended vacations, and jointly completing household chores are much less common than in years gone by.

Interviews with teenagers and young adults indicate that the security of knowing those routine activities would take place or the emotional satisfaction of engaging in such activities as a family unit have been lost on the emerging generation. The family routines they have matured with are less meaningful—for instance, watching television at the same time. More often than not, the behavioral patterns with which they are most familiar are not of regularly shared experiences but of isolation and survival.

The cause of this change may be our obsession with maximizing and protecting our time. When life was less hectic and complex, parents were expected to and typically did spend considerable time with their children. Today, estimates of the amount of time a typical parent spends with his or her child ranges from six minutes to ninety minutes a day. No matter which standard is relied upon, the bottom line is that children these days get cheated out of the time they need if they are to absorb the sense of personal value and societal responsibility that is viewed as healthy and beneficial. The message being sent to our children, loud and clear, is that they are not as deserving of our time as are other people and other pursuits. The only way they can arrest more of our attention is by competing, which means learning the world of big people and playing the game their way.

A DIFFERENT ATTITUDE AMONG PARENTS

Many parents feel threatened these days by youngsters who want a traditional childhood. Most parents admit that they are straining to juggle the numerous opportunities and crises that demand their time, attention, and energy. Slowing down to accommodate the various needs of their young ones creates all types of internal conflict for many parents. In our materialistic, image-conscious, mile-a-minute world, children can become vulnerable, lost in the shuffle.

It often seems as though the two worlds—that of adults and that of our children—simply cannot be reconciled. Millions of parents have concluded that the world of the child and the world of the adult cannot peacefully coexist; one or the other has to compromise. Parents then have to make some tough choices. As they experience the innocence and vulnerability of their off-spring, some parents convince themselves that those are not qualities which enable people to get ahead in the world. They conclude that innocence and vulnerability (sometimes known as tenderheartedness) are the very qualities that allow an individual to be exploited by unscrupulous beings who scout for opportunities to take advantage of the unsuspecting or the unprepared.

Such a parent's natural response, then, is to prepare his youngsters to do battle in the war zone in which adults operate. He persuades himself that causing his children to surrender some of the joys of growing up for the security of surviving in a dangerous and heartless world is an unfortunate but necessary transaction. In the end, he sees pushing his kids to grow up quickly as compassionate parenting. It is in the child's best interests, and it meets the parent's needs better, too.

Sadly, one journalist who researched the changing nature of childhood concluded that we have crushed the ability of our children to dream and to revel in the fun of childhood. "The steady drip of economic pressure, commercial greed, parental absence, and overprogramming eventually robs children of their innocence and later, of their maturity. Encouraging children to be children allows them to mature at a steadier, more natural pace, as opposed to imposing whatever commercial facsimile of maturity is in vogue at the moment."[5]

PARENTS, CHILDREN, AND THE FAMILY

As mentioned in the previous chapter, the shrinking of time in which we allow children to be children is only one symptom of the besieged family of the nineties. Redefinitions of family; new perspectives on marriage, divorce, and cohabitation; changes in childbearing patterns; revised gender roles; and sexual promiscuity all are putting pressure on quality family life in America. These changes reflect more than a sense of confusion, feelings of desperation, or mere self-deception. These dubious outcomes have long-term consequences that must be heeded.

One might argue that redesigning the roles of men and women and repositioning childhood in the scheme of human development are reasonable changes to pursue; after all, change is inevitable, even healthy and helpful, and America became a great nation by taking risks, by innovating, by questioning the norms.

A proper view of our history, though, shows that healthy growth requires change to be tied to a well-conceived, balanced strategy for the development of individuals and families. At every juncture in our nation's history, progress has been the product of a logical combination and extension of our Judeo-Christian values, our human capabilities, an equitable distribution of available resources, and a clearly understood sense of purpose carried out with unity under strong leadership.

The changes that are restructuring the American family today do not come from such a mold or operate within such an environment. Sadly, the problems we see emerging so broadly today are the product of emotional, spiritual, cultural, and intellectual anarchy.

As the traditional family has been undermined, so has our basic model for healthy relationships. Our children grow up but lose the ability to learn how positive and intimate relationships develop and are nurtured. That is not a lesson that can be gleaned from textbooks. It is best learned through personal exposure to such relationships in a natural setting.

A primary reason so many relationships are described as dysfunctional these days is because we have allowed the traditional family to dissipate before our very eyes. Such family bonds produce the primary emotional stability we rely upon as the base for our personal growth. Once the stability of the family has been lost, we surrender much of our personal emotional consistency and security. We have not filled the void left by the traditional family system with an alternative that can be counted on over the long haul. Though some have sought satisfaction in family realities by substituting the fulfillment of selfish desires (such as childbearing without marriage or divorce due to "lifestyle differences"), they have ignored the hard work and sacrifice required to build lasting and meaningful family relationships. And, as noted in this chapter, the consequences impact children as much as parents.

Perhaps the lesson is that there are no shortcuts for anything worthwhile. Marriage as a sacred commitment requires work and perseverance. Maybe the lesson is that God's plan for the family is the only viable plan for the family, and He has made

His views on family clearly known through the Bible. Perhaps our current family travails will help us to reestablish the family as a priority in our lives. Or it could be that the purpose of today's family chaos is to underscore the necessity of a comprehensive worldview that places God at the center and that instills His values as the foundation for our decisions and actions.

Whatever the lesson is, we must learn it quickly, before our families are no longer able to reap the benefits of the insights gained.

NOTES

1. This estimate is based on statistics from the U. S. Department of Education cited in Mary Jordan, "Summit Searches for Cease Fire in Violence Enveloping Children," *Washington Post*, 22 July 1993, 1. Looking at the high school population alone, about 20 percent of students—one of every five—carry a weapon to school on a regular basis. (See William Bennett, *The Index of Leading Cultural Indicators* [New York: Simon & Schuster, 1994], 31.)

2. John Silber, *Straight Shooting* (New York: Harper Perennial, 1990), 228.

3. Karl Zinsmeister, "Raising Hiroko," *The American Enterprise*, March/April 1990.

4. Barbara Dafoe Whitehead, "Dan Quayle Was Right," *Atlantic Monthly*, April 1993.

5. Richard Louv, *Childhood's Future* (New York: Anchor, 1990), 113–114.

THE SEARCH

1. *What are the main differences between the children's games and amusements popular in the fifties compared to those popular today?*

2. *List three ways that violence is penetrating the mind and circumstances of young people (see pages 157–159). What can we as adults do to protect children from these forces?*

3. *How are the choices so much more difficult for teenage girls who have become pregnant? What do they stand to lose?*

4. *The changing attitudes of parents toward children are undercutting the development of positive and intimate relationships in the family. In what areas have parents' attitudes covertly changed toward children (review pages 161–162)? As an adult, do you at times carry any of these attitudes toward children?*

5. *By allowing the traditional family to dissipate, what are we giving up as individuals?*

POINT OF ACTION

Let your child choose an activity that he or she enjoys and then schedule time to do it together on a regular basis. If you are unmarried or childless, volunteer to spend time once a month with a neighbor's or relative's child in a playful activity that the child chooses.

PART 3

HOPE FOR THE NATION

. . . .

A fter reading about the state of the nation in Part 2, one thing should
be clear: Those who look at our nation and boldly proclaim that we
are the envy of the world, the mightiest power on the face of the earth,
are taking a superficial look at reality. When we explore the heart and
the hope of the country, we find little in which to take pride or for which
we may hold much hope.

That does not mean that matters cannot be significantly changed,
though. If we were to concentrate our ability to work hard, our desire to
do good, our capacity to understand complex conditions and respond
intelligently, and to maintain an enduring interest in spiritual matters
toward solving the crisis in which we live, we can find hope for the future. The problems are extensive, ingrained, and complicated, but they
are not beyond solution.

In this part you will read about five critical responses we must
make to American culture as it stands today. Like everyone else, you
must either agree to be part of the solution or admit that you are part of
the problem. The five responses, explored in the next four chapters, are
the following: (1) developing a viable worldview that will enable us to see
things clearly and have a useful decision-making filter; (2) changing our
expectations of the world; (3) addressing and filling the leadership vacuum that is sucking the life out of our future; (4) knowing and interacting
with the only true source of power: God (through the appropriate use of
the spiritual practices that God ordained for our use, we can restructure
our reality, leaning on His power); and (5) achieving personal wholeness
through personal service and giving. (The latter happens only when we
focus on something other than ourselves—God—so this will also be discussed in chapter 13, "Faith That Matters.")

This is the question: What will you do about the decline of America? You can neither wait for someone else to do the job, nor expect
someone else to carry your weight in the process. Each of us must play a
role in the rehabilitation of America.

. . . .

CHAPTER 10

A COHERENT WORLDVIEW

If you embrace any of the following three worldviews, by definition you have a certain attitude toward the meaning of your existence. But you also will behave according to a certain pattern that reflects your perspective of life. The relationship of behavior and worldview can be seen in four leaders who promoted distinctive perspectives of the world. These perspectives of our world are important, for if any one is true it holds hope (or despair) for changing our nation.

THREE NOTABLE VIEWS OF OUR WORLD

"I think; therefore, I am." René Descartes opened the doors for a naturalist point of view with his classic statement. Descartes professed to be a Christian, but his breakthrough insight was the intellectual stepping-stone to a unique conclusion: God was the maker of the universe who had since discharged Himself from any further relationship with that creation. In this view, nature has its own set of laws and dynamics which guide the world, apart from any theistic intervention or concern, and which is void of any overriding reason or purpose.

Unlike naturalism, existentialism says meaning is elusive. "Every living thing is born without reason, prolongs itself out of weakness and dies by chance," said the philosopher and existential advocate Jean-Paul Sartre. Later, German philosopher Friedrich Nietzsche made this philosophy user-friendly by boldly proclaiming, "God is dead." Sartre and Nietzsche determinedly argued that all human activity is of little value, is of no distinction, and leads to no particular end. In short, life is meaningless.

A more optimistic viewpoint came from Jerusalem. Jesus of Nazareth offered a third view of our world when He provided his followers with tangible hope and a sense of purpose in life. "I am the way, the truth and the life." Because of the nature of the God who created the world and its inhabitants, Jesus claimed that life has meaning and purpose. There are absolutes, drawn from God and His character, that can be known and used for the common good. Followers of the Christian worldview believe that through reliance upon Jesus Christ and adherence to the principles He taught, both temporal and eternal fulfillment can be received as God's gift.

MODERN VOICES

The debate has raged throughout the ages as to which philosophical view is right. Many of the voices that continue the debate today echo those views. The arguments may be more sophisticated, but the perspectives have changed little. Consider, for instance, the words of a scientist and a singer/composer.

The scientist, Carl Sagan, struck the publishing mother lode with his book *Cosmos*, an essay on the meaning and order of life. It is an ode to naturalism, and he eruditely promotes the naturalistic view with such statements as "the cosmos is all that there is, or ever was, or ever will be."[1] The naturalist view of the wonders and powers of a godless universe suggest that there is cause and effect, but without any grand purpose or direction.

Billy Joel, popular musician and an articulate spokesman for the views of millions from his generation, has recently written of the skepticism engendered by the Enlightenment and akin to existential thinking: a life without certainty or absolutes. In his song "Shades of Grey," he advocates moral relativism, a worldview that characterizes a majority of Americans. There may be right and wrong, Joel says, but the singer sees only "shades of grey;" no one can say some action is right or wrong, or that his or her view is better than someone else's view.

In the relativist perspective, there are no absolutes, only those responses that seem right to the individual at the moment.

The best we can hope for is to peacefully coexist and gain some modicum of satisfaction from life—assuming that our efforts do not conflict with those of others in our midst, as they attempt to extract their due measure of satisfaction from life.

Kurt Vonnegut, Jr., the best-selling novelist, writes of God creating the world, surveying His work, and requesting the man He created to figure out some reason because He can't see any purpose to His own creation.[2] Through Vonnegut's popular and engaging prose, the existentialist view has been captured (and widely exposed) in a humorous and endearing manner, one that blunts the heavy consequences of a world without purpose or direction. This view has been summarized in a recent advertising headline: "So much activity, so little meaning."

And everyone's favorite reincarnate, entertainer Shirley Mac-Laine, has assumed the mantle of spokes-entity for the elusive but inescapable New Age movement. In her best-selling book *It's All in the Playing*, MacLaine explained that she had created everything in her world. She concluded from her revelation that she was one with everything and was, in fact, everything: "I was my own universe."[3] The Eastern-influenced views of those following New Age thinking contend that we are our own gods, we dictate what happens in our lives, and we can experience whatever is necessary for ultimate significance.

GETTING FROM CONFUSION TO CLARITY

Countless individuals—scientists, religious leaders, philosophers, politicians, educators—have proposed their philosophy of life for the world to embrace. The issue has not been finding new philosophies of life from which to choose but evaluating the ones that have already been proposed in light of whether they will enhance your life because they reflect the wisdom and security of real truth.

Some two thousand years ago, a Roman officer named Pontius Pilate confronted Jesus Christ in the court chambers and, after asking the world's Savior for self-justification, rhetorically asked, "What is truth?" That question remains a timeless challenge to us in our struggle to justify ourselves, the ways in which we live, the goals we set for ourselves, and the virtues and conditions we hold dear. The answer to Pilate's question is the key to insight into the meaning and purpose of life. Your answer to that question will determine who you are, how you behave, and the nature of your destiny. It is a question—and answer—whose importance is impossible to overestimate.

The practical response to the question is to size up our existence and embrace a worldview that helps us answer Pilate's query. A worldview is the group of assumptions a person possesses that defines his understanding of, and responses to, the world. It is essentially a person's philosophy of life, a holistic perspective built incrementally over the entire course of his life and derived from the sum of his experiences, insights, beliefs, observations, expectations, dreams, and relationships. A person's worldview is the filter through which he accesses all information about life and possibilities, screening that data to arrive at conclusions as to how to respond to conditions in ways that are consistent with his mind and heart.

It may sound simple, but it's difficult to identify your worldview. Can you articulate it in a few words or a handful of sentences? Probably not. Even those people who have worked hard to develop and refine their worldview do not reduce it to a simple phrase or expression. The world in which we live is complex. Of necessity, the worldview we adopt must address the various dimensions of that complexity to arrive at a perspective that organizes, provides meaning, and offers us direction in relation to the world in which we live. A viable worldview contains assumptions that are relatively consistent with each other, intentional and consciously identified, and verifiable.

A life philosophy or worldview is needed by all people. In fact, whether we can easily define that perspective or not, each of us has formed some semblance of a worldview that serves as the basis for our attitudes, opinions, values, beliefs, words, and deeds. For some adults, that philosophy is intentional; for most Americans, the filter through which we see the world is a tacit lens, in place by circumstance rather than design.

Some people possess a worldview that is solidified and unchanging. They are confident that they have evaluated what needed to be studied to arrive at a correct understanding of reality and eternity, and they stand firm on the conclusions they have drawn until other exigencies push them to rethink their standards. Others have a more fluid worldview. Their dominant perspective changes as their environment changes. Their standards are not firm but temporary and meant to be flexible. Their philosophy is not really a definitive outlook that filters and organizes their reality so much as it is a defense mechanism that enables them to contend with the rush of influences, opportunities, and demands made on them. Their philosophy changes in response to transformations in the culture, in knowledge, or in personal responsiveness to external (and, sometimes, internal) realities.

Some people are quite articulate in describing their worldview, having spent many hours reflecting on what they believe, why they believe it, and how those beliefs and perspectives should be integrated into the total fabric of their lives. They are able to articulate their outlook because it is settled in their minds; there is virtually no shifting of their core insights, values, beliefs, and assumptions. Our research suggests, though, that such introspection and clarity is unusual. Most Americans do not have a coherent philosophy of life, and most of those who claim they maintain such a view are unable to clearly define it upon request. That is partially because their views are not consistent. They change with the shifts in the world around them, making clarity difficult to achieve, either for themselves or in response to the inquiries of others.

It is the absence of a true worldview that plagues the nation. Our moral problems, ethical crises, and personal confusion regarding the direction and realities of living are directly related to our failure to develop a foundational wisdom and moral base that will shape our responses to our environment.

The development, articulation, and reliance upon a well-established worldview is not simply a matter of academic interest. From a personal perspective, you derive tremendous value from having a specific, detailed, and consistent worldview. In practical terms, it is the mental grid through which you examine options and alternatives related to the myriad of challenges you face in life. Your philosophy of life and your perspective of the world around you will produce certain character traits, relationships, lifestyle decisions, and spiritual perspectives that would likely have been different in the absence of that worldview. Your choice of what to believe about the important matters of life—summed up in the word *truth*—will define who you are, how you perceive your life, and how you respond to the world you encounter.

But what worldview will you choose? There is a philosophical menu with numerous options available to you, each vying for

COMPETING WORLDVIEWS*

Naturalism	Nature has own laws governing world apart from God's intervention; no overriding purpose. Carl Sagan
Existentialism	There is no God, activity is of little value, all is by chance and ultimately meaningless. Jean-Paul Sartre
New Age	We are gods shaping our own lives, and can experience ultimate significance. Shirley MacLaine
Nihilism	Nothing really matters, life is fruitless, amoral with the will to power over others. Friedrich Nietzsche
Secular humanism	Science defines reality, humankind is the creative energy and nucleus of all that matters.
Relativism	No absolutes, everyone has personal truth for their circumstances.
Christian theism	Absolute truth determined by sovereign, infinite, personal God revealed in His Son Jesus Christ, to whom we are responsible to obey as His creatures.

* Some of the worldviews overlap in concept or practice.

your attention and selection. Each carries with it a different series of assumptions, implications, and consequences.

CONTENDERS FOR YOUR CONSIDERATION

Many philosophies or worldviews are evident in America as we approach the new millennium. Among those are *nihilism* (the view that nothing really matters, that life is a fruitless, absurd play without a significant conclusion); *secular humanism* (the view that science can tell us all we can and need to know about reality; that whatever is not scientifically verifiable is not to be trusted or considered; that humankind is the creative energy behind the world today and the nucleus of all that matters); *relativism* (the view that everyone possesses his own brand of truth, and nobody can contradict that truth, since there are no absolutes); and *Christian theism* (the view that there is one God, the Creator of the universe, who exists in relationship with humankind and has provided the absolute principles and personal resources necessary for purposeful and fulfilling living in the created environment).[4]

One way of looking at these competing outlooks is to examine what each of them considers to be important. To the nihilist, nothing is really important since everything is part of a grand cosmic charade. To the secular humanist, that which is scientifically proven is important. To the relativist, whatever he or she thinks is important is important. To the Christian theist, that which God defined as true and significant is of the utmost importance.

Today, the two dominant views that characterize American society are relativism and Christian theism. In days gone by, most people would have been Christian theists. Today, however, about three out of every four adults is a relativist—even though more than half of those individuals label themselves "Christian." *It is my wholehearted conviction that the crisis of values, purpose, and direction that is undermining America is directly correlated with the increasing acceptance of relativism as an appropriate worldview.*

The issue of which worldview to embrace spans the theological gamut. My research has discovered that a majority of adults whose religious beliefs categorize them as born-again Christians nevertheless reject the possibility that there is any type of absolute truth.[5] In other words, people who are "hard-core Christians" are every bit as divided and confused on issues of truth and practical life philosophy as are others. You could even make a strong argument that within the church world there is an even greater split on beliefs and perspectives related to truth than you would find outside the Christian church. Among adults who attend mainline Protestant churches (i.e., United Church of Christ, Episcopal, Evangelical Lutheran Church in America, United Methodist, and Presbyterian Church in the U.S.A), more than three-quarters do not believe in absolute truth but have developed other truth perspectives that act as the fulcrum of their worldview.[6]

RELATIVISM CONSIDERED

The crux of the relativist position is that all reality is subjective. To those who approach life from this perspective, nothing can be known with certainty; all views are equally valid; culture influences what is appropriate; and there is no consistent common ground from which decisions can be made, since everyone's opinion is equally valid.

From a logical point of view, relativism doesn't make sense. And, in fact, that is why America is becoming emotionally, morally, and ethically paralyzed: its basic philosophy is seriously flawed.

In the world of relativism, two conflicting and irreconcilable views may exist—but neither is allowed to be rejected, because that would infer the existence of an absolute. Although the logic of life would suggest that two conflicting and irreconcilable views cannot both be correct, in the world of relativism, they are equally valid. In this way of thinking, all standards are transient and personal. They change according to time, place, circumstances and people.

"Because I Said So"

In the relativist scheme of life, everything is subjective. Morality is a matter of personal preference. Ethics vary from situation to situation. Covenants and agreements may be changed on a whim. Values shift from day to day, as we experience unforeseen consequences, encounter novel concepts, or realize that our existing values stand in the way of enjoying a greater degree of satisfaction. People demand rights but ignore the corresponding responsibilities.

The outcomes of a system riddled with internal conflict are obvious. People often become frustrated and angry because they cannot get their own way. Nobody listens to anyone else because the opinions of other people don't really matter and there's nothing of value to learn from others. Arguments based on facts are refuted because we can choose not to accept the veracity of the underlying data. In fact, data are comparatively useless since all ideas are equally valid, regardless of the supporting statistics. Arguments based on intuition, however, cannot be refuted because you cannot challenge someone else's feelings; all feelings are similarly valid.

Consider some of the potential outcomes of a relativistic perspective. Suicide is a reasonable response to life because the person decided that life was not worth living—and nobody can reasonably argue otherwise when there is no absolute value placed on life. Rape is not a criminal act as long as the rapist had a need or reason to engage in such behavior, or perhaps felt that the victim "was asking for it." Theft is an acceptable response to poverty, since the poor person who steals from another person is simply trying to get by in life, meeting a viable, tangible need that society admits should be taken care of. Lying to someone is justified by the liar's desire to protect his own best interests. Terrorism can be justified by the intense desire or needs of the terrorists. Anarchy, in which chaos and lawlessness prevail, must be accepted as the equal of democracy. Racial prejudice is esteemed as a viable reaction to people of different races, as would be slavery, prostitution, and peddling illicit drugs (if, of course, there could be such a thing as an illicit drug), simply because the individuals engaged in those activities defined them as personally desirable.

This is pure madness, of course. No sane society would permit such a philosophy of life to be pervasive. But that is exactly what has happened in the United States over the past twenty-five years. We have abandoned our mores and traditions—the values-ladened perspectives that shaped the legal, familial, spiritual, economic, and cultural character of the United States—in favor of a patchwork of inconsistent personal freedoms deployed without accompanying responsibilities. The Pandora's Box of fulfillment-without-consequences was opened wide, and now we can't get the door shut. Worse, it seems as if nobody's even trying.

Perhaps the most devious legacy of relativism is that it precludes meaning. Because it eschews standards and accountability, the only possible result is chaos and selfism. A culture based on relativism is a culture doomed to dissipation and collapse. It is a people who will be defined—and devastated—by moral bankruptcy, ethical turbulence, spiritual degeneration, and interpersonal pain. Relativism can only result in a culture crippled by extreme selfishness and the inability to rally around a common cause. In such a society the only common cause is self; there is too much competition for primacy to allow for anything more than an uncomfortable state of survival of the most selfish.

Frustration in America

Relativism is a no-win philosophy. Since there is no place for compromise, common good, or a societal ethic that esteems something other than self, frustration becomes our constant emotional companion. We believe that our conscience is infallible and become irritated when others do not follow the dictates of our conscience. And we just cannot understand why others don't see things our way. Our own standards and values make decisions and directions rather clear, but other people just don't seem to get it.

In a relativistic culture, there are no heroes because there is no one who possesses or defends exactly the same values system and lifestyle that characterizes us. And, indeed, our studies show that few Americans today have heroes. Worse, those in the youngest generation bemoan the fact that they do not even have role models whose examples they can learn from, whose successes they can emulate. Instead, they have role repellents: examples of how not to act, without a sense of what the appropriate and viable alternatives might be.

In a relativistic culture, the only limit on ethical behavior is what you cannot get away with, in light of the prevailing laws of the land. Cheating is not cheating if nobody realizes you have cheated. Lying is defensible as your means of protecting your own needs and best interests, which are always superior to the needs and interests of others. Crime is just another way of equalizing reality and getting that which you innately feel you deserve.

In a relativistic culture, there is no real value to hard work. Work is just a means to an end, anyway, so as long as the paycheck keeps coming or your needs are otherwise taken care of, there is no need to invest yourself in a career or profession. What's more important is that you have the self-esteem, the personal enjoyment and the sense of fulfillment you need. If that comes from hard work and thrift, fine. If it doesn't, fine. The touchstone of relativism is that the activity must fit the outcome; if work meets your personal needs for satisfaction and enjoyment, then it's worth the investment.

In a relativistic culture, people are a means to an end, not an end in themselves. Relationships are critical—and they will last as long as they provide more value than they consume in personal emotional resources. Respect is something to be received rather than given. Tolerance is highly valued because it reduces the need to prove the superiority of your own claims, perspectives and behaviors; you may simply endure others while realizing that you have a better way.

In the end, a culture that accepts all truth as being relative is one in which the individual is always right, the other person always wrong. Immorality, by traditional measures, abounds because there are no remaining standards, no means of accountability to a model, no sense of purpose that produces parameters that foster the achievement of meaning. The thought of accountability offends those in the relativist mode since it requires the introduction of moral and ethical standards.

What Is Truth in Relativism?

In the culture of relativism, truth is whatever we say it is. Our opinions are elevated to the status of perfect wisdom.

Amazingly, in a system where relativism reigns, absolute tolerance is the only rational response. Thus, even a madman is given the same courtesies and opportunities as the savior and servant, because we cannot be truly certain who, if anyone, is correct in his or her assessment of the character of those two extremes. In the absence of absolute moral and ethical standards, people are actually *required* to demonstrate tolerance of all views and behaviors. Under such conditions, perception *is* reality.

Yet, in a relativistic society, decisions still get made and life goes on. How? Compromise becomes critical. Political policies become laws that do not reflect the best interests of the society, only the ways that provide for maximized acceptability at the time. Discipline of the children is not based on the long-term positive effects on the child, but on the momentary satisfaction of everyone's immediate needs. Spiritual principles that are unpopular—regarding hot issues such as divorce, adultery, deception, homosexuality, and war—are tempered so that a majority rule situation may prevail, leaving the maximum number of people feeling good about the outcome.

THE REALITY OF ABSOLUTE TRUTH

As offensive as it may be to secular minds that have been polluted by the thought that they have total freedom and cannot be deemed erroneous, the only means to a fulfilling, orderly, and proper life is to accept and live in accordance with absolute standards.

There are three strong arguments you can make for the need for accepting moral, ethical, and spiritual absolutes. One argument is that because we all have an inner need for order and meaning in life, establishing and holding fast to the factors that will remain predictable and unchanging is a natural cornerstone for a society. In this scenario, absolutes represent the best option we have for making sense of reality and knowing how to intelligently and confidently make good decisions. In a world in which everything is relative, there is nothing that you can count on, resulting in rampant unpredictability, confusion, fear, and disappointment. Life becomes a game of chance, a daily gamble in which we never know what to expect, how to react, or who we are. With absolutes, we can know that certain truths will be in place, and we can build our responses to life around those foundations.

A second reason for embracing absolute truth as a wise strategy has to do with historical facts. Relying upon empirical evidence, we can trace how people's decisions in the past have led to specific outcomes. As we examine the moral, ethical, and spiritual patterns of thought and behavior over the last two millennia, a clear pattern emerges. Undeniably some perspectives have yet to be proven false; others have yet to be proven true. Yet even if we were to use only past experience as the basis of creating a system of truth, we would find that a body of perspectives does exist that we can identify as truth in all known cases. Certain behaviors (e.g., murder, intentional disregard of God, commitment to interpersonal accountability, intensity of communication in relationships, sexual promiscuity, establishing vision for your life, dishonesty) always result in certain, foreseeable outcomes. Certain conceptual views (e.g., all people are valuable, money is a means not an end, saving resources is foolish, morality need not be consistent, the proper decision always results in public favor) also result in life conditions that are identifiable in advance. Thus, developing a life view based on the predictable outcomes borne from hundreds of years of human experience is wise.

But the most compelling argument is that God Himself has ordained that there are truths that are inalienable. Because He is the embodiment of truth—that is, we only know of a concept we call absolute truth because it is a reflection of His core character as He has allowed us to know that character—we must take this perspective seriously. In some ways, we then are relying upon faith in Him. Those who read the Bible, who understand that it is the only book that claims to be God's inspired Word communicated through men, and that it reflects His values and His direction for people, a clear portrait of pure truth is found. But this is not a blind faith; the prior pair of arguments for this acceptance of God as the embodiment of truth, and as the One who has laid out truth for us to understand, to own and to live by, attest to the fact that God's principles are absolutely true and valid, even according to our finite senses and means of measurement.[7]

Accepting the existence of absolutes in the moral, ethical, and spiritual arenas is logical. A fundamental flaw in the concept of relativism is that conflicting perspectives must be given the same weight and cannot be resolved. In the absolute perspective, conflict will occur but there will be viable resolution in line with truths that exist and are acknowledged as being valid. It may feel good or be emotionally seductive to claim that everyone's views are of equal value, but that does not mean that they truly are of equal veracity. Moral, ethical, and spiritual truths are no more subjective than are the truths related to the tangible world (e.g., a rock is hard, water weighs more than air, all people die physically, a mile is longer than an inch). We only have trouble accepting the less tangible absolutes because we have rejected the standards set by the One who made those intangible but significant realities in the first place, substituting our own imperfect and selfish ideas for those of God.

TAKE IT OR LEAVE IT

The fact that we may choose to believe something does not make it true. Many times people have believed that the world was going to end on a certain date in history, but their beliefs were wrong because they were based on feelings and subjective interpretations rather than absolute truths. Many Americans believed that providing every person with the opportunity to have a free education would eradicate poverty. This belief has proven to be false because the premise was not based on an absolute truth, but upon a cultural belief or assumption. More simplistically, millions of people believed in Santa Claus or the Easter Bunny—or, from a more contemporary vein, the Loch Ness Monster or the talent of Milli Vanilli—only to realize eventually that all these beliefs were just instances of misplaced trust or faith.

In the same way, if we choose not to believe something that is absolutely true, our refusal to accept that truth does not negate the reality of the truth principle. This is the major hurdle for a society leaning so heavily upon relativism. The underlying assumption is that if we collectively ignore or reject a principle, then it is not true, whether or not reality proves it to be true or otherwise. Thus, the relativistic culture may boldly proclaim that adultery is a natural and reasonable behavior that will not cause permanent damage. But the absolute truth is that because of God's design and dictates for human beings, adultery leaves permanent emotional scars in the lives of all who have been involved in such a rejection of God's truth about human relationships. Our wanting our own way does not make it right, no matter how forcefully we promote the dismissal of God's truths. We may anesthetize ourselves to the side effects, but those side effects will exist in spite of our best efforts to deny them.

As Americans, the ultimate achievement-based society in the world, we struggle against the idea that truth is to be discovered rather than created. Our natural inclination, emerging from a culture in which innovation, creativity, incremental development, and hard work are esteemed, is to believe that anything we need, we create; that anything we create has value; and that anything we value is valid and true. This view simply is not accurate. Because moral, ethical and spiritual truths come from God, the best we can hope to do is discover them. Any other perspective insinuates that God needs our help in defining the appropriate parameters of human thought and behavior. The absurdity of such a view is monumental and is abundantly clear either from reading the lessons contained in the Bible; from evaluating how well we have done at defining our own brand of truth over the years; and upon an honest recognition of the known limitations that human beings bring to the moral, ethical, and spiritual realms. Fortunately, the God of Israel is a Creator who wants us to discover them, because He created them for our own good.

Whether we accept or reject the truth created by God for our good, it exists and has consequences, both for those who accept it and for those who reject it. His truth principles, because they show us the inner being of an omnipotent, omniscient, holy, and loving spiritual Father, transcend cultural circumstances and personal desires. His truths are based upon rationalism; full knowledge of past, present, and future; order and structure; and ultimate goodness. Human truth cannot compete with that standard because our own truth emanates from a nature that is imperfect, limited, selfish, and distorted.

Through the ages, we have also experienced the foolishness of attempting to separate truth from its imprint on morality, art, politics, science, and law. Every aspect of our lives is influenced by our perception of truth; to make false lines of separation is mere illusion that causes a distortion of reality. Truth is unified in itself; it cannot be compartmentalized into the different pigeonholes we humanly devise to better delineate and comprehend the complexities of life. The central truths of existence run consistently throughout all of those aspects of life.[8]

GOD'S TRUTH BRINGS DIFFERENT RESULTS

Absolute truths, once accepted, produce very different outcomes than what we experience in America today as a result of our investment in relativism. Although some may choke on the very notion of a black-and-white system of examining reality, God's truth lends itself to that type of analysis in many cases. Because absolutes enable us to determine right from wrong and good from evil, we may identify some of the reigning falsehoods that plague our nation. God's truth is not the result of compromise or consensus; it is the result of perfect standards that apply to all cases, across all time and space, and which result in the optimal outcomes when followed strictly. His truth is not measured by the outcomes they produce, but by the purity with which they are adhered to.

For instance, in relativistic America, we revere tolerance and eschew judgment. Naturally, in some instances, judgment is unwarranted. Often, we may judge a person's total character on the basis of a faulty behavior. That is untenable and improper. However, tolerating all behaviors and points of view out of the belief that everything is right and nobody can be judged to be wrong brings on innumerable crises. All leaders whose strategies and actions were indefensible, from Stalin, Hitler, and Mussolini to Jim Jones and David Koresh, suddenly are shrouded in the approval wrought by the mantle of tolerance.

Sincerity may be upheld by relativists as a mark of truth. Certainly, the wonderful truths promoted by people such as Martin Luther King, Jr., Mohandas Gandhi, and Mother Teresa are outgrowths of the sincerity with which they held their personal convictions. But people who possess and promulgate errant philosophies as if they are truth are often passionate and sincere too. Adolph Hitler was sincere in wanting to create a master race. Thousands of plantation owners who hung blacks because of their color were sincere. Hollywood producer Steven Bochco is sincere in creating television programs designed to push the edges of standards of decency in what children may watch. The emotional fervor of these people does not certify the validity or correctness of their views any more than the emotional energy of the crowd that demanded Jesus' execution were legally, ethically, or morally justified in their call for His death.

Those who look at individuals seeking to uphold God's absolutes often call them, as did Billy Joel or former presidential candidate John Silber, arrogant. They often criticize those who strive to live according to established absolutes because their consciences may lead them astray in the determination of those absolutes. But that is why it is imperative to acknowledge that the source of absolutes is not human conscience because a human source could easily produce subjective, inappropriate standards.

WHAT ARE THE ABSOLUTES?

To establish a base of absolute moral, ethical and spiritual truths, we are fortunate in that the source of all truth—God—has graciously provided us a manual on truth, which we know as the Bible. This book not only identifies the principles, but also provides lessons regarding the application of those truths and the consequences for refuting or acting in opposition to them.

The Bible also distinguishes between values and truth. We are given an idea as to what virtuous values might include: respect, kindness, fairness, forgiveness, love. The values we possess should be the bridge between our attitudes, opinions, and beliefs and our behavior. But the basis of even our values must be truth.

The Bible provides many truths we can see are both true and absolute. They are verifiable, in history; they are reasonable, logically; they are defensible, in terms of human circumstance and expectation; and they are biblically valid. Some of those absolute truths include the following:

- The Bible is the inspired Word of God and is infallible in its content.
- Jesus Christ is God, who became man, ministered on earth, and continues to reign over the world today.
- People are inherently evil and that evil is manifested through the commission of sins against God. Our only hope for eternal life is by intentionally seeking and accepting God's gracious forgiveness of our sins, a grace available to us through the substitutionary death and subsequent resurrection of Jesus Christ.
- The Ten Commandments, given by God to Moses, remain a valid set of parameters for life today; failure to comply with those parameters will produce negative consequences for the individual. These commandments establish critical principles such as the sanctity of human life; the significance of honesty and integrity; the centrality of God in all manner of life; and so forth.

It is not within the scope of this book to provide a comprehensive discourse on all absolute truths we can derive from Scripture. Others have written more extensively on these matters. Making a personal commitment to know the God who is the source of all truth; to become intimately acquainted with His truths; and to apply those truths to our lives in all situations is a central necessity for our lives.

Also realize that some might wonder about the distinction between belief and truth. For instance, many say that they believe the only way to have eternal life is through accepting Christ as their savior and by confessing their sins to God as a means of accepting His grace. Is that belief or truth? Because this has been specifically given to us as a life principle in the Bible, it moves out of the realm of belief, into the realm of truth. We may believe it to be true, or we may choose not to; but, bottom line, because God has dictated that this is reality, it is an undeniable truth about our relationship with Him and our future after physical death.

How we deal with God's truths is a matter of faith. Arthur Holmes explains the relationship between truth and faith:

> Faith, then, is man's response to God, the opening of our lives to Him. Faith is more than assent to true propositions (credal assent). . . . Faith, then, is not itself a source of new information or a mysterious kind of learning process, but openness to what is already revealed; it internalizes what we already know. It enlivens knowledge; it is likely, therefore, to produce both conviction about and obedience to what is otherwise a detached sort of knowledge.[9]

As Holmes points out, faith is a practical response to truth. It is the content of truth in which we place our faith; ultimately we can have confidence that such faith is justified because the source of the truths to which we subscribe is God.

PRACTICAL REALITIES

Think about the implications of a culture in which there was a prescribed body of truth principles which formed the parameters of thought, word and deed.

It would be a culture in which justice prevailed, because there would be no qualms about right and wrong, or about the importance of the preservation of valid rights. Rampant crime would not be likely, or perhaps even possible, because people would understand their personal responsibilities in light of the truths that create a just and orderly environment in which everyone's behavior is free within specified limits.

It would be a society in which the family was a priority in people's lives, because we would recognize that any other design for male-female-child relationships would invite disaster. Efforts to tamper with the basic family design established by God from the beginning of humanity would be seen as perversions of truth, and social pressure would prevail upon the wayward to recognize the objective restraints provided by their loving Creator.

It would be a culture in which poverty would not exist, except temporarily, because God's people would recognize the needs of others and respond lovingly and compassionately to those needs. In light of God's truths about the role of money, the value of care and the importance of community and service, expensive and unwieldy government programs would not be a political football kicked back and forth between political parties; the issue would be resolved quickly, quietly and personally by the church.

It would be a culture in which people accept the responsibility for their actions, thus reducing instances of verbal deceit, tax fraud, physical violence, substance abuse, and the like. Rather than placing the blame on others, or seeking to blame the victim, individuals would recognize that in light of the absolute standards against which we are judged, actions have consequences, and we must accept those consequences when they are pertinent.

There are numerous ways in which the culture would be revolutionized if we simply took God at His Word. The blueprint for a life based on truth exists. The missing link is simply our arrogance in thinking that we can develop a better way than that proposed by God.

Don't misunderstand. Even under the best of conditions, we know that life in America will never reach utopian heights. Because of the fallen nature of human beings and the propensity to disobey God's truths, there would always be struggles to maintain a righteous response to the whims and lures of the marketplace and the human heart. But with the order, wisdom and sensibility provided by a deep understanding of God's profound truths, it would birth a culture in which the higher moral, ethical and spiritual virtues and values would be common and overt. The very nature of the culture—the heartbeat of the people— would be so fundamentally different as to produce a new world.

However, because God's truth is personal, it would transform the culture by transforming those individuals who devote themselves to His principles. As a personal reality, truth changes the inner character of the individual toward more closely mirroring the image of God. In this manner, as we become more synchronized with His nature, so would our culture reflect more of the righteousness and beauty that resides within the being of God.[10]

Ultimately, then, we would be a culture of substance, escaping the present disease from which we suffer, so aptly labeled "hollowness" by Os Guinness. Rather than a focus on style, feelings and image, we would emphasize the content of life, centered on truth. We would recognize that the majority opinion is not truth, but consensus; and that God's truth is quite separate from public opinion. And whereas relativism reigns supreme in America because it permits individuals to retain control over their own lifestyles and life experiences, God's truth puts control squarely in His hands.[11]

In the end, we have a choice to make. We can accept God's truths and endeavor to conform to them, or we can flaunt our human weakness and deny their absolute authority. Because we have the opportunity to decide—theologians call this "free will" —we can blame no one but ourselves for the consequences of our preference. It is our decision to make. And the consequences, which are knowable in advance, are ours with which to contend.

NOTES

1. Carl Sagan, *Cosmos* (New York: Random, 1980), 4.
2. Kurt Vonnegut, Jr., *Cat's Cradle* (New York: Dell, 1970).
3. Shirley MacLaine, *It's All in the Playing* (New York: Bantam, 1987), 192.
4. James Sire, *The Universe Next Door* (Downers Grove, Ill., Inter-Varsity, 1988).
5. George Barna, *Virtual America* (Ventura, Calif.: Regal, 1994), chapter 5.
6. Ibid.
7. See passages in the Bible such as John 8:32 (regarding being able to know the truth); John 14:10–11 (concerning the verifiability of the truth); John 14:6 (to suggest God is the embodiment of truth); and Acts 14:15–17; Psalm 19:1–6; Romans 1:19–20; John 1:6–8 (that we can observe God's truth in the world).
8. Arthur Holmes, *All Truth Is God's Truth* (Grand Rapids: Eerdman's, 1977), chapters 1 and 3.
9. Ibid., 71–72.
10. Ibid., 34.
11. Os Guinness, *The American Hour* (New York: Free, 1993), 290–303.

THE SEARCH

1. Can you distinguish the existentialist, naturalist, and Christian views of life? Contrast them.

2. Of the three worldviews mentioned above, which do you think best fits the realities of life and why? Give reasons to refute the other two views.

3. Summarize in a few sentences your own worldview—that which organizes, provides meaning, and gives direction in the way you live.

4. Nihilism, secular humanism and the other views mentioned in question 1 proliferate in our society. But relativism plays a critical role. Why is relativism so accepted and what can be done to counteract it?

5. In a culture that submits to absolute truth, how could our lives change for the better? Give examples.

POINT OF ACTION

Identify three areas in your life where your worldview and practices don't match well. Take concrete steps to make the two compatible.

CHAPTER 11

REASONABLE EXPECTATIONS

W hat do the following stories have in common? The 1980 U.S. Olympic ice hockey team capturing the gold medal. Jimmy Carter emerging from a better-known, better-financed pack of contenders to be elected president of the United States. Bo Jackson making a successful comeback in baseball after what doctors assured him would be a career-ending hip injury. David defeating Goliath. The miracles of Jesus. Jesus rising from the dead. Japan rebuilding its nation and its economy in the wake of embarrassment and physical devastation in World War II.

If you said they fulfilled unreasonable expectations, you'd be right. They all exceeded others' expectations; some would say "they beat incredible odds." And these well-known stories can be echoed in scores of lesser-known and yet impressive stories of people who exceeded our expectations. Maybe you know someone like that—a person who overcame the odds to ward off defeat. Maybe it was someone who courageously fought off cancer; a couple who refused to give in and were able to make their stormy marriage work; someone who persevered and was able to meet an impossible deadline; a person who, through sheer determination and effort, raised incredible amounts of money for charitable work; or perhaps it was a child who worked for years to overcome a physical or mental disability.

PEOPLE WE REMEMBER

We remember these people and incidents because they overcame expectations[1] when pure logic raised reasonable doubts about their ability to perform a specific deed: they captured our heart, imagination, and respect because they refused to accept external doubts as the final word, but instead defied the prevailing expectations.

Such people are our versions of Rocky Balboa, the wildly popular movie character who won a heavyweight boxing title and then defended it successfully in three sequels. Rocky consistently (and unbelievably) did what others deemed to be impossible. Most of us know individuals who have performed incredible feats of courage, commitment, and perseverance that both awe and inspire us in our own daily struggles.

You may carry memories of meeting less challenging but still important expectations. In our driven, achievement-based society, goals, standards, and objectives are all different routes to establishing expectations.

Expectations are a powerful force in our lives, even though we may pursue them without acknowledgment, without testing, and often without giving them a second thought. Theoretically, we base our expectations upon our values, beliefs, and experiences, in concert with our analysis of conditions and possibilities.

Expectations are a response to preexisting emotional and intellectual impulses within us. More often than not, however, we reverse the process. Instead of basing our expectations on our character and core perspectives, we design our lives around the myriad of expectations that emerge in our daily affairs, subtly and not so subtly demanding that we meet them.

AMERICA'S EXPECTATIONS

This backwards approach to defining how we will interact with our world has resulted in some unusual priorities and behaviors. What follows is a list of the expectations embraced—some boldly, some secretly—by a majority of American adults. A simple gaze at the list confirms that our expectations encompass many inconsistencies, as well as many anticipated outcomes that are, perhaps, absurd. Yet, our research reveals that these expectations are a large part of the core of achievements and experiences that most Americans are gearing their lives toward satisfying. How many of these expectations do you hold dear?

1. Escalating salary and position, with decreasing levels of responsibility and anxiety on the job

2. Good physical health, aided by an awareness of (but not necessarily the application of) the value of exercise and good nutrition

3. Loyal friends who will always forgive and will be sensitive to your needs, without demanding much in return

4. A loving family that accepts you for who you are and gives you the freedom to pursue those dreams that are most important to you, without judgment, condemnation, or expressions of doubt

5. A comfortable lifestyle, based on owning a large, well-appointed home in a safe neighborhood, with good schools and convenient services, and the full inventory of modern appliances and home media, such as a color TV and a stereo receiver

6. An accepting and compassionate God who will spare you from suffering on earth, and will provide eternal security in response to your being a nice person, trying your hardest most of the time, believing that He exists and acknowledging that He is powerful

7. Social institutions will provide excellent services, available without question whenever you feel you need them, with a minimum of resources expended to receive those services

8. High integrity among other people; they will be honest, trustworthy, respectful, moral, ethical and fair, and they will forgive your lapses of integrity without a fuss

9. Objective reporting of events by the media, in which facts are thoroughly verified and there is no subjective interpretation of events, just an unbiased description of the events that transpired, and representative quotes defining the experiences under investigation

10. National safety from foreign attack, without being heavily taxed for such protection

11. Public services that continually improve in quality and scope while the cost for those services decline

12. A marriage that endures, thanks to your partner's willingness to sacrifice his or her personal desires and needs in favor of providing for your best interests

13. Being able to retire financially secure and live a comfortable retirement life in a desirable location

14. Career opportunities for anyone who wishes to work and to rise in the ranks; career success requires desire and hard work, but those who really want to get ahead can certainly do so if they are sufficiently industrious

15. Fulfillment that comes from personal achievement, as determined by the satisfaction of the goals and desires you have set for yourself

16. Technology that enhances the quality of your life and makes your daily activities easier and more efficient

17. Confidence that any problem can be solved if sufficient resources are devoted to finding the solution; thus we can, with enough time and effort, cure cancer, AIDS, birth defects, world hunger, and air pollution

18. Friends who accept any of your failures without condemnation, and who provide you with the encouragement and understanding needed to sustain you through your dejection

19. Prayers will be answered by God according to our needs and desires, as long as we are sincere and reasonable in our requests

20. Anyone who truly desires to be happy can be happy; every day should be enjoyable and rewarding

You probably have more than twenty expectations. Even so, most of your expectations might be classified into just a handful of categories: those pertaining to fun and joy in life, those related to the achievement of wealth, those associated with living in comfort, and those tied to personal acceptance by others.

If you read the list and felt it was excessively long, be assured that this is not even exhaustive. The twenty expectations represent only a down payment on the hundreds of expectations that each of us use to guide our lives. In addition to the expectations commonly held by Americans, each individual maintains a substantial number of expectations that are unique to that person and help to define their unique character and lifestyle.

HOW EXPECTATIONS AFFECT US

Expectations have a powerful pull on you. When you satisfy them, you feel pleased and fulfilled. When you meet expectations that others said could not be achieved, you gain a special sense of pride and vindication. When you exceed expectations, you develop a deeper sense of self-confidence and may even reestablish loftier goals and dreams for the future.

Failing to match your expectations, however, can have damaging effects. Emotionally, you may become irritated, frustrated or angry. Falling short may produce self-doubt and diminish your self-esteem. It is common for those who have failed to live up to expectations—whether self-imposed or dictated by others—to become embarrassed, isolated, discouraged, disillusioned, cynical, and even physically or emotionally impaired.

Other people may also react to our inability to accomplish what was expected. We may be fired, demoted, receive a pay cut, become the butt of jokes, lose friends, become an outcast, suffer a damaged reputation, and so forth. Expectations become something that we and others count on to portray a future reality; when that reality does not come to pass, all of those involved feel cheated and respond in whatever ways seem appropriate.

As alluded to earlier, expectations also serve as a guideline in the development of personal and societal values and goals. For millions of adults, their attitudes are shaped by what they feel is expected of them. Often we exhibit an "if, then" approach to our circumstances: if they expect this of me, then I'm entitled to think or act in a given manner.

You may know a co-worker, for instance, who says, "If they want me to work extra hours, then I'm eventually entitled to a raise, more respect, recognition, and eventually a promotion." (Those are expectations 1, 8, and 14 in action.)

EXPECTATIONS IMPACT OUR CULTURE

The expectations versus the actual outcomes from one generation to the next have affected twentieth century American culture. After World War II, civilians and returning G.I.'s alike expected more goods and services after a war that required rationing, long hours of work (and for G.I.'s, fighting), and delayed dreams. With a successful positive economy, many of those expectations were met. A baby boom ensued, and those "boomers" received much attention. Later as adults, Baby Boomers saw many of their expectations unmet, and other expectations only partially fulfilled.

Today the next generation entering adulthood, the Baby Busters (or the so-called Generation X) have lowered their expectations greatly in a period of economic constraints. In fact, our nation is struggling with a generation of people whose expectations are so low that they have little faith in the future and limited desire to push the boundaries of achievement and wisdom. The Baby Busters have seen the consequences of the preceding generation (i.e., the Boomers) set lofty, self-absorbed expectations and doggedly pursue those, ignoring the long-term costs of their selfishness. Busters generally feel that the future is likely to be a disaster for them: that means they will never reach the lofty heights aspired to or achieved by the Boomers. This sentiment has created dissonance and disappointment on a massive scale—a magnitude of disillusionment that will radically impact the social, economic and spiritual health of America for decades to come.

The Busters have a point. Our consumption-based lifestyles have depleted much of the balance that was designed into the universe. Americans constitute less than 5 percent of the world's population, but we account for more than one-third of the planet's annual depletion of natural resources. Consider the fact that the average person living in America today is 4½ times richer than were his or her grandparents who lived at the turn of the twentieth century—and yet we're convinced that we're losing our economic edge and capacity. Even compared to adults in 1950, the typical American today owns twice as many cars, drives nearly three times as far, consumes more than twenty times the volume of plastic, is more than five times as likely to have a home fitted with central air conditioning. We live in a home complete with many devices that did not even exist forty years ago but which have become "indispensable" today, including microwave ovens, video cassette recorders, cordless telephones, and color television sets. We pursue these riches, regardless of the environmental, interpersonal or emotional consequences of such usage, because we believe they have the power to fulfill our desires.

Yet research by the National Opinion Research Center over the last forty years shows that the proportion of Americans who are "very happy" with life has generally remained unchanged or decreased in spite of this materialistic bonanza. In the analysis of Alan Durning, "If our wants are insatiable, there is simply no such thing as 'enough.'"[2]

Yes, expectations have a powerful influence on individuals and on nations. The American culture is being redefined by the satisfaction and the inability to satisfy past expectations.

WHAT'S REASONABLE?

A central question must be posed, though: Are our expectations reasonable? The answer to that question is no. Our *unreasonable* expectations are a key reason we feel so bad about ourselves. In many instances we have failed to meet our expectations because they were incapable of being met.

Think about some of the expectations that we typically embrace. Many of them are inconsistent with each other. Some of the conflicts could represent simply a healthy tension that produces balance. In most instances, however, people take a black-and-white approach to life conditions and opt for one or the other.

- *Possessions vs. sacrifice.* We treasure both our desire for material gain with the Christian call for sacrifice. Most of us support capitalism because it dangles before our faces the carrot of receiving what we want. In contrast, one of the benefits of the Christian faith is that we embrace the needs and hurts of others and thus strive to give away what we have. How do we reconcile such opposing expectations?

- *Cultural norms vs. character.* We embrace the American culture as one that is second to none, claiming that its strength and vitality are at least partly attributable to the Christian principles on which it is founded. However, a careful examination of these realities shows that Christianity commands us to be gentle, forgiving, loving, and sacrificial. We are to display humility, as Christ did. In contrast, progress and achievement in contemporary American culture require you to be aggressive, competitive, selfish and impersonal.

197

INCONSISTENT EXPECTATIONS	
WHAT WE WOULD LIKE	**WHAT IS RIGHT**
More possessions	Sacrifice what we have
Follow the cultural norms	Uphold Christian character
Personal advancement	Uphold community
Seek profit	Care for people
Please others	Make tough personal choices

- *Community vs. individuality.* We uphold the value of our democratic form of government and the ideals that undergird this system. We cherish this system because it promotes the common good. However, from an individual's perspective—my expectations and your expectations (and some of those placed upon us by others)—we ignore the common good in favor of personal survival.

- *Profit vs. personal care.* Most Americans accept a business philosophy that pushes them to do whatever is necessary to be financially profitable. At the same time that we accept profit, we try to promote a social ethic that mandates that we help people, even if it means some sacrifice.

- *Self-determination vs. social pressure.* In our quest for personal freedom, we have come to embrace the belief that we, alone, are capable of intelligently dictating how to live and what constitutes personal success and fulfillment. Yet, we conscientiously attend to and then pander to the standards of consumption and image set by others. We accept those standards based on the ambiguous notion that they work and are meaningful in the eyes of others—those whom we unconsciously seek to impress.

Naturally, life will always confront us with complicated choices. There is nothing inherently wrong in permitting the existence of incompatible perspectives—as long as we have a filter. A filter provides internal clarity as it points us in a direction which is consistent with our values and beliefs. Such tension between competing needs and desires is acceptable; however, reacting in ways that can only be described as muddled and schizophrenic caused by attempting to carry out mutually exclusive ends is mere foolishness.

HOW DO YOU DEFINE SUCCESS?

We may also wish to raise questions about the very goals and definitions we embrace. Success is one of the goals of most Americans. We define success in terms of our material achievement and emotional comfort. Sociologists have concluded that most of us think of success in terms of achieving wealth, power and prestige. We expect to grasp success by accumulating any or all of these three elements.

The ways in which we regard these factors is quite telling, though. Many Americans view wealth as a sign of God's blessing, of personal superiority or righteousness, and as a symbol of our own self-sufficiency. Power is a means of control, and thus enables us to dictate the activities which bring us desired outcomes (i.e., success). Power, however, is typically reflective of ego gratification, selfishness, and an attitude of dominance, rather than servanthood. Prestige or status is a means of demanding respect from others, a mechanism for stroking our ego rather than exuding humility. Prestige often produces overt pride.[3]

Many have gone a step further, wrapping this definition of success in spiritual principles they allege are biblical. For decades, we have endured the religious ramblings of individuals who claim that God wants us to be wealthy, and any goal or condition short of affluence is a reflection of our lack of faith or a heart which has not sufficiently repented of sin, thereby shackling God from the ability to shower material blessings upon us as He is anxious to do. Some of the more recent proponents of this doctrine (sometimes known as the "prosperity doctrine" or "name-it-and-claim-it" theology) have gone so far as to suggest that God wants Christians to have riches so that they can redistribute that wealth in His name.

A careful study of the Bible, however, clearly indicates that while God may, and at times does, bestow material wealth, such wealth does not constitute a complete rendering of His perspective on success, nor His teachings regarding the means to achieving true success. His view of success is founded upon the transformation of our hearts and minds resulting from the acceptance of His offer of eternal salvation through Jesus Christ.

In God's eyes, the material stuff we so cherish is transient. Jesus once asked the rich man, "What good will it be for a man if he gains the whole world yet forfeits his soul?" (Matthew 16:26). "You can't take it with you" is the earthly expression of the emptiness of material riches. When a person seeks to serve God and focuses on lasting, eternal gains instead of earthly gains, he has two personal transformations: a new source of joy (that is, by serving others in Christ's name) and an altered lifestyle (one of reduced anxiety and enhanced comfort through simplicity).

THE SOURCES OF CONFUSION

For most of us, though, unrealistic expectations dominate. In a nation as highly educated and so extensively wired for communication, how could we have arrived at a place where inappropriate expectations run rampant? There is no single explanation, but a confluence of reasons which have created the condition.

Mass Media

The mass media in America produce incredible distortions of reality, leading to equally incredible expectations. Television, movies, radio and other media provide a filtered view of reality that cannot help but draw people to improper conclusions. Sometimes, these media accomplish this through entertainment that portrays reality in ways which alter our perceptions. Sometimes it is through advocacy journalism whose purpose is to manipulate our perceptions. Geraldo, Oprah, Phil, Sally Jesse and a growing cast of performers transmit mutant information and ideology as if it were representative of something other than the most bizarre and aberrant of the human condition. Their debates about sexual mores, money, and power at times create dissatisfaction and even envy among viewers.

Meanwhile, magazines and newspapers feed expectations about social issues and morality. National magazines such as *Cosmopolitan* pushed women to expect more from the workplace, reconsider their roles as wives, and challenge expectations about clothing, men, and marriage. *People* magazine seems to rewrite reality with its portraits of the rich and famous. Newspapers from coast to coast spotlight new analyses of humanity, based on essentially errant views. And in many cases, the media—from TV to newspapers manipulate us through the transmission of advertising messages that are designed to reshape our perceptions and redirect our behavior.

Family Training

Many of the cues we get come from family. Whether they were bred in us as children or are responses to the reactions we get from other family members as adults, we are conditioned by those whom we love to pursue specific courses of thought or action in light of family expectations.

Public Education

Our public (and many private) schools convey values and expectations to our children. Those lessons are then carried into life. The expectations go far beyond academic achievement, delving into behavioral patterns, relational practices, lifestyles and roles, career aspirations and other personal perspectives. Expectations can range from a well-paying job and job security to life as a community leader or loner in the countryside. Attend any high school graduation ceremony next June and listen to some of the expectations the graduates articulate in the commencement speeches.

Religious Education

Many Americans have had a period of exposure to religious education, often during their younger years. The marks of that training can be seen in most adults, although the adults themselves often have a difficult time tracing the impact of their religious training. Many of the errant expectations held by Americans can be related to their views on God, faith, their church and the Bible. God may be the God of miracles or the God of revenge; church may be the church of rules or the church of love without standards.

For many, such expectations of God or church come from their misunderstanding of authentic Christianity, whether due to their own faulty interpretation of valid teaching, or due to unbiblical teaching. In some cases, negative expectations arise not from teaching at all, but from poor examples of supposedly Christian teachers or fellow students whose attitudes or behaviors are unfair or selfish.

Political Hyperbole

Getting elected to office has become big business, a sophisticated game in which the more believable the hyperbole, the better the chances are of getting elected—and of hurting people through dashed dreams and hollow visions. Some promise diminished—or eliminated—criminal activity or schools with smaller class sizes; they raise voters' expectations of what is reasonable in their communities and the nation. In spite of our halfhearted calls for campaign reform and truth in advertising, we continue to fall prey to the charms and persuasion of those who run for political office.

Human Nature

Perhaps the greatest source of unrealistic expectations is our own human nature. Throughout human history, people have lived with unrealistic and inappropriate expectations. This seems to be one outgrowth of the imperfect, sinful, selfish nature of people. Many will not acknowledge their own faulty thinking about expectations, as politicians and best-selling motivational authors tell us that we can have anything we want, if we stick to it. This Horatio Alger mentality also appears in television and newspaper profiles of successful overcomers.

We want to accept that view, for it implies we have control over our future and that people are basically good and care for others' interests. Christianity and especially the Bible, however, portray men and women as basically selfish and sinful, prone to selfish, and unrealistic, and often unhealthy expectations.

THE POWER TO CHANGE—OR BE CHANGED

Identifying each of these sources as core influences on our expectations raises a pair of issues. First, it reminds us that we each play a role in the development of other people's expectations. That brings with it a responsibility to be sure that we are promoting expectations that are reasonable and rational. We have the power to change others for good or bad. Whether our role is as a parent, a friend, a boss, a co-worker, or some other role, through our interaction with others we will either establish expectations or respond to preexisting expectations in that person's life. We ought not take this lightly.

Second, this listing of influencers also reminds us that every one of these sources with which we have contact is likely to change us in some way, unless we are prepared to resist unwanted influence. Thus we not only have the power to change others, we have the power to be changed. It is up to us, individually, to sift through the multitude of messages communicated by these influencers in order to accept those which fit with our life's vision, our personal values, and our religious beliefs.

For instance, some viewers who watch television five hours a day say, "It's just entertainment. It can't change me. Sometimes it stays on in the background; other times I watch, but it doesn't affect me much. I go to bed at night and forget it." But many argue in the area of televised violence alone that people have come to tolerate, even accept, violence as a way of settling disputes. When young people witness more than 10,000 violent incidents on TV by the time they graduate from high school, that leaves a mark. Even Congress recognizes that truth, as Senator Paul Simon convinced cable TV to monitor itself; cable TV now will sponsor a study of the effects of such programming.

Certainly when young adults watch prime time TV and see the clergy and other religious people portrayed as buffoons, that makes a lasting impression. We cannot wholly blame the television networks: we both allow them to air such programming by watching it, and we err in not clearly identifying the potential negative ramifications such information intake may have on our lives.

In the end, the fact that we have developed expectations derived from each of these sources is a tribute to our failure to screen the messages we receive, as well as to our own deceitful hearts. Indeed, virtually every subgroup of the American population struggles with some forms of deception and misunderstanding when it comes to expectations. Boomers have always seen themselves as a special generation whose dreams could not be denied. Busters have seen themselves as victims, whose dreams will never materialize. Immigrants have accepted the fantasy that America remains the land of opportunity in which their dreams will come true.

THE PATH TO TRUE SUCCESS

How can we restore sanity to our expectations? The answer is to redefine the source of those expectations. History shows again and again that when we, as finite human beings, try to define reasonable and fulfilling expectations, we invariably err. Even our best efforts are usually compromised by faulty assumptions and a nature that leads us astray. As the prophet Jeremiah noted more than two thousand years ago, "The heart is deceitful above all things and beyond cure" (Jeremiah 17:9). Left to our own devices, we will likely fail to develop expectations that can be counted on to result in true success—especially if we are to embrace God's standards of success.

Even the people who have accomplished the material ends they set out to reach have found those outcomes to be empty. Our research underscores that wealth does not produce complete satisfaction. At best, material affluence allows the possessor of such wealth to be sufficiently insulated from reality and so profoundly distracted from his or her real needs and desires as to ignore the implications of chasing the things of the world rather than committing to the things of God.

This makes the pursuit of biblical expectations—and biblically-based expectations alone—so inviting. In our studies, those individuals who appear to have achieved a state of relative contentment tend not to be affluent, highly educated, popular, or sophisticated. They do tend to be deeply spiritual and to live a comparatively simple life. Whereas most Americans worship success, they are fulfilled by worshipping God; while most adults seek fame and fortune, they seek anonymity and opportunities for service. They live largely according to God's expectations rather than their own. (For a biblical study of God's expectations for His people, see "Nine Great Expectations" in the appendix.)

Perhaps we delude ourselves by thinking that we can create happiness in our lives. *I am increasingly convinced that happiness is not created; it happens as a by-product of values and beliefs which produce a heart, mind, and lifestyle that are unconcerned about making happiness happen.* Aspiration is certainly one of the personal qualities that distinguish the typical American from other people on the planet. But our aspirations are too often ill-conceived and ill-pursued.

FINDING INNER PEACE

How, then, do those who have reached inner peace and a true fulfillment with life get to that point? Conversations with our respondents[4] have led Barna Research Group to conclude that those who are sold out to exploring life's possibilities have a unique reply to a fundamental question that most Americans ignore: i.e., what is the purpose of life? Among those who find deep satisfaction with life, their answer typically relates to having a deepening faith in, and relationship with God, in which His ends become their own ends, and His means shape their behaviors. The focus is upon the development of individual character, rather than upon the accumulation of life's material treasures and images.

Our primary focus, then, ought to be God's will. This, of course, is a simple but biblical perspective. And while it may be conceptually simple, its achievement, especially in a material-crazy culture, is anything but simple. The keys to achievement in this biblical model are antithetical to what our culture esteems: allowing God to define and shape us and our driving purposes in life, and striving to achieve an integrity of character that reflects the character of God and brings peace with Him.

Pursuing peace and a deeper relationship with God through knowing, loving, and serving Him and His creation, not only reflects a substantial swath of expectations but will also facilitate outcomes that make life less stressful and more fulfilling.

NOTES

1. Expectations are defined here as that which is looked forward to or anticipated to occur, as something that is reasonable, due, or necessary.
2. "Asking How Much Is Enough," Alan Durning, in *The State of the World—1991*, ed. Lester Brown (Washington, D.C.: Worldwatch Institute, 1991), 153–54, 161
3. This has been nicely summarized by Anthony Campolo in the first chapter of his book *The Success Fantasy* (Wheaton, Ill.: Victor, 1980).
4. *OmniPoll*, 1-94, and *OmniPoll*, 2-94, reports of national surveys conducted by the Barna Research Group and published in January 1994 and July 1994, respectively.

THE SEARCH

1. List seven of the twenty expectations (pages 193–194) that are most important to you. Why are they at the top of your list of expectations?

2. Examine your major expectations in the following areas: joy in life, achieving wealth, living in comfort, and acceptance by others. Are these reasonable in today's world? Why or why not?

3. All the conflicting expectations listed (possessions vs. sacrifice, etc.) can be reduced to the basic tension between the needs of the person and our society. If this is true, what solution to our conflicting expectations would apply to all five conflicts?

4. The media, family, education, religion, and politics help create false or distorted expectations. List a few ways these institutions can be made to foster healthy, realistic, and biblical expectations.

5. If wealth and success do not satisfy deep needs, what are the key ingredients for those who have found true happiness and purpose? How do these "secrets" work, whereas the former do not?

POINT OF ACTION

Read the appendix, "Nine Great Expectations," to learn of how we can fulfill God's expectations. Then, during the next week, daily fulfill one expectation for God or others, however large or small. Each day, renounce at least one false expectation related to self.

CHAPTER 12
VISIONARY
LEADERSHIP

A mong the world's great civilizations and nations, not one rose to prominence and left its mark on humanity without having strong, visionary leadership at the forefront.

That's a strong statement but an accurate one. Many nations have had tremendous opportunities and great desire, but failed to make a lasting difference. Analyses of such peoples indicate that a common reason for their inability to reach their potential was the lack of effective, foresighted leadership. The presence of strong leadership within a culture is not, by itself, sufficient to carry a nation to greatness; but its absence is sufficient to preclude the possibility of such a lasting influence.

A study of history also shows that societies characterized by mediocre leadership tend to dissolve into a chaotic mixture of competition based on greed and other base human motives. In contrast, inspiring leaders, driven by a great cause and a firm character, focus the attention and energy of the people upon the greater ends of the world at-large and away from their personal needs. Such leaders motivate people to commit to something that is bigger, more significant and more fulfilling than just their personal agendas.

BEWARE THE PETER PRINCIPLE

If we as Americans feel so bad, one reason may be this truth: at the end of the twentieth century we are a nation bereft of strong, visionary leadership. We lack vision. Our government features leaders who lack the character, temperament, resources, and vision of true leaders. Their performance is verification of the Peter Principle. In the late sixties sociologist Lawrence Peter articulated a principle he said infects business and government: people rise to their own level of incompetence; eventually many people assume jobs beyond their capabilities and the public suffers as a result. "The cream rises until it sours," Peter wrote in 1969; a quarter-century later, America is drowning in a sea of soured cream.

In government the Peter Principle shows with leaders performing duties one step beyond their highest level of competence; rather than doing what they do best, they are conducting business at their highest level of incompetence. We have individuals whose leadership skills are second tier, at best, but whom are operating at the highest levels of leadership.

Is there a flaw in the reproductive system that has resulted in the failure to produce new, skilled, capable leaders who are competent to master the challenges of this complex, fast-paced, ever-changing culture? Absolutely not. For every era, there are many who have the gifts and abilities; the problem lies elsewhere.

I believe the major problem is that we have succumbed to the pitfalls of a lack of vision, largely because we have lost our sense of purpose and drive. All great societies had great leaders; all great leaders inspired people through the communication and passionate pursuit of a great vision for the future; and all great visions for the future have been founded upon the alluring challenge of a great cause. Americans are no longer compelled by a great cause that motivates and unifies the collective resources of the people. Decades of comfort, physical security, and prolific participation in leisure activities have softened the national will to press on and to do much beyond expand the comfort zone.

This widespread lethargy has made it difficult to motivate people to reach for new goals and to stretch the horizons. What we experience, instead, are temporary bursts of energy, attributable to the charismatic and inspiring words of a high profile leader. But no leader can long sustain such emotion-based zeal or passion; lacking a cause worthy dying for, people who invest in a leader's program eventually will weary of the demands of sacrifice and soon will veer off to the next alluring opportunity. The effects of charismatic leadership are becoming more short-lived with each passing year.

IDENTIFYING THE CORE CAUSE

Historically, Americans have been a cause-driven people. In the early years of the nation, people looked to America to become the new promised land—a country offering a new type of society, characterized by religious fervor and freedom, economic and lifestyle independence, and personal input into the public decision-making process. People accepted the responsibilities associated with such goals. Naturally, occasional crises arose as people's desires and tendencies clashed with the needs of the larger collective. But resolution was invariably reached as a result of the common goals maintained by the public. People were committed to reasonable boundaries.

These days, there seem to be comparatively few goals we have in common, even if individuals embrace the same terminology for their conceptual framework. *Freedom* means so many different things to people that it is hard to capture the unifying thread in the word and in our country. One man's freedom is another's limit. Freedom to smoke cigarettes for one person becomes freedom from smokers to his neighbor. Freedom of religion for one person can be attacked by someone else as harming his freedom from religion. Meanwhile, *responsibility* now has a score of meanings, ranging from an extreme sense of patriotism and service to others to personal satisfaction and fulfillment at the expense of others.

The book of Proverbs foretold the consequences of such limited leadership: "Without a revelation, the people cast off restraint" (Proverbs 29:18 NKJV). Other translations of the same ancient text render it just as startling in its message: "Without a vision, the people perish" (KJV). The kernel of wisdom emerging from this text is that people, left to their own devices, will meander aimlessly, striving for things of little long-term value, unless a deeper purpose and outcome is brought to their attention and promoted as a corporate reality to which they can commit themselves. It is vision for the future that provides motivation, direction, and logical parameters toward filling life with meaning.

WHAT VISION IS

In *The Power of Vision* I described vision as a mental portrait of a preferable future, communicated by God to His chosen leaders. Such a future is based upon an accurate understanding of God, self, and circumstances. In response to such vision, leaders can bring people to places they would never have reached without the emotional and intellectual power that comes from seeing a better future and having the common determination to make that vision a reality.[1]

True Vision Comes From God

But there are several truths we must underscore in this definition of vision to understand why it seems absent these days and what we can do to achieve a vision-driven society. First, notice the source of significant vision: God. Of course, people can concoct their own vision for the future, and use that vision to inspire others to unusual levels of activity and achievement. Hitler, for instance, was a visionary leader who drove millions of people to passionately pursue his vision; but there is no denying that the vision he provided was simply his personal vision for the world. Mao Tse-Tung was another visionary leader, but his, too, was a personal vision which lacked any sense of God's purposes or directives. His leadership capabilities were strong but ultimately vacant as a result of the emptiness of the foundations of his vision.

Vision Without Ego

Visionary leaders are driven by the higher values of life, rather than by personal ego or opportunism. Visionary leaders are flawed individuals, to be sure; but they achieve unusual heights, through the efforts of their followers, because of their unique blend of leadership abilities and visionary capacity. They motivate not for their own glory but for the people's well-being.

Leadership Versus Management

Often, we confuse management with leadership. The two roles are crucial but distinct, and the people who fill them are quite different, too, in temperament, perspective, talents and focus of performance.

A leader inspires, motivates, encourages, directs, and empowers people. A manager develops structure and systems, carries out the vision provided by the leader through efficient planning and the wise use of resources, and runs the operational machinery necessary to make progress. A manager also provides consistent evaluation of progress in light of the vision that has been set forth by the leader.[2]

WHERE ARE THE LEADERS?

We would like to believe America has visionary leaders. Remember, such leaders will achieve unusual heights. They will rise to the top. Yet many Americans agree that the U.S. has few leaders of vision. Why haven't more risen to do what they have been gifted to do? Why is it that at a time of such expansive opportunity that those whose natural inclinations are to help people maximize those opportunities are not champing at the bit to provide true leadership in government, business, and the church?

There appear to be three primary reasons. The first of those has to do with inappropriate vision. Bad vision produces bad results. The second involves the unwillingness of capable leaders to do battle with society for the privilege of leading. Although some innate leaders are compelled to lead in very high profile ways, most are reasonable people who can get by just fine by carrying out other functions. Third, Americans are not good at taking direction these days. You can't lead unless somebody follows; in a society built upon getting one's own way, from the manner in which we define truth to the lifestyle parameters to which we are willing to submit, coalescing followers is a daunting task.

Bad Vision

First, we must acknowledge that many potentially strong leaders are in key positions where their leadership gifts could make a difference. However, many of these capable individuals are failing because their vision is based on their own brand of truth, rather than upon God's desires and direction for the coming years. They have the right abilities, but not the right perspective. They possess the proper techniques, but not the appropriate heart. Consequently, when push comes to shove, they will be (or have been) shoved out of the path of lasting influence because they are seeking to bring the wrong vision to fruition.

When leaders base their strategies and their call to a better future upon values and priorities that are purely of human desire, it is inevitable that something less than the best possible outcomes will be achieved. The great causes to which people arise must be those that square with God's purposes and intentions; anything less loses its power when the going gets tough, or when other worthy alternatives arise. Thus, it is not simply enough to be a leader who casts a vision for a better future. The vision must reflect God's values and His focus.

A Bad Deal

A second reason for the dearth of strong, visionary leaders rising to their ultimate level of competence is that many capable leaders have looked at the landscape and decided that the circumstances in which they would have to lead are not adequately attractive to justify what they must endure to make a lasting difference. A key dimension of effective leadership is endurance, but endurance can exist only if the individual is willing to pay the price of leadership.

The cost of leadership is considerable these days. In the past, leaders always generated attention and sometimes stirred people's ire or disenchantment. But today, in the age of instantaneous media and the no-rules school of reporting, constant public opposition and intense scrutiny is a virtual guarantee. Especially in our society today, in which investigative journalism is confused with inappropriate muckraking and unjustifiable emotional intrusion and interrogation, many individuals foresee the toll that leadership will (often unnecessarily) take on them and their families, and they conclude that they have a different set of priorities. As risk-takers, they know when to risk and when to rest. They see a mass media intent upon second-guessing leaders, resulting in the cruel and persistent ridicule of leaders as a national sport.

And it is not simply the mass media that make them leery of providing leadership. The demise of spiritual depth and the lost sense of security and fair play in our society have created a public that is increasingly hostile to the leaders on whom they depend for strength and guidance. The public consistently contends that a leader's long-term track record or personal motivations are less critical than the quality or outcome of his most recent decision.

The potential for quality leadership is further undermined by a public that is divided on matters of purpose and guidance. Americans have lost their unity and their willingness to sacrifice for the benefit of the common good. Leaders may be expected to heal the brokenness of the nation, but they must do so in an environment of aggressive doubt, skepticism and challenge.

For many leaders, then, the bottom-line analysis is that this is not an attractive time to maximize their personal talents and abilities. Consequently, many devote themselves to business ventures or intellectual pursuits where their abilities enable them to escape much of the harshness of public evaluation. They are unavailable for government service at the very time when their gifts are most needed to refine and reshape people's perspectives and individual foci in life.

But aren't individuals who are natural leaders always going to strive for the highest possible position of influence and impact? Can someone who is truly a leader resist the urge to take the tough stands and lead people in ways that will promote the self-interest of those who initially resist?

Not always. I have found that leaders are not only strong individuals whose intellect, drives, and emotional composure enable them to survive even the most unlikely of circumstances. They also call upon their wisdom to count the cost of leadership before jumping into the fray. They are not so impulsive as to embrace no-win situations simply to grasp the opportunity to be the number one person. As a result, many good men and women forgo public service.

Few Followers

The third barrier to having strong visionary leaders is the unwillingness of Americans to follow their leaders. This is no small difficulty; a primary element of being a leader is to have people who follow.

Even though less than one-fifth of the population describe themselves as leaders, few people are willing to follow the vision, the plans, the methods, or the exhortations of leaders on a consistent basis. Most people "cherry pick" the rules they wish to follow, the standards to which they will be held accountable, and the people to whom they will pay their respect and attention. In

WHY PEOPLE DON'T........

LEAD	FOLLOW
Loss of purpose and drive	Complaining, creating obstacles
Confuse management with leadership	Loss of fair play and team work
Vision based on our own truth	Wanting our own way
Criticism from populace, media	Feeling we have the right to judge
Unwilling followers	Not understanding the role of support
Doubt, skepticism, challenge	Thinking we are joint decision makers

essence, America has become not just a diverse culture but an unruly one, as well. There is little sense of unity among the people, a limited willingness to sacrifice for the common good, and a growing distaste for those who strive to impose any types of limitations or obligations upon the individual.

For the past fifteen years, I have observed Americans become increasingly control-oriented. Fewer and fewer adults demonstrate good citizenship, which has traditionally meant placing the health and welfare of the nation ahead of personal desires and hopes. And the denial of traditional Christian virtues, such as serving others before serving self or seeking to heal relationships through reconciliation and forgiveness rather than vengeance, has been even more overt and pronounced.

For America to get back on track as a nation, we must allow leaders to lead and we must create conditions in which those who are not leaders are ready, willing, and able to follow. You may be a leader or follower; it does not matter. Either way, you have a responsibility to God, to yourself, to your family, and to the community at-large to carry out your prescribed function to its utmost level.

RESTORING THE BASICS

Changing Our Attitudes

To answer the question "Why do I feel so bad . . . about leadership in America," let's look at ourselves before we look at our leaders. When we change our attitudes and actions, strong visionary leaders will be able to govern. To start with, let's support our leaders. This means letters of support and our prayers even when we disagree with their decisions. We must be united in purpose. This does not mean we should not disagree with specific decisions; but we should encourage our leaders in seeking after wise rule that strives for the common good. We should seek for their spiritual, mental and even physical alertness for the tasks they must perform.

Accepting Our Role

Second, let's accept our roles as followers. As previously mentioned, most Americans are not primarily leaders, although we generally have at least one or two aspects of our lives in which we are expected to provide some type of leadership to others, such as parenting. Leaders typically get the most attention, but their effectiveness depends wholly on how their followers— that's most of us—respond to their visions and strategies. When we follow, we give leaders the opportunity to make things happen. No matter how outstanding the chief, unless the Indians are ready and willing to take orders and put the plan into action, the leader is simply a one-person armada. If we are to restore America to a nation in which order, purpose, and joy are evident, then each of us must take seriously our duties as a team member who follows the lead of another person.

Providing support for leaders is a significant task. Sadly, research and the daily course of events show that many followers have lost their sense of fair play and teamwork. Often, we read of individuals who seem to get a bigger kick out of tearing down leaders than from supporting them through verbal encouragement, intellectual understanding and acceptance, personal sacrifice of resources, or even the willingness to give the leader the benefit of the doubt in questionable circumstances.

Perhaps this is a reflection of our collective ego gone astray. Maybe it is due to our lack of comprehension of the roles of leaders and followers, and what it means to be a team player. Beyond a doubt, this condition may be partially attributed to our ignorance of the fact that God has required us to *willingly submit* to the leadership of those whom He has ordained to lead. Our obligation is not to approve of God's choice of leaders, or of those whom He has permitted to fill positions of leadership, but to voluntarily commit to their service.[3] Followers who second guess, complain, and create new obstacles only make matters worse. There is no defense for destructive criticism of leaders; there is only limited justification of constructive criticisms; there is a great need for the general support of our leaders.

Revising Our Definition of Leadership

Third, let us revise our definition of leadership. As we seek and elect leaders, let's remember leadership is not about public manipulation, establishing dominance, or persuading people to do what is against their natural inclinations. Leadership, in essence, is the art of communicating a vision for a preferable future, and thinking and behaving in ways which inspire, direct, and enable others to put forth their best efforts toward cooperatively bringing that vision to fruition.

Therefore, as followers let us look for leaders who have a coherent and consistent group of thoughts and deeds that serves the best interests of the people. Such ideas should be consistent with God's truths and principles, and should move toward maximizing fulfillment and meaning while minimizing pain and suffering.

Creating the Right Environment

The way to attract such godly, visionary leaders is to make it possible and attractive to lead people. This means that we must esteem our leaders. We show our regard for them by compensating them tangibly and fairly for their efforts, whether the compensation be financial, psychological, or otherwise. We must delegate both the responsibility and the commensurate authority to make decisions and carry them out, without undue interference.

MARKS OF A GOOD LEADER

As we try to recognize good leaders, it is valid to ask about character traits. What are the marks of a good leader? We have already referred to leaders needing coherent thoughts and deeds and having ideas that are consistent with God's principles. Here are several additional traits to look for in prospective leaders—and traits we would encourage every would-be leader to develop. (A good leader will have various innate qualities, which he or she can refine through training and experience, to become an effective leader.)

Traits of High Character

The biblical principle seems appropriate in the selection of leaders: those who have done justice to the small duties assigned to them deserve the opportunity to prove themselves with greater responsibility (Matthew 25:21). In more cases than not, we will discover that such individuals possess a series of character attributes common to most godly leaders: vision, integrity, constant devotion to learning, humility, and spiritual maturity and growth. In addition, effective leaders will display top-notch communication skills as well as team-building and decision-making skills. Those who lack these components are probably not gifted to be leaders.

A Servant's Heart

Leadership is an earned privilege conveyed to those who have the character to provide guidance to those in need of a leader. The heart of leadership is the practice of servanthood: doing for others what they could not do for themselves, for the best interests of all involved, in concert with biblical standards. That which is done for personal gain is not leadership but selfishness. That which is done to protect or ensure the best interests of a select few is not leadership but manipulation.

Thus, we are seeking individuals who know God, know His ways and His perspectives, and who are devoted to serving others. This is the leadership legacy of Jesus: to enhance the lives of others through determined and complete servanthood. As we can identify people who view leadership in this manner, it is our duty to provide them with responsibility and authority, increasing those levels as they prove themselves worthy.

Courage and Integrity

A visionary leader is sensitive but does not acquiesce to every request. This implies that some of the means by which many of our contemporary leaders gain their sense of propriety must be altered. We need leaders who major on substance and minor on style; who focus on people and then create procedures; who balance what comes from head and heart, but filter all of their reasoning and feeling through the perfect screen of Scripture. This will result in a very different form of decision-making than has been typical in the past quarter century.

Leading in accordance with public opinion polls, for instance, is not so much leadership as it is cowardice. While survey data may enable a leader to remain aware of people's needs and sensitive to their values, attitudes, experiences, and desires, such data cannot confirm what is truly best for the people, nor what is right according to God's dictates. This is where the courage, the integrity, and the character of the leader must emerge to make the tough decisions on behalf of a people who cannot be counted on to make the same difficult decisions on their own.

Compromise may be the heart of politics, but it is far from the heart of God. Thus, leaders whose chief claim to fame is their ability to achieve consensus through the art of compromise may not be strong leaders so much as they are terrific negotiators. Naturally, there are times when negotiation and compromise are warranted and are perhaps the most viable means to progress. However, as many biblical stories attest, God's principles are not up for grabs; they are to remain unchanged, uncompromised, and unashamedly pursued by those who seek to serve people by remaining true to God. Truth is not something to be pursued via a lowest common denominator series of interpersonal strategies.

Godly leaders make the tough stands and stick with them. It would be better to lose a fight on the basis of principle than to bend toward a common will that is clearly an affront to what God wants.

Our leaders should return to the central repository of all truth to determine how the nation ought to be led through the bewildering complexities of the new age in which we live. This will require courage. Such beliefs, based on biblical truth, will be challenged. For instance, Ronald Reagan's stands in favor of school prayer and other expressions of public faith were savagely ripped by the media as the inappropriate and old-fashioned musings of an intellectually soft old man; his opposition to federal funding of abortion reflected his understanding that the Scriptures regard unborn life as valuable as the life of a newborn.

Those who have been willing to stand tall for righteousness in the past two decades have received severe criticism for their standards, whether Republican or Democrat, congressman or president. Prior to Reagan, President Jimmy Carter was laughed at by the nation's comedians after he publicly paraphrased Jesus' admonition that lusting after an individual in your heart is as serious a sin as consummating such lust in the flesh. (He then admitted that he, a married man, struggled with lust, bringing more ridicule and nervous titters.)

Such courage was displayed in biblical times, and the result was the visionary leadership of three of the most inspiring men the world has seen. Moses brought his people back to the Law whenever there was a doubt as to how to rule on a problem. David followed suit. When Jesus established the new covenant with humankind, the apostles claimed His teachings time and time again as the central tenets of their decision making.

We have the model; the challenge to our leaders is to demonstrate the courage and the discipline to adapt that model to each day's needs.

THE EFFECTIVE FOLLOWER

We have seen the qualities of an effective leader and looked at the need as followers to change our attitudes, accept our roles, and create a positive environment. But now we must consider other elements. For being an effective follower means more than merely seeking to stay within prescribed parameters and avoiding conflict. We must *embrace* the leadership of others; we must *devote* ourselves to carrying out that which the leader has determined to be viable; we must model for others the joys and blessings of being followers.

A true follower does not regret that someone else is a leader. Instead, the follower appreciates that someone else has accepted the heavy responsibility of leadership. Keep in mind that leaders will be judged by a different standard by God. The significance of that realization, alone, underscores one benefit of being a follower.

But followers are not without obligations. Like supporting players on an athletic team, we must carry our certain duties if we are to maximize our potential and the leadership is to achieve a winning effort. As valuable team players, followers apply these truths to their words and actions:

- Nobody can always have things his or her way; this is especially true for followers, who must trust the decisions and determinations of those in charge.
- Once agreement has been reached regarding the basic direction in which the people will move, the effective follower will not constantly question the thinking, the planning,

or the implementation by the leader. The one exception would be exposing spiritual or moral improprieties that would undermine a plan.

- Like their leaders, followers should be held accountable for their performance. Followers, like leaders, have a responsibility to improve in their ability to play their role; each of us, regardless of the duties we have, are being counted on to perform at optimal levels for the greater good.

- Difficult as it may be, living in community (which is inescapable, but also beneficial) requires that we operate in the hope of accomplishing the greater, common good, rather than merely focusing upon our personal outcomes. This may require sacrifice on your part in some cases.

- Followers respect leaders as mentors from whom they can grow. But mentors also ask tough questions and challenge us followers frequently. If we can see life as a journey, rather than a destination, it will be easier to accept some of the probing and occasionally uncomfortable inquiries made of us.

As mentioned earlier, we must remember to encourage our leaders through various ways, including prayer and letter writing. Such activities remind us that our leaders are responsible to impart vision, values, priorities, and goals to us, and we should support them in those efforts.

THE POWER OF POSITIVE
PRAYERS AND COMMITMENT

One effective way to encourage your leader is to replace heartfelt criticisms with prayer for him or her. Another is to reaffirm an honest and meaningful commitment to whatever the leader has determined to pursue on behalf of you and your fellow followers. In what ways have you affirmed your loyalty to those who lead you? This type of support is not only biblical, but can go a long way toward freeing your own spirit and the leadership process itself.

Such support for our leaders can cause the mass media to offer a more productive view of society and its leaders. The media are like any other business: they will market the product most likely to sell. Only when we stand up and assert our desire to see leaders treated fairly will the media retreat from their jaundiced investigative reporting. It is our responsibility to demand such a transformation.

Naturally, there are times when it is appropriate to take a tough stand against a leader. But when is such opposition justified? When the leader is seeking to implement something that denies God's truth or His principles. Otherwise, we are called to submit to the authorities who reign. We may do so with a clear conscience knowing that this is God's will for us, and that ultimately all authorities come under His authority.

Until we, as a nation, are able to minimize our penchant for criticism and skepticism, leaders will be unnecessarily hampered in their effectiveness. No matter how magnificent the leader may be, unless the followers consent to be led, an environment of anxiety and gridlock will persist. In such an environment, nobody wins. That is the American environment today.

LEADERSHIP FOR A NEW ERA

Can the United States get back on track? Absolutely, but not without some significant changes in leadership and followership. These changes are not so much related to techniques and performance standards as they are to our perspectives and attitudes about our individual role in the unfolding of our culture.

Our leaders must embrace God's truth as their own set of guiding principles and standards. Anything less may reflect good intentions but will fall short of the mark of impact with virtue. When secular analysts such as Warren Bennis and Burt Nanus speak of leaders as people who "do the right thing," they are echoing God's sentiments without using His words. What could be more proper than leading people in God's ways?[4] The "right thing" implies that there is a set of objective standards to which we ought to adhere; those standards must come from a source of truth, of which God is the point of origin.

We must remember that leaders perform certain responsibilities because God has allowed them to possess those duties. When we do, we will respect our leaders and desire to help. If you are a leader, you should appreciate the trust and opportunities that such selection implies, and have a healthy fear that God is your ultimate leader whom you are called to satisfy and by whom you will be evaluated.

The above attitudes can open the decision-making and behavioral bottleneck and move America toward realizing its potential. In developing such attitudes we—as followers and leaders—must be stretched to refine our character. Among those higher qualities which research shows to be absent but which would benefit both followers and leaders are: loyalty; gentle honesty regarding motives and concerns; commitment to a common cause and purpose; sharing our personal resources unselfishly; demonstrating a heart of understanding; and being willing to be held accountable for our actions and words. When these attributes are in full bloom, we have the potential to emerge as a team working together for a higher good. The refusal to mature into such a character condition can only intimate the potential for hardship and failure to maximize our potential.

An objective assessment of the American condition today can lead to only one conclusion: releasing the power of strong, godly, visionary leadership is a key—if not *the* key—to restoring health to American society. And such leadership cannot occur without some fundamental changes in the ways in which the mass of followers think and behave. Thus, whether you are a leader or follower, you can—and must—be part of the solution.

NOTES

1. For a more extensive discussion of vision, especially in relation to church leadership and spiritual development, see George Barna, *The Power of Vision* (Ventura, Calif.: Regal, 1992). Other useful resources related to vision include Burt Nanus, *Visionary Leaders* (San Francisco: Jossey-Bass, 1992); Warren Bennis and Burt Nanus, *Leaders* (New York: Harper and Row, 1985); and part 3 of James Kouzes and Barry Posner, *The Leadership Challenge* (San Francisco: Jossey-Bass, 1990).

2. Ideally, leaders and managers form a hand-in-glove relationship. They need each other; one without the other produces imbalance and generally creates a situation in which either chaos or stagnation prevails. For a more extensive discussion of the differences between leaders and managers, see George Barna, "Pastoral Leadership in the Church," part of the video series "The Church in a Changing Culture," produced by Word (1994).

3. This is captured most succinctly in 1 Peter 2:13–17.

4. See Bennis and Nanus, *Leaders*.

THE SEARCH

1. *The author lists three reasons for a leadership vacuum in America today: lack of character, resources, and vision. What do you think are the root causes for this vacuum?*

2. *What are the three main barriers obstructing leaders from taking the helm at present (see pages 213–216)? How might we overcome each of these obstructions?*

3. *How does knowing God promote effective leadership? What characteristics differentiate the godly leader from a mere effective worldly leader?*

4. *Why is support for leaders such a significant task?*

5. *List five specific ways in which you can become a better follower.*

POINT OF ACTION

If you are a leader, define or further clarify your main vision to your followers. If you are a follower, think of three ways you can better support the goals of one of the people who is a leader in your life. Then act on those three ways.

CHAPTER 13
FAITH
THAT
MATTERS

When Charles Colson, founder of Prison Fellowship, received the 1993 Templeton Prize for Progress in Religion, he told listeners at the University of Chicago that every member of this planet, and Americans in particular, needed to realize in the technological nineties that progress sometimes can be found in the past.

"Progress does not always mean discovering something new. Sometimes it means rediscovering wisdom that is ancient and eternal. Sometimes in our search for advancement, we find it only where we began. The greatest progress in religion today is to meet every nation's most urgent need: a revolution that begins in the human heart. . . .

"The God of Abraham, Isaac, and Jacob reigns," Colson declared. "His plan and purposes rob the future of its fear."[1]

That noble statement is lost to most Americans, who reject the notion that religious beliefs can play a significant role in the healing and restoration of this nation. In Barna Research interviews with adults concerning their religious beliefs and the importance of religion, we consistently discover that spirituality mostly gets lip service; few people can speak intelligently or passionately about their faith views and the relationship between their religious beliefs and their lifestyles and values. Most are unaware of how their generic dismissal of the importance of the spiritual dimension in their life has serious and long-term implications for their life—on earth and beyond.

BLOCKED HEARTS

The consequence of such an attitude, however, is that Americans no longer are consistently standing up for spiritual insight, integrity, and stability. Most Americans are living without seeing the need for personal spirituality, even though we were created to operate with both physical and spiritual experience and depth. Dismissing either one of those renders us incomplete and fragile.

To deny the influence of true spirituality is like living with a heart in which all but one of the valves is hopelessly clogged: your heart may still beat, but it will leave you virtually paralyzed, incapable of reaching the potential you would have had if the heart had been operating at full capacity. Without a commitment to understanding and living in harmony with your spiritual nature, your potential is severely limited; the spiritual ignorance and paralysis that sets in cannot help but impact the rest of your life.

Here is the key antidote to feeling bad about ourselves: the hope and peace that emanates from true faith—from a spiritual commitment to the true God and to personal growth. Such growth comes from a faith that is rich in practical substance. Only in this way can we enjoy the fullness of life.

In his Templeton Address, Charles Colson reminded his audience that sometimes we move forward by looking backward—not *moving* backward, but looking back to learn from history so that we will be better skilled to create a preferable future that is based on truth and consistency. He argued that there are no new theological truths which need to be discovered for us to become a whole people.

Colson is right. There may be new applications of those historical insights, or new methods of making them relevant and real to modern seekers of truth, but the wisdom of God was displayed for humankind ages ago; it cannot be improved upon, nor does it need to be enhanced. The spiritual truths that have been valid and useful in the past remain just as legitimate and utilitarian today as they were centuries ago. God's core principles, like God Himself, have not changed and will not change.

Colson also is correct about the practicality of the Christian faith. It transforms people—both their attitudes and actions—through the power of God. But the Christian values and lifestyles cannot be assessed as proper simply because they result in desirable or favorable ends. True faith is about doing what is right in God's eyes because He commands it and He deserves it. Because we serve a God who is eternal and perfect, what was right in God's eyes centuries ago remains right in His eyes today.

The consistency He represents allows us to build on what the pioneers of the faith discovered millennia ago, and remains pertinent to us as we enter the twenty-first century. We must embrace the historical truths and basic Christian principles, not because they are the most appealing options available to us, but because they are His truths and His admonitions to us; they are eternal and relevant to all cultures in all places.

THE WAR FOR RIGHTEOUSNESS

Previous chapters in Part 3 have addressed the need for a revolution of the intellect (that is, discovering and committing to God's truth), a revolution in leadership and modeling, and a revolution in people's core expectations and attitudes. But none of those battles, if won, will be sufficiently significant, by themselves or even in tandem, to win the war for meaning, purpose and righteousness in life. The ultimate victory cannot be achieved unless we have our spiritual core at the center of this cultural reformation.

Because of the manner in which God designed humankind and the nature of the universe in which we live, we cannot accomplish the ultimate task of transforming the culture, through the cumulative transformation of individuals, without such a change being anchored in a deep, powerful faith system based on the ultimate Truth. This revolution of the heart must extend beyond religious ceremony and the mouthing of traditional prayers. The faith revolution must be holistic and authentic to have the power to reform a rotting culture.

If you are not a Christian, understand that ultimate Truth, according to the Scriptures, is realized through Jesus Christ. Although He is God, He willingly came to earth, where He appeared in a body, died for people's sins, mastered both sin and death, and then returned to heaven.[2] Accepting those truths can begin the faith revolution in you.

If you are a Christian, realize that God's call to you is not to create heaven on earth, but to improve our world (until Christ returns) by godly living. Until Jesus brings His followers home, however, we have been called to work toward the development of a better society, where truth is endorsed and revered. Let's look at how Christians can influence their culture for good.

A THEOLOGY OF CULTURE

Some church leaders are recognizing the need for a theology of culture. If we understand culture to be the organized ways in which people relate to each other, and theology to refer to our knowledge of God and His ways, then those church leaders are advocating that we properly understand—from God's perspective—the value of, and the appropriate means of interacting with, our society.

In practical terms, a theology of culture pushes us to answer some penetrating questions. What is the role of culture in our lives? What is the role of the Christian in influencing the culture? What methods are most appropriate to impact the world and respond to its challenges? Perhaps the key question to pose is: Can people of orthodox Christian faith best serve God by treating the world as an evil and insurmountable foe, and thus becoming intentionally isolated from that offensive culture—or can they best serve God by viewing the society as potentially mindful of God's ways, and adapting modern ways (that is, to "contextualize") of presenting His principles so they are understandable?

Retreat . . .

The first approach—regarding the world as an evil foe—has an inherent problem. If Christians view the culture in which they live as hostile and unsalvageable, and choose to insulate themselves until God returns, the gospel weakens itself. This strategy of isolation means that the gospel does not have willing individuals to influence and help to transform individuals and entire nations. Instead, those who embrace the Word of God are, in effect, in danger of being transformed by the power of the prevailing world system. By retreating into the safety of Christian enclaves where we preach comfortable theology and doctrine to the already-convinced and allow our good works only to impact those already saved by Christ, God's glory is muffled by human disobedience.

How often do we take this defeatist position, though? All too often. Many churches refuse to take risks to help the lost understand God's truths, fearing they will be defiled. Millions of individual believers shrink from confrontations related to their faith out of fear of being alone, or embarrassed, or confused.

... Or Advance

Biblically, our theology of culture must point us in the direction of saying that every culture is fallen, since it reflects the collective heart of the people that comprise that culture; but that the individuals who have been regenerated by the grace of God through the death and resurrection of Christ represent the true hope of instilling positive values and perspectives in that culture.

Christians who wish to advance the gospel—and that should be all of us—must adopt a practical theology of culture. Here are some of the questions we should address for a proper theology of our culture:

- How do we raise the issue of sin in relation to cultural activity, and what does accountability for such sin look like?

- How do we handle affluence and poverty, in light of God's expectations and principles?

- What is the role of the church in a culture which has other values preeminent?

- How are roles to be handled: male versus female, young versus old, white versus nonwhite, educated versus illiterate, leaders versus followers?

- What is the appropriate means to establishing meaningful societal change: relief, development, structural change, and/or prayer?

- How should faith and religious values enter into the decision-making equation? What degree of influence should faith views have upon the conduct of daily events in a culture in which religious freedom and faith pluralism are deemed vital to the heartbeat of the culture?

A FAITH FOCUS

In order to apply a relevant faith to a modern culture, we initially must confront our priorities. What must our focus in life be? Our focus will largely direct our personal resources and dictate how we influence the culture—or how we allow that culture to influence us. Our focus will also determine how central our faith becomes in our life.

The so-called "new age" religions, which promote man's goodness and supposed ability to improve himself, are growing in acceptance for several reasons. The foremost reason is their focus upon personal primacy and power. These faiths concentrate upon who you are and what you can accomplish through the force of your personality, your intellect, and your determination. Using the power of positive thinking, self-realization techniques, and other perspectives, these faith groups esteem the individual above all else. The focus is on self, in the full belief that all else is tangential.

The Christian faith, however, is remarkably different. Its primary focus is upon the person and the principles of God, as manifested through an individual relationship with Jesus Christ. The purpose of Christianity is not to draw attention to ourselves, or to exploit spiritual power and authority for our own ends, but to worship and serve the one God of the universe.

As you think about your personal faith journey, ask yourself on whom you focus: yourself or the Creator who has requested that you devote your energy to knowing and serving Him.

Developing Our Inner Person

Spirituality is not meant to be confused with religious activity. Spiritual development connotes inner growth—drawing closer to God so that we become more like Him; we want to develop our inner person. Ultimately, because we aim to discover and embrace truth, our commitment to personal faith development is not about ceremony, ritual, control, or emotional comfort. As God is the embodiment of absolute truth, and we are called to embrace both His character and His perspectives, we need to commit to a path designed to continually discover and respond to that truth. Again, we must constantly challenge our actions to determine the underlying motivations: are they to facilitate a new character, to draw us closer to the example of Christ, or are we motivated by other purposes?

A focus upon spiritual maturity intimates that our religious journey is to reflect not mere observation of religious rituals and activities, but to energetically participate in the pursuit of God.

The focus of true spirituality is active pursuit of God's ways. One does not arrive at a higher level of spiritual maturity by merely watching others engage in the struggle to find and emulate God. That development requires an enthusiastic and expectant pursuit of the Creator.

Becoming a Godly Person

Authentic spirituality also shifts our focus from the need to do the right things to the necessity of becoming a godly person. A primary purpose of the earthly ministry of Jesus Christ was to show that with even our best efforts, we could not earn a place in God's presence. Our sole hope is to gain His acceptance through our reliance on Christ as our savior; and then that we will reflect the significance of that relationship through our changed heart.

What, then, is the reason for focusing upon God and His will? In the most basic of terms, we do this because He commands it; it is right. But we also do this because such focusing on God provides us purpose in life, defines values and benefits that are personally meaningful, and enables us to be the type of person in whom God takes pleasure.

As you examine your own focus, how would you describe it? Is it driven by a passion to be obedient to God, or by a fear of His reprisal for doing the wrong things, or a cultural leaning toward religious involvement and association?

Back to the Basics

The Barna Research Group has found compelling evidence that one reason why the Christian church, and why most individual believers, have little influence is because most Christians do not understand even the most basic realities of their faith. I am constantly astounded—and dismayed—to discover the shallowness of the faith of American Christians. Until we can easily and convincingly articulate—for ourselves, if not for others—what we believe and why we believe it, we are not likely to have much of an impact on the thinking or behavior of other people. And without a return to knowledge of the basics, a faith focus that directs our personal modes of thought, word, and deed is not likely.

A Shallow Faith

To have a faith focus and go beyond playing a religious game, each of us must be able to articulate our core beliefs clearly

KEY QUESTIONS IN THE CHRISTIAN FAITH TO STUDY

Achieving peace with God	Good works and salvation
Determinism and prayer	Nature of the Trinity
Miracles of Jesus	Role of the Holy Spirit
Reliability of the Bible	Separation from God
Nature of Satan	Eternal judgment
Relevance of church tradition	Christianity and other religions
Responsibilities in church	God allowing pain

and persuasively. Until we can unhesitatingly define the nature of our beliefs, our religion is without substance; it is simple mythology, a religious illusion, void of personal truth and meaning. Such shallow faith cannot exert influence in human endeavors. We would be better off devoting our energies to other matters than to tinker with a heartless form of religion.

But how can you get to a place where you have a substantive faith that you understand and can articulate to those who pose honest inquiries? There are no shortcuts. It will take a commitment of time, energy, attention, and emotional devotion to truly gain a grip on the Christian faith.

Most Americans have been raised with some background in Christian beliefs and principles. But it is an incomplete background—and that incompleteness is dangerous. You may think you are a Christian because of some knowledge of Bible stories or characters. Similarly, many genuine Christians are satisfied that they have a strong faith because they read their Bible and go to church.

A Strong Faith

But a strong faith will flavor every dimension of our lives for a more godly outcome. Such a faith begins by asking basic questions about the trustworthiness of the Bible, our relationship with God, and the power of Jesus and the Holy Spirit in our lives. If we come up short on some of these central elements, we must then commit to learning the answers and integrating them into the fabric of our daily life.

- How can you achieve peace with God? What confidence do you have of "eternal salvation"? Can a person, once saved, lose his salvation?
- Do you view God as personal and caring? Why should people pray if God is in control and has already determined the outcome of the human struggle with sin?
- Did the miracles of Jesus really take place, and why? Does God still perform miracles today?
- Do you believe the Bible is reliable? Is it inerrant or infallible, or merely interesting and influential?
- Is Satan a real being or just a symbol of evil? What are the origin and the powers of Satan?
- Where did the church's traditions come from, why are they important, and how are they relevant today?
- Why should a person be part of a church? What is each person's biblical responsibilities within that church?
- What is the role of good works, if not as the basis of salvation?
- What is the relationship of God, Jesus Christ, and the Holy Spirit? Do you believe Jesus is active in your life through the indwelling Holy Spirit?
- What are the roles of the Holy Spirit in people's lives?
- Do you believe in the presence of sin in the world, and its potential to weaken your testimony for God? What caused our separation from God?
- What happens to people after they die if they meant well and lived a decent life, but never accepted Jesus Christ as their savior? Will they be judged as unworthy of heaven?
- How does Christianity differ from other major world religions?
- Do you believe God is just and holy, as the Bible describes Him? If God loves and cares for His people, why do bad things happen to Christians? How can a God of love allow pain and suffering?

Certainly, there are other queries that you, personally, might find to be interesting, compelling, or valuable toward being a confident Christian. Take this practice seriously. You cannot be a credible and influential representative of Jesus Christ until you have shown your own commitment to understanding your faith, and pursued the answers to these important realities.

Knowing the Great Statements of Faith

Another practice that might aid you in getting greater insight into your faith would be to study the various creeds of the church. Over the ages, the leaders of the Christian church developed prayers for people to recite which encompassed many of the most basic truths of Christianity. The Nicene Creed, the Apostles' Creed, the Westminster Confession, and other great statements of faith are packed with core truths. Read them, recite them, and think about their great truths. Becoming fully comfortable in defending the principles embedded in them is another means of clarifying what and why you believe and strengthening your faith.

A WHOLE WORLDWIEW

In chapter 10 we described several worldviews, including Christianity. Those Christians who clarify the basic truths of their faith can create a vibrant life view. When you understand and fully embrace the Christian worldview, this perspective of life can become a reliable decision-making filter. It will enable you to aid those who are struggling with the purpose of life; you can help them to make sense out of the daily chaos and turbulence of life.

That is how you and I become agents of transformation for God's glory. Unless America has a sufficient cadre of such agents of influence, the hope of the nation being restored to any kind of righteous character is slim.

A FAITH THAT SERVES

Making Our Faith Complete

Another central factor in the development of a substantive faith is to recognize that Christians are not called to be served by the world, but to serve it. This act of humility should be an expression of a contrite and broken heart, a reflection of a people who know that just as Christ modeled service to those who did not deserve such service, so are we to influence the world by our demonstrations of concern and caring (Philippians 2:4–8).

One way we make our faith complete is by serving other people—both Christians and nonbelievers. As we subject ourselves to God, we realize that He desires to use us as a means to fulfilling His ends. We are the conduits through which His grace and love flow; Christianity is made tangible to others through our obedience to His call, and through the visible results of our efforts on His behalf. Significantly, Christian service is not good works done for the sake of doing good; it is good works for the sake of Christ. Our good works flow from heartfelt concern for God's creation and in obedience to the Creator.

Evangelism and Social Action

Service to others is a means of making our faith holistic. A holistic faith displays a balance between evangelism and social action. In his book *One-Sided Christianity?* Professor Ron Sider observes that most churches are heavily skewed toward either evangelism or social concern, as if one were more appropriate than the other, or being effective in one could compensate for ineffectuality in the other. Our findings at Barna Research support his conclusions. A more biblical model of church activity, Sider argues, is a body of believers that places equally fervent emphasis upon evangelism and social-concern ministry. Such service to the world provides opportunities for evangelism and displays the tenderness of a truly broken heart. In addition, Sider writes, joining evangelism to social-concern ministry permits the establishment of true community, and it facilitates the healing of the world's problems through a concerted trust in Christ—and Christ alone.[3]

Types of Service and Spiritual Gifts

Naturally, there are many types of service that permit our faith to be reflected and perfected. Those types range from simple volunteer activities at a church or hospital to personally engaging in evangelistic conversations with nonbelievers to committing your life to missions work in a foreign country. None of these is more holy or important than any other, if done with a servant's heart and the goal of pleasing God. The key is that we view our lives as being designed to serve God and other people, rather than waiting for or expecting to be served by Him and His creation.

In this process, recognizing your spiritual gifts and temperament type can help you determine the specific types of service you are best prepared and skilled to perform. By using spiritual gifts tests, you can identify the types of special abilities and interests God has placed within you, and make a concerted effort to use those particular abilities in your serving. Likewise, understanding your temperament type can alleviate much of the emotional stress of wondering why you do not process information, interact with people, and make decisions in ways that are similar to (or different from) other Christians. A temperament analysis test such as the Myers-Briggs Temperament Analysis can be very helpful. (Myers-Briggs, a personal favorite, is easy to score and has much written on its applications in a ministry context.) Because each of us is unique, it is valuable to identify the uniqueness that God designed into our lives, and to determine ways of maximizing the benefits of those special qualities.[4]

Significantly, our service must be motivated by compassion and be of practical help; lectures or nice platitudes are not service. In his book *Involvement*, theologian John Stott recounts a poem written by a homeless woman to the pastor of the church she had attended. In paraphrasing the beatitudes, preached by Jesus in the Sermon on the Mount, the woman sadly described the nature of the Christian response to her tangible need.

> I was hungry and you formed a humanities group to discuss my hunger.
> I was imprisoned and you crept off quietly to your chapel and prayed for my release.
> I was naked and in your mind you debated the morality of my appearance.
> I was sick and you knelt and thanked God for your health.
> I was homeless and you preached to me of the spiritual shelter of the love of God.
> I was lonely and you left me alone to pray for me.
> You seem so holy and so close to God. But I am still very hungry, and lonely and cold.[5]

Jesus' service of people was never for show; it was for the purposes of healing, feeding, saving, or other practical purposes. He called upon every follower to imitate His lead of serving those who are not worthy to be served. It is through this overt demonstration of love and humility that Christianity draws people's attention, provides real substance to an invisible faith, and brings skeptics to their knees when they are touched by the love of Christ manifested in the good works of Christ's devotees. Imagine the power of Christian service in a culture as hurting, as cynical, and as confused as ours.

NEW CHURCH MODELS

Churches throughout America also have the opportunity to demonstrate the power of Christianity to a skeptical world. Millions of people are closely watching Christian churches to sense whether the people who enter there—and exit into the neighborhoods of America—have what they are looking for—meaning in life, joy, and the power to make a difference for a purpose greater than survival. The church possesses the answer—the embodiment of Jesus Christ in each of us—but often members do not reflect the risen Savior in a meaningful fashion. Just as many of us pray that individuals will be converted from the shallowness of life without Christ to fullness in Him, so must many of our churches be converted from the emptiness of routine and ritual to the fullness of His power and substance.

The Gospel for Modern Times

Many churches shun presenting the gospel in a modern context, fearing that it will result in compromising the faith. This concern is unnecessary, however. In the same way that marketing a church is not inherently evil, although it can be done improperly, so must we understand that the contextualization of the gospel is a biblical principle that permeated the ministries of Jesus, Paul, Peter, Luke, and virtually every saint whose ministry is described for us in Scripture.[6] The gospel can certainly be stretched beyond recognition by those who have their own personal ends in mind, but we must not let the possibility of errant behavior stop us from ministering with biblical principles simply because of the potential for abuse. If we took that approach, no ministry would ever take place; the fear of corruption would totally paralyze us.

How can we make the Christian faith accessible through the local church; that is, contextualized without being compromised? First, we must examine the style of ministry we offer and ensure that it is relevant to the culture. Notice that this suggests the style, not the substance, of the ministry must be designed to connect with the culture. The substance of our faith is given to us by God; and so is the freedom to design methods that will enable that content to have meaning to people. Our language, the songs we sing, the format of the service, the types of outreach activities we sponsor, how we personalize the message—all of these matters may be designed in ways that speak loudly and clearly to our society without undermining the truth of the Bible.

Contextualization and relevance can be achieved in other ways, too. The relationships we build with people to deepen their understanding of Christianity and their sense of being supported by a family of faith are also important. Increasingly, churches are rediscovering that facilitating personal mentoring relationships (sometimes known as one-on-one discipleship) can greatly enhance the faith journey of individuals. The learning process becomes personal and people can get closer to God and leap forward in their Christian development in such settings.

The Powerful Pull of Unity

Churches are also finding that they have greater influence in the community when they intentionally seek unity both within their own fellowship as well as with other ministries. In a world divided by animosities and doubts, any group that displays contentment and solidarity is odd—but intriguing. People naturally want to be associated with something that has the potential to accomplish great outcomes, and which is based on an abiding sense of togetherness and mutual love. When churches can lay down their denominational or ecclesiastical differences in light of the common beliefs we possess and the common goals we are striving to realize, outsiders take notice. As long as doctrinal basics are not compromised, such unity is appropriate and powerful. In fact, such unity often enables churches to reap results that would not have been achieved through solitary efforts.

Consider the example of the urban churches in South Central Los Angeles in the wake of the riots after the Rodney King beating. Several dozen churches banded together to promote after-school programs, family reconciliation projects, gang alternatives, and neighborhood pride efforts. The results have been affirming and hopeful. But these outcomes are not likely to have been realized had these churches each utilized their own limited resources of volunteers, ingenuity, space, and money to attack the problems ingrained in this strife-torn section of Los Angeles. The power of

Christianity has been seen in a new way by local residents not because there are 150 churches in a key area of the city, but because dozens of those congregations showed the unity that comes from faith in Christ and a commitment to godly rather than strictly human purposes.

Ultimately, churches must be true to the vision that God has given to their leaders to define and sustain the ministry.[7] No single model for church development is "right" or even appropriate in all circumstances; we need a multiplicity of models to reach such a fragmented and diverse society. One church strategy is not necessarily better than another; it is simply different and perhaps better attuned to reaching different types of people more effectively and efficiently. When Christians are willing to strategically design a church or ministry to reach desired outcomes most quickly and powerfully, they are putting wisdom into practice. It means taking risks and trusting that God is in the venture.

America needs individual Christians who are willing to personally grow in ways which enable them to allow churches to take new approaches, to experiment with novel strategies and to learn from those experiments so that the future may see even greater results for Christ. The Church does not need innovation for the sake of change; it does need change for the sake of penetrating a constantly evolving and shifting culture with the relevance and power of the gospel of Christ.

FAITH BEYOND THE WALLS

The bottom line is that America needs a faith revolution. We do not need a religious revival, for religion is not the missing ingredient in our culture; if anything, we have too much religion and not enough of Jesus Christ and authentic faith to address the emptiness and diverted focus of this culture. We sorely need an injection of God's love, Christ's saving power and the leading of His Holy Spirit to resurrect a faltering nation.

But our faith can no longer be compartmentalized. The Christian faith is made whole when it becomes the wellspring of our lives, the centerpiece of our hearts and minds, informing every endeavor we undertake. Unless our Christian faith resides at the core of our decision-making, our lifestyles, our perspectives, and our relationships, our faith has become sterile. The only way to guard against such spiritual impotence is to invite Christ to transform every aspect of our character and our lifestyle so that our faith becomes evident in all that we do and say. When His ways are preeminent in us, He will create the revolution that is so badly needed in America.

Is your Christianity so real, so vibrant, and so deep that America is on the verge of being transformed through your own individual contribution to a cultural revolution?

NOTES

1. Charles Colson, "The Enduring Revolution," the Templeton Address, 2 September 1993, as reprinted in *Religious Broadcasting*, February 1994, 138–43; statement from page 142.

2. The gospel of Jesus is based on the eyewitness accounts and the reliability of the Scriptures. Jesus Himself declared deity and being truth incarnate when he declared "I am the way and the truth and the life. No one comes to the Father except through me" (John 14:6). The apostle Paul describes the incarnation and sacrificial death of Jesus as "the mystery of godliness" in 1 Timothy 3:16.

3. Ron Sider, *One-Sided Christianity?* (Grand Rapids, Mich.: Zondervan, 1993).

4. For information on the Myers-Briggs test, see Roy Oswald and Otto Kroeger, *Personality Type and Religious Leadership* (Washington, D.C.: Alban Institute, 1988); and Otto Kroeger, *Type Talk at Work* (New York: Delacorte, 1992). For more on spiritual gifts, a useful book which includes a spiritual gifts test is C. Peter Wagner's recently revised book, *Your Spiritual Gifts* (Ventura, Calif.: Regal, 1994).

5. John Stott, *Involvement* (Old Tappan, N.J.: Revell, 1985), 41.

6. Paul's greatest explication of the principle of contextualization is found in 1 Corinthians 9:19–25. Numerous examples of this can be seen in the New Testament. I have discussed these in other places; see Appendix 1 in *Church Marketing* (Ventura, Calif.: Regal, 1992), and *Marketing the Church* (Colorado Springs: NavPress, 1988).

7. Vision is absolutely essential for churches but also for each of us as individuals striving to be obedient servants of God. For a deeper discussion of the role of vision in our lives and especially in the life of the church, see George Barna, *The Power of Vision* (Ventura, Calif.: Regal, 1992).

THE SEARCH

1. *In interacting with your culture, you may have chosen a policy of isolation or accommodation. Which approach do you tend to practice?*

2. *How do spirituality and religious activity differ? What are the benefits of a mature spirituality that even strong religious observance cannot provide?*

3. *Pick from page 235 a few of the key questions related to our faith. How can the answers relate positively to some of the problems of our culture?*

4. *In addition to service as a volunteer (see page 237), there are many opportunities to serve people daily. Talking with and helping the homeless we pass on city streets, writing government officials who shape public policy toward the needy, and donating money to relief agencies are just three ways to contribute. List two things you can do in your community as acts of service.*

5. *Recall the poem mentioned by John Stott. What other ways do we avoid practical service, yet retain good intentions?*

POINT OF ACTION

Find a problem in your local area and apply your church's resources to provide a unique, gospel-based solution.

EPILOGUE
....
AT THE CROSSROADS

I have a strong distaste for hyperbole. Social commentators who label each emerging world event "an international crisis" turn my stomach. Sportscasters who term every other player on the team a "superstar" lose my respect. And political candidates who grandly proclaim that they will usher in "sweeping reform that will transform the nation" are, in my eyes, merely hot air merchants.

It is with great hesitation, therefore, that I make the following statement. It seems too catastrophic. Yet I believe it is true. *Within the next decade, America will experience one of two cataclysmic outcomes: widespread spiritual revival or absolute cultural anarchy.*

REVIVAL OR ANARCHY

The more desirable of these outcomes, of course, would be a spiritual reawakening akin to the Reformation. Certainly, such a renewed heart would bring with it some major personal and societal consequences, as true repentance always does. But think how exhilarating it would be to live in a society in which God's ways were our ways. Not only would we bring joy to the heart of God, but we would radically reform the very nature of life in America. Tender hearts, open minds, sacrificial living, mutual consideration, purposeful existence—life would be utterly changed. I have no doubt that such a sweeping revival is the fervent prayer of many Americans.

And why shouldn't it be? Consider the alternative. A culture in which anything goes. A society that is morally corrupt and bankrupt, largely because we will only rise to meet the expectations placed upon us, and modern expectations have sunk below the level of detection. A nation disheartened emotionally because of the selfishness and depravity of the people, with no mitigating philosophy or institutions in place to resurrect the nation. A new America—one characterized by gridlocked government, a bankrupt economy, lifestyles shaped by fear and mistrust, hearts harboring faith in little besides futility and despair.

Without a spiritual revival in America, the trends in leadership, worldviews, families, relationships, and the distribution of wealth all suggest a downward path to anarchy. Cultural anarchy may be first, but it will lead to socio-political anarchy. Waiting in the wings, then, is the virtually inevitable conclusion to our foolishness—the dismantling of the order and stability that has made America a great nation for more than two hundred years.

Cultural anarchy seems more likely than ever. We are already so far down the road toward this outcome that only a conscious, well-managed, intensive movement will alter this course of deterioration. I am not sanguine about the prospects of a cultural revival taking place.

AN OPPORTUNITY TO LEAD

In this book we have considered why things are so bad in our personal lives as we have looked at the downward spiral of American culture. Now we must consider how we can change the culture, both as individuals and as a group. Christians do have that ability, through the power of God that continues to transform lives. Rerouting the course of our culture will require that the Christian body arise, in unison, to lead the way to a better tomorrow. This is the one existing group that has the motivation, the history, the resources and the calling to mastermind and to undergird this revolution.

A CALL TO REVOLUTION

The Christian church is the last hope for the survival of a vibrant America. I admit that sounds hyperbolic. Yet I am convinced that Christians can help to save America—and that any goal short of this will simply contribute to the ultimate demise of this country.

The magnitude of our goal clearly makes the matter of paramount importance. If we set our sights low and hit the target, we will lose the war. If we aim high and miss, we can rest easier in the knowledge that we tried our best, even if it was too little, too late. Only if we aim high and hit the mark can we emerge victorious. And if we are engaging in this war with the full expectation that we fight it for God's purposes, based on His strength, why would we set our sights any lower—unless, of course, we lack faith or commitment.

I urge you to carefully consider what it means to aim high so that we might win the war for the character and future of American society. Like the people of Israel, who waited expectantly for a political savior, we must not fall into the same trap; our goal is not to create a political revolution. Our aim is to be used by God as catalysts in a spiritual revival that transforms all aspects of the culture through the renewed minds and hearts of the population.

The Revolution Within

How could such a revival occur? First, you and I must be *personally gripped by genuine spiritual renewal.* Before we can hope to change the world, we must be personally changed so that we reflect the character that God wishes to establish throughout the world. Unless we reflect the heart that God wishes to establish in us, our words of warning and exhortation have no power. America needs Christians who will boldly model third millennia Christian character. Before God can work in the world, we must allow Him to renew us.

There is a way out. It is not a formula; it is a response to our Creator. It starts not with grand plans for America but with personal renewal in hearts—yours and mine. Revolution on a small scale can become revolution on a large scale. When our hearts are broken by the evil and shallowness of our culture, and when they fill with the love and hope that comes from our relationship with Jesus, people cannot help but take our urgent and passionate pleas for repentance seriously.

A Closer Relationship

Second, realize God can use you and me only as we develop our relationship with Him. That means *concerted prayer* for personal transformation (not just cultural transformation). Our relationship also grows through a well-honed *understanding of God's Word*, especially in relationship to human depravity, cultural perversion, and the essence of renewal. This will compel us to see our own dependence on God and to draw closer to Him.

The Roles We Play

Third, realize that God is calling you and me to each play a different but equally significant role in the restoration of this nation's people to God. Our roles differ because our spiritual gifts, natural abilites, and stations in life differ. Where do you live? What skills do you have? What is your education? Your marital and economic status also will affect your role. Start with a self-assessment of these and other areas. Then use your unique position to influence those in your particular world to follow the Savior who restores us to well-being.

Total Commitment

Fourth, we must show evidence of being sold out to God's values. On the surface, it appears that our nation is waging a war of values and lifestyles. Beneath the surface, though, is a savage war for the soul of a nation and the souls of the individuals in that nation. As His foot soldiers in multilevel, hand-to-heart combat, we must be able to demonstrate what we proclaim through our own actions and conviction. When we are fully committed to God's values, we will be ready and willing to defend what we preach through sound doctrine and the relevant articulation of His principles.

If we are soldiers in a spiritual battle, such commitment means we will endure through the challenge and derision we face. Like the apostle Paul or like Jesus Himself, we can expect to be mocked, slandered, threatened and physically assaulted. To endure in such a battle—to be fully committed to a movement of restoration—we must believe sufficiently in the power of God and the cause of Christ to take an immovable position and face the consequences with total faith.

THE FUTURE OF THE AMERICAN CHURCH

As a family of those committed to faith and unity in Christ, Christians must see this day as that which calls the church to take a firm stand or to fade into oblivion. The Bible clearly tells us that God will ultimately prevail in human history and that His will is going to be accomplished through the remnant of faith, the church which He established through Christ. But that is no guarantee that the American church is going to last or be greeted with cheers in the heavenly places.

No person can earn his way into His presence. But those of us who have trusted Christ for our salvation also know that once we have entered in relationship with Him, we are to "work out" and demonstrate that salvation with the blood, sweat, and tears that make our faith real to a doubting world. We have been placed here for the purpose of reclaiming America, if not the world, for Christ. Are you committed to the call?

. . . WHY DO I FEEL SO BAD?

Clearly we have seen that America's golden glow has faded. But Americans do not feel badly primarily for reasons of lost opportunities; their real aches come from losses on the inside—the loss of peace and contentment. Such a sense of loss makes sense when we recognize God says we build upon a rotten foundation of selfishness and sin. That loss must be replaced. The transformation begins with a spiritual revival among Christians.

If you feel bad about the state of the world—and the state of your *private* world—rest assured that it is the Holy Spirit prompting you to wake up and partake in the most significant revolution this nation has ever seen. Your uneasiness with the culture is a sign of personal health. It is God's way of saying that He wants to use you to help others see some of the very challenges and opportunities that we have addressed in this book.

The choice before us is clear: will we pursue spiritual revival or permit cultural anarchy? To which end will you commit your life?

About the Barna Research Group

The Barna Research Group was started in 1984 by George and Nancy Barna to provide full-service marketing research capabilities to Christian ministries. During its decade of service to Christian organizations, the company has assisted numerous ministries, including churches of all sizes, denominations, and parachurch ministries involved in various outreach activities. Barna Research Group has also served a wide range of secular clients, especially those in the non-profit realm and media organizations.

The vision at Barna Research is to enable Christian leaders in America to make better decisions for ministry by providing current, accurate, and reliable information in bite-sized pieces and at economical costs. Toward this end, BRG provides a variety of services and products, including research studies, standardized diagnostic tools, syndicated reports, books, and audio and video tapes. Other services are live presentations and seminars.

For further information about George Barna or the Barna Research Group, please contact them at P. O. Box 4152, Glendale CA 91204 or call 818-241-9300. A full listing of resources currently available will be provided upon request.

APPENDIX

······································

NINE GREAT EXPECTATIONS

What are some of the expectations that God has identified as being crucial to our personal development, toward achieving fulfillment, and toward bringing Him joy and honor? These expectations are embedded in the Bible for us to understand and carry out. Chapter 9 addressed our faulty personal expectations, but God has superior expectations for those who follow Him.

Here are His nine great expectations. In broad strokes, each of us must apply them to the specific circumstances in which He has placed us. As you read below, review your unique, God-given gifts and special circumstances. As you put these into practice, you can make a genuine contribution to your culture.

First, we are called to regard the blessings we receive as a means to blessing others. We are not to hog the blessings, but to pass them on to other people as God's agents of blessing (Genesis 12:1–3).

Second, our character is to reflect the highest of human qualities, described as those traits required of elders (see 1 Timothy 3) or of individuals whose lives are "bearing fruit" (described in Galatians 5:22–23). Such attributes include being loving, joyful, a peacemaker, kind, faithful, gentle, self-controlled, hospitable, and humble.

Third, God expects us to follow the Ten Commandments—not as a hollow routine, but as a heartfelt expression of our care for Him and His creation. Adhering to these guidelines is not a prerequisite to gaining entrance in heaven, but their application would certainly lead to a lifestyle that pleases and glorifies God and meets His expectations for our lives (Exodus 20:1–17).

From the parables of Jesus we find many lessons regarding what God expects of followers of Christ. For example, (4) we are called to view our faith as a source of ultimate joy and fulfillment, not as a series of restrictive and discouraging rules and regulations; (5) to model proper behavior and values for other people (Matthew 18:6–7); and (6) to keep troubles in relationships from festering and developing into animosities; instead we are to address them head-on, aiming for resolution and a restoration of the relationship (Matthew 18:15–17). You may wish to study Jesus' parable for other insights into God's expectations.

We can find three more of God's great expectations in the Sermon on the Mount. This message, given on the Mount of Olives in Jerusalem, is perhaps Jesus' most famous single teaching, and it contains many expectations. Here are three you can study: (7) we should accept suffering for our faith as a means to greater eternal blessing (Matthew 5:11–12); (8) our lives should be a compelling reflection of God's ways (5:13–17); (9) we are not to worry about the future, for if we trust God He will take care of us (6:25–34).

Undoubtedly, you can locate additional expectations as you search the Scriptures, as you search your heart, and as you pray to Him for wisdom. Hold firm to understanding that God's ways are not our ways (Isaiah 55:8–9) and that His wisdom differs from the world's wisdom. You have a choice to make: follow His admonitions for your life, or pursue the best the world has to offer. You have a distinct advantage in making that choice: we have decades' worth of research that shows which route is most productive, most fulfilling, and most meaningful. On a pure cost-benefit analysis, the evidence overwhelmingly points to the wisdom of accepting God's expectations as the best plan for your future.

Even more important than the practical benefits, though, we have His Word, which tells us that success is not based on what you produce in this life, in this place. In His perfect vision, success is determined by your character—the character you build in response to His prompting and to your dedication in following His mandate.

Making God's expectations your expectations may not correspond with your dreams of worldly success. But following His expectations is a matter of obedience, which He will ultimately honor. If Americans were to return to a commitment to pursuing the character God expects of us, the concerns and struggles outlined in this book would not be issues.

BIBLIOGRAPHY

Anderson, J. Kerby. *Signs of Warning, Signs of Hope.* Chicago: Moody, 1994.

Barna, George. *Virtual America.* Ventura, Calif.: Regal, 1994.

_____. *Baby Busters.* Chicago: Northfield, 1994.

_____. *Absolute Confusion.* Ventura, Calif.: Regal, 1993.

_____. *The Future of the American Family.* Chicago: Moody, 1993.

_____. *America Renews Its Search for God.* Ventura, Calif.: Regal, 1992.

_____. *What Americans Believe.* Ventura, Calif.: Regal, 1991.

_____. *User Friendly Churches.* Ventura, Calif.: Regal, 1991.

_____. *The Frog in the Kettle.* Ventura, Calif.: Regal, 1990.

Bartlett, Donald and Steele, James. *America: What Went Wrong?* Kansas City, Mo.: Andrews and McMeel, 1992.

Bellah, Robert, *et. al. The Good Society.* New York: Knopf, 1991.

_____ (editors). *Individualism and Commitment in American Life.* New York: Harper & Row, 1987.

_____. *Habits of the Heart.* New York: Harper & Row, 1985.

Bennett, William. *The Index of Leading Cultural Indicators.* New York: Simon & Schuster, 1994.

_____. *The Devaluing of America.* New York: Summit, 1992.

_____. *Our Children and Our Country.* New York: Simon & Schuster, 1988.

Bennis, Warren and Nanus, Burt. *Leaders*. New York: Harper & Row, 1985.

————. *On Becoming A Leader*. Reading, Mass.: Addison-Wesley, 1989.

Bork, Robert. *The Tempting of America*. New York: Touchstone, 1989.

Brown, Lester, et al. *State of the World, 1991*. New York: Norton, 1991.

Carter, Stephen. *The Culture of Disbelief*. New York: Basic, 1993.

Colson, Charles. *The Body*. Dallas: Word, 1993.

————. *Kingdoms in Conflict*. New York: William Morrow, 1987.

Dionne, E.J., Jr. *Why Americans Hate Politics*. New York: Touchstone, 1991.

Drucker, Peter. *The New Realities*. New York: Harper & Row, 1989.

Etzioni, Amitai. *The Spirit of Community*. New York: Crown, 1993.

Gallup, George, Jr. and Castelli, Jim. *The People's Religion*. New York: MacMillian, 1989.

Gilder, George; *Life After Television*. Knoxville, TN: Whittle Direct Books; 1990.

Greeley, Andrew. *Religious Change in America*. Cambridge, Mass.: Harvard Univ. Press, 1989.

Gross, Martin. *A Call for Revolution*. New York: Ballantine, 1993.

Guinness, Os. *The American Hour*. New York: Free Press, 1993.

Holmes, Arthur. *All Truth Is God's Truth*. Grand Rapids, Mich.: Eerdmans, 1977.

Hughes, Robert. *Culture of Complaint*. New York: Oxford Univ. Press, 1993.

Johnson, Alan and Webber, Robert. *What Christians Believe*. Grand Rapids, Mich.: Zondervan, 1993.

Kanter, Rosabeth Moss. *When Giants Learn to Dance*. New York: Simon & Schuster, 1989.

Kosmin, Barry and Lachman, Seymour. *One Nation Under God*. New York: Harmony, 1993.

Kouzes, James and Posner, Barry. *The Leadership Challenge*. San Francisco: Jossey-Bass, 1990.

Lewis, Hunter. *A Question of Values*. San Francisco: Harper Collins, 1990.

Lutzer, Erwin. *Twelve Myths Americans Believe*. Chicago, Moody, 1993.

Mouw, Richard. *Distorted Truth*. San Francisco: Harper & Row 1989.

Nanus, Burt. *Visionary Leadership*. San Francisco: Jossey-Bass, 1992.

Newman, Katherine. *Declining Fortunes*. New York: Basic, 1993.

Richards, R. Scott. *Myths the World Taught Me*. Nashville: Thomas Nelson, 1991.

Roof, Wade. *A Generation of Seekers*. San Francisco: Harper Collins, 1993.

Ruggiero, Vincent. *Warning: Nonsense Is Destroying America*. Nashville: Thomas Nelson, 1994.

Schillebeeckx, Edward. *Church*. New York: Crossroad, 1990.

Sider, Ronald. *One-Sided Christianity?* Grand Rapids, Mich.: Zondervan, 1993.

_____. *Rich Christians in an Age of Hunger*. Dallas: Word, 1990.

Silber, John. *Straight Shooting*. New York: Harper, 1990.

Sire, James. *The Universe Next Door*. Downers Grove, Ill.: InterVarsity, 1988.

Steele, Shelby. *The Content of Our Character*. New York: Harper, 1990.

Stott, John. *Involvement*. (Vol. 1); Old Tappan, N.J.: Revell, 1985.

Sykes, Charles. *A Nation of Victims*. New York: St. Martin's, 1992.

Taylor, Daniel. *The Myth of Certainty*. Grand Rapids, Mich.: Zondervan, 1992.

Thomas, Cal. *The Things That Matter Most*. Grand Rapids, Mich.: HarperCollins/Zondervan, 1994.

Toffler, Alvin. *Power Shift*. New York: Bantam, 1990.

Wilson, James Q. *The Moral Sense*. New York: Free Press, 1993.